FIVE SEATS OF POWER

FIVE SEATS OF POWER

DISCOVERING THE BEST YOU CAN BE THROUGH THE MAHABHARATA

RAGHU ANANTHANARAYANAN

HarperCollins *Publishers* India

First published in India by HarperCollins *Publishers* 2022

HarperCollins Publishers India, Cyber City, Building 10-A, Gurugram,
Haryana-122002, India
www.harpercollins.co.in

2 4 6 8 10 9 7 5 3 1

P-ISBN: 978-93-5489-231-8
E-ISBN: 978-93-5489-553-1

The views expressed herein are the author's own and intended to trigger a self-reflective process. They are meant for informational purposes only and are not intended to hurt any person's beliefs or sentiments. The views expressed in Part 4 of this book are those of the respective leaders.

Typeset in 10.5/14 Adobe Caslon Pro at
Manipal Technologies Limited, Manipal

Printed and bound at
MicroPrints India, New Delhi

MIX
Paper
FSC FSC® C218906

This product is made of FSC®-certified and other controlled material.

HarperCollins Publishers, Macken House, 39/40 Mayor Street
Upper, Dublin 1, D01 C9W8, Ireland

Dedicated to
my Gurus Yogacharya T. Krishnamacharya and
Shri T.K.V. Desikachar, as well as Na Muthuswamy, who opened
my eyes to the depth and beauty of the Mahabharata Koothu
performance tradition.

Contents

Foreword

ix

Introduction

xi

The Mahabharata Revisited

xxv

Part 1: Tales of Power from the Mahabharata

1

Part 2: The Five Seats of Power in their Contemporary Avatars

121

Part 3: Discovering the Best That You Can Be

174

Part 4: Inspiring Leadership Journeys

200

Appendix

237

Acknowledgements

251

Foreword

India is a collage of many strands of philosophy, science, and many ways of engaging with the world. It has been able to weave a tapestry where these strands flow into each other. Science and spirituality, the philosophical and the pragmatic, blend together in many subtle ways. These are very relevant in an emerging global context, where society is impacted by vast changes in technology.

Leadership processes that can mobilize the natural genius of people and shape powerful organizations lie at the core of success. Raghu Ananthanarayanan has engaged with this enquiry for over four decades and made unique contributions to the fields of leadership development and organizational transformation. He has enabled organizations and leaders to anticipate the future and build capabilities through frameworks derived from traditional Indic wisdom.

Raghu uses design principles drawn from Vaastu Shastra to study organizations and facilitate their growth. He has also effectively used insights from the Yoga Sutras and the Mahabharata to enable behavioural transformation and inspire people to perform to their potential.

I have had the opportunity to appreciate his methods over the years through his association with Tata Consultancy Services (TCS). His leadership development programme, 'A Leader Prepares', has enabled over 2,000 people in leadership positions to gain a new perspective into themselves and their roles.

Through this book, Raghu offers a bridge between one's inner potential and its outer expression. It can be used as a mirror to reflect upon yourself and put into practice its pragmatic recommendations. It can be your first step on the inner voyage to become the best version of who you can be.

Natarajan Chandrashekaran
Chairman, Tata Sons

Introduction

Since time immemorial, man has been on an eternal quest to know oneself. But why is this quest important in the first place? It's because if we do not understand the process through which we make meaning of ourselves and the world, we will lack the clarity to use our skills effectively.

Defining oneself is an integral part of all the philosophies of the world. In the East, we have Vedic scriptures, the Yoga Sutras and Buddhist traditions that focus on the subject. In the West, the dominant idea of scientific proof and validation took over with the birth of psychology as a major field of study. Freud approached looking into one's own mind from a scientific perspective. This became more prominent in the work of Swiss psychiatrist Carl Jung. Having studied and referenced the Vedas and Upanishads in his work, Jung had a deep appreciation of the wisdom of the East.

At its extreme, this journey led to the birth of Skinnerian behaviourism, which shrugs off any attempt to understand the self. It is only concerned with behaviours that are to be operationally conditioned to control the behaviours one wants the other to exhibit.

Some of the recent advancements in psychology have emerged from meaningful engagements with Buddhist and Yogic traditions.

Dialogues with the Dalai Lama and a deep study of the Bhagavad Gita have informed the emerging practices of psychology.[1]

And despite all of this, Western psychology is mired in the question of consciousness. It is a chicken-and-egg situation. How did consciousness emerge? Is it a result of the brain and mental processes, or is it the other way around?

The Eastern tradition, unlike the West, posits the primacy of consciousness and considers it the substratum of all existence and therefore of human intelligence. When subjectivity becomes valued, one's sense of self doesn't need any validation from anchors outside. The Eastern tradition offers a range of methods to understand the self without getting caught up with theories and other forms of self-deception.

The Mahabharata is one such powerful and evocative tool to mirror and observe yourself, and this book draws its framework from the epic to bring out your heroic potential. In essence, this book asks the question: How can you discover the best that you can be? Through the story of the five Pandava heroes who won the battle of Kurukshetra to reclaim their kingdom, we will examine each of the Pandavas as an archetype of a particular power.

When seen through an Indian lens, a story is never linear. The journey never ends with a 'happily ever after'. It is more complicated than that. Even though the Pandavas win, they also pay for the expedient choices they made. The journey of a hero in the Mahabharata is an inner journey, where the impediments to the unfolding of one's true self are identified to be dissolved. And when that happens, the person's actions reflect Divine Intelligence.

---

1 See Subhash C. Bhatia, Jayakrishna Madabushi, Venkata Kolli and Vishal Madan, 'The Bhagavad Gita and Contemporary Psychotherapies', *Indian Journal of Psychiatry* 55 (Suppl 2): S315–21, 2013, https://www.researchgate.net/publication/249648667_The_Bhagavad_Gita_and_contemporary_psychotherapies; and Tapas Kumar Aich, 'Buddha Philosophy and Western Psychology', *Indian Journal of Psychiatry* 55 (Suppl 3): S165–70, 2013, https://www.ncbi.nlm.nih.gov/pmc/articles/PMC3705677/.

You are free to draw your own lessons from these stories and the discussions. However, you should be aware of this: the evocations, provocations and internal dialogues that get triggered by the stories all reflect your own psyche. There is no single truth out there. How you define yourself is not just your truth but also a reflection of who you are.

While examining the Pandava heroes and drawing out lessons that would be relevant today, we will draw upon Carl Jung's ideas of archetype and shadow.

What Is an Archetype?

The idea of an archetype was popularized by Jung, who used it to describe the patterns of behaviour held deep in a person's mind. These unconscious patterns determine the ways in which people perceive their world and shape their identity. For simplicity's sake, I will use the masculine pronoun to describe these archetypes, although archetypes are universal and transcend gender boundaries.

These patterns have a brighter side that energizes a person's behaviour. They also have a dark, or 'disowned', side, which causes loss of energy and triggers compulsive behaviour. The disowned part of the archetype is called the shadow. For a person to mobilize his heroic potential, he must transform the dark and compulsive energies. This transformation is essential for a leader to be the best he can be.

Jung suggested that archetypes are models of people, behaviours or personalities. Archetypes are universal human tendencies that play a role in influencing human behaviour. He believed that each archetype played a role in one's personality but felt that most people were dominated by one specific archetype. The actual way in which an archetype is expressed or realized depends upon several factors, including an individual's cultural influences and uniquely personal experiences. Jung believed that archaic and mythic characters from traditional stories that make up the archetypes reside within all people from all over the world. It is these archetypes that symbolize basic human motivations, values and personalities.

Joseph Campbell, one of the most influential thinkers in comparative mythology and comparative religion and the author of *The Hero with a Thousand Faces* and many other books on world mythology, says while speaking about mythology, that archetypes describe what is true and enduring in the human psyche. Myths speak to us through symbols that 'do not refer to historical events: they refer through historical events to spiritual and psychological principles and powers that are of yesterday, today and tomorrow, and they are everywhere'.[2] The archetypal energies are the quintessential patterns of unique types of talents, capabilities and propensities that manifest as behaviours.

While examining the Pandava heroes, I am not going to try and map them on to Jungian archetypes, but rather borrow the idea and view the five Pandavas as archetypal energies that manifest in the way we play our roles in life. The five Pandava princes are symbols through which we examine and enquire into the principles and psychological patterns of power. These Mahabharata heroes are committed to the *dharmic* path and symbolize the responsible ways of deploying power and occupying leadership positions.

In most Indian languages, the word *svabhaava* is used to mean the unique self that determines the ways in which a person behaves. *Svadharma* is another word that is used almost synonymously, but with a different nuance. It refers to the ethical essence of the persona. I use the word archetype here to encompass both *svabhaava* and *svadharma*.

The meaning and import of these words can be understood more clearly if we contrast a stereotype with an archetype. Stereotypes are, for example, the way Bhima would be portrayed in a film: a big, musclebound and impulsive person. An archetype is much deeper; it is the quintessence of a psychological pattern.

The Bhima archetype can be understood as the inner urge for passion and adventure. This manifests as readiness for action and an ability to venture into spaces that are dangerous and challenging. It is deeply internal to the person.

---

2 Joseph Campbell, *Goddess: Mysteries of the Feminine Divine*, ed. Saffron Rossi, Joseph Campbell Foundation, 2013.

It is the seed that manifests as a tree. All mango seeds will grow into mango trees, but each tree will have its own distinct features. However, no one will mistake a mango tree for a teak tree.

But before we understand the seed, let us understand the key concept of *dharma*.

Dharma and *Adharma*

Our actions can be viewed through the filter of the concept of *dharma*. The Mahabharata was written to enable a common person to reflect on the ideas of *dharma* and *adharma* by contemplating the struggle between the Pandavas and the Kauravas. Our talents and propensities can be deployed in *daivic* or *asuric* ways. When we hear the word *asuric*, we associate with it undesirable and immoral behaviour – *adharma*. And when we hear *daivic*, we associate with it the desirable and respectable – *dharma*.

It is essential for anyone in a leadership position to be anchored in *dharma*. A simple but powerful way to apply *dharma* as a filter to our behaviour is to ask ourselves: is our action going to enhance life in our context, in the others with whom we are engaging, and ourselves simultaneously?

Any action that benefits ourselves at the expense of others and the context is *adharmic*. *Dharma* is never absolutist. It is contextual, and we must make a choice to deploy our propensities in ways appropriate to the larger context.

Anger is not *daivic* or *asuric* per se. Do you deploy anger in *dharmic* ways that enhance life or do you deploy it in *adharmic* ways that are self-centred and exploitative? When it is repressed and disowned, perhaps due to social conditioning that unfairly views anger as wrong in all circumstances, it festers deep in the recesses of your mind.

The disowned and repressed side of oneself triggers action that is compulsive and self-centred. The Jungian idea of shadow describes this process deeper.

What Is a Shadow?

When we grow up, through a process of acculturation and socialization, we internalize ideas that our community and society hold as good and appropriate (*daivic*). We therefore learn to reject and repress behaviours that our community and society describes as *asuric*. However, these behavioural impulses don't simply disappear. All of us hold parts that we don't like or that we think society won't like. We eventually push those parts down into our unconscious psyches.

The concept of shadow was first coined by Carl Jung to refer to this collection of repressed patterns of ourselves. When we distance ourselves consciously from those behaviours, emotions and thoughts we find dangerous, we push them into our shadows. *Asuric* behaviour is often triggered by our shadows.

The shadow impacts the whole personality and disturbs our sense of self. The disowned aspects of feeling, thought and action impact the processes through which we make choices and give meaning to things. This way, they contradict our idea of self.

We cannot become conscious of the shadow without considerable psychological effort. To become conscious of it, we have to recognize the dark aspects of the personality as present and real. Violent emotions, shameful experiences, immoral impulses, urges and taboo desires, fears and irrational wishes are a few examples of the shadow aspects of the mind. Rather than confront something that we don't like, our minds pretend that it doesn't exist.

How have these behaviours manifested among the Pandavas and the Kauravas?

Heroic and Shadow Behaviours in the Mahabharata

In the Mahabharata, the Pandavas are juxtaposed against the Kauravas. Each of the Kaurava characters is endowed with all the capabilities of the Pandavas. However, they are caught in choices that come from their shadows.

When I use the idea of counterpoint, I am contrasting the characters who reflect the *dharmic* and *adharmic* aspects of an archetype in their psychological patterns. I am using the words 'shadow' and 'disowned' to refer to the repressed and submerged energies of the archetype that become compulsive drives in them.

To illustrate, let us examine Bhima with his counterpoint Duryodhana. While Bhima seeks to find a *dharmic* response to the challenges he faces, Duryodhana laments that his envy overpowers him, and he struggles to do the right thing even when his rational mind knows what the *dharmic* choice may be. The Mahabharata is full of such plays between the two sides of the same coin and therefore provides a fascinating study of human behaviour in all its complexity.

In Yudhishthira's commitment to role appropriateness and discipline, he represses his spontaneity. This energy explodes through compulsive gambling in one of the most tragic and well-known episodes in the Mahabharata, which we will explore in more depth in the second chapter. This is his shadow – his disowned side. Nevertheless, it is a part of him.

I will use the following terms to refer to different levels of subtlety of the archetype that manifests through the hero:

- Archetypal energy to mean the quintessential seed that contains all the possible behaviours that can be exhibited by that archetype.
- Propensity to mean the more tangible and cognizable possibilities of action that emerge as the archetypal energy manifests in a context.
- We will use terms such as 'A Yudhishthira will act/think/feel' as a shorthand for 'Yudhishthira's archetypal energy will manifest through action/thought/feeling in the following way'.

Introducing the Five Powers

This book is founded on the key premise of exploring the five powers that are essential for the growth and evolution of any organization. These are:

1. to set out the policy and regulatory framework and enforce it;
2. to defend its boundaries from competitors and expand these boundaries;
3. to create a sense of in-group solidarity among the members of the organization;
4. to create knowledge and technology that is unique to the organization;
5. to question the current paradigm and enable the organization to discover a more powerful paradigm.

When we give these powers a human form, they become the quintessential ways in which the archetypal energies play out in an organizational context.

The Pandavas as Archetypes

What do we mean by archetypes in an organizational context?

Let us digress for a moment to understand this more thoroughly. In the game of cricket, there are three generic roles: the batter, the bowler and the fielder. When we read these terms, we can easily picture the kind of actions each one performs and the relationship they have with others. We also have an idea of the overall set of rules of the game, so we know that a player can be a batter at one point of time, a fielder at another and a bowler at another. These players engage with the game as it is being played.

They innovate on the ways of bowling or batting to enhance their efficiency and effectiveness so that their winning average goes up. Beside these roles, there is another important role that doesn't receive as much spotlight as the game itself. There is someone who may not be playing the game, but quietly studying the viability of the game in the longer term.

When the popularity of the five-day Test match was waning, limited-overs cricket was introduced. This was made more exciting by creating a World Cup tournament. These were paradigmatic changes in the game of cricket, which was until then a gentleman's game played in white flannels. Limited-overs cricket also fitted well with a television audience. It created a lot of excitement among the viewers, increasing the commercial value of the game. Thus, the long-term sustainability of cricket was assured.

In an organizational context, I refer to these roles played by the Pandavas as an archetype, a specific way of using your power, to distinguish it from the idea of a role as a title: vice president, executive, management trainee and so on. These are positional descriptors. I am also distinguishing the idea of the archetype from the idea of functional roles such as finance, marketing, etc.

Let me return to our original premise, where I listed the five powers of an organization:

- Setting out the policy and regulatory framework and enforcing it: this evokes the archetypal pattern of a king or a judge.
- Defending its boundaries from competitors and expanding these boundaries: this evokes the archetypal pattern of a warrior or an explorer.
- Creating in-group solidarity among the members of the organization: this evokes the archetypal pattern of a healer or a nurturer.
- Creating knowledge and technology that is unique to the organization: this evokes the archetypal pattern of a researcher or a scholar.
- Questioning the current paradigm and letting the organization discover a more powerful paradigm: this evokes the archetypal pattern of a questioner or a meditator.

The five Pandavas represent these five archetypes in an embodied way – in ways a person chooses to play a role. The various stories in the Mahabharata enable us to understand the nuances of these archetypes in detail.

- The archetypal role of a king or a judge is personified by Yudhishthira.

- The archetypal role of a warrior or an explorer is personified by Bhima.
- The archetypal role of a healer or a nurturer is personified by Nakula.
- The archetypal role of a researcher or a scholar is personified by Sahadeva.
- The archetypal role of a questioner or a meditator is personified by Arjuna.

Let me illustrate this using the example of a head of finance in a large organization.

He has to enforce rules and policy, and study the balance sheet to suggest ways of growing the organization. He needs to create a sense of team cohesion and examine the efficacy of the technology his team uses. This will ensure the smooth and effective functioning of the finance department. In this, he must awaken the power of Yudhishthira.

If he is an astute reader of the business context and observes how it is evolving, he might suggest new ways of looking at the function so that it becomes more closely linked with strategy and goes beyond the traditional boundaries of accounting and reporting. This head of finance has to go beyond the frame of being just his job title, and look at the whole business and its relation to the external environment. He must participate in the process of building alternative scenarios. For this, he must awaken the power of Arjuna.

In order to select the best scenario and evolve a strategic plan, it is critical to have detailed number-crunching and thought experiments based on data and research. To do this, he must awaken the power of Sahadeva.

To nurture his team and facilitate collaboration and a sense of belonging among the team members, he must awaken the power of Nakula.

Finally, as a member of the core management team, he needs courage to pursue bold strategies, take risks, propose aggressive goals and arouse the passion of the organization. For this, he must awaken the power of Bhima.

Thus, in order to be a great leader, this head of finance has to be proficient in all the five aspects of the business that I have listed. He has to understand and embody the five role archetypes in himself and deploy them appropriately in the appropriate context.

This is where the intrinsic capability of the individual and the situational demands placed by the role archetype is critical. Individuals become more or less proficient in one or more of the five role archetypes, but the emerging context could demand any of the five or a combination of them.

In the start-up phase of an organization, the warrior archetype is obviously very important. Until the organization is stable, you cannot really set out policy and rules. If the head of finance wishes to make a great career in this start-up, he has to evoke each of these role archetypes within and balance it with others in an appropriate way. When the consolidation phase emerges, he cannot run his team the same way as he did during the early phase.

The Mahabharata is an invaluable resource for a leader because it provides a sandbox: an intellectual and emotional playground in which to test himself. It acts as a mirror and provides a lens through which he can study the context and explore how others play the game of business.

Each of these role archetypes is an inherent power within us that can be mastered.

- Yudhishthira embodies the Power of Order and Stability
- Bhima embodies the Power of Passion and Action
- Nakula embodies the Power of Compassion and Service
- Sahadeva embodies the Power of Knowledge and Curiosity
- Arjuna embodies the Power of *Dharma Sankata*[3] and Integration

---

3 A *dharma sankata* is the decision-making dilemma that a person faces when confronted with alternatives that seem equally compelling but have mutually opposing outcomes, as well as contrary ethical pulls. A *dharma sankata* can be resolved only through deep introspection and re-examination of one's assumptions and conclusions about the nature of man and the nature of the world.

These archetypes represent the ways in which you can play leadership roles. The Mahabharata also portrays people with heroic capabilities who play leadership roles in dysfunctional ways.

This book explores this basic premise and offers you a way of studying your own relationship with these forms of power. It will therefore enable you to embark on a journey of how to master yourself.

The Mahabharata as a Playbook to Discover Your True Self

The Mahabharata is a treasure trove of archetypal stories. When you enquire into the behaviours of the heroes and their counterpoints, it provides you with an invaluable lens through which you can examine and understand power. You can also understand the misuse of power and its consequences to yourself and others whom you lead.

There are three reasons that make the Mahabharata an ideal playbook to discover your true self. Firstly, it presents five types of power, each personified by the five Pandava brothers. Secondly, through its stories, it delves into how each Pandava explores all the facets of the power they are gifted with, till each of them become the best they can be. They make mistakes and the shadow sides of their gifts derail them, but they take on the shadow fully and emerge as stronger human beings and heroic warriors. Thirdly, through a clever juxtaposition of the behaviours of the Kauravas, the Mahabharata shows what happens when you are endowed with gifts but are driven by the shadow aspects of the archetype. It shows the destruction that is wrought when you deploy power without facing up to your shadow side.

The Mahabharata looks into the perennial wisdom of the Indic tradition through an intense and archetypal human drama. It becomes a handy vehicle for us to understand the human drama as it unfolds in an organization. Though the Mahabharata is thousands of years old, basic human emotions and inner needs and desires have not changed. We still enact dramas that are similar to those the Mahabharata characters went through.

How This Book is Organized

We started with an overview, where we came to a fundamental understanding of heroes and archetypes. We explored why the Mahabharata is an ideal laboratory for this learning and also looked at some of the ways in which you could play with the Pandava archetypes as five kinds of power and propensities.

In Part 1, we will take a detailed look at the Pandavas and go into the nuances of each of the propensities through stories from the Mahabharata. We will follow the old Indian tradition of storytelling followed by reflection and dialogue. The evocation that the story triggers gets situated in our reality, helping us explore many facets of the hero archetype and examine their contemporary relevance. We will enquire into the ways in which the feeling, thought and action propensities of each archetype can be deployed. This will enable us to understand the use of power with responsibility.

In Part 2, we will go through a distillation of the enabling and derailing behaviours of each Pandava archetype. I will share with you a few case studies to explore how the framework of the five seats of power can be used to understand your own style.

In Part 3, I offer self-reflective exercises to help you discover your own abilities by asking the question: *In doing what I am doing, what am I really doing?* Asking oneself this question with great seriousness is the essence of the Bhagavad Gita. This is the burden of Arjuna's dialogue with Lord Krishna.

We have been fortunate to get reflections from some iconic leaders of our times. In Part 4, I share interviews with leaders in which they recount their amazing journeys. I hope this will provide you with another window to examine leadership.

In these interviews, these leaders share their perspectives on leadership as a process of discovery, their reflections on decision-making dilemmas and critical turning points in their journeys. You will have a glimpse of the seats of power that each is predisposed to and the power and propensities deployed.

As mentioned earlier, this book is meant to be a field book rather than a point of view. I invite you, dear reader, to enter the book as a participant in a dialogue. It is only through discussing and playing with several possible meanings that you understand your own life journey. This is essential for self-reflection and self-discovery.

Every point of view and interpretation we have of characters and the story reflect us; they are *our* projections. This is what makes the Mahabharata a window to our inner world and a source of perennial wisdom.

A Word of Caution to the Reader

In my four decades of work as a leadership coach and consultant, I have felt that my *dharma* is to offer tools that allow leaders to discover the wisdom hidden inside themselves. This book is about leadership, and yet, it is quite different from other books in the same genre. It is not a compilation of lessons from the Mahabharata packaged in a set of how-to capsules for you to apply to your work and life. This book is not a philosophical discourse.

Even the most profound idea, when applied without sensitivity to your context and a realistic assessment of your capabilities and limitations will only invite disaster. Using lessons from the Mahabharata, I will teach you methods to discover the best you can be and become contextually aware. Anything less would not respect your unique genius and your unique circumstances!

Also please keep in mind, in this book, whenever I use the names of the characters from the Mahabharata outside the context of the stories from the epic, it refers to the specific archetypes. E.g., when I say a Yudhishthira or a Sahadeva, I refer to their respective archetypes, not Yudhishthira or Sahadeva as characters from the Mahabharata.

The Mahabharata Revisited

Here is a quick retelling of the Mahabharata in order to appreciate its nuances and the secrets of human behaviour. This retelling is based on my discussions with Sashikanth Ananthachari,[1] a storyteller and filmmaker who has been working on the performance traditions of the Mahabharata in his oeuvre of three films, two books and an installation for his 'Epic Performance Traditions Project', for which I have been a sounding board and which I hope has been mutually beneficial to both of us.

---

1 Sashikanth Ananthachari is a filmmaker and writer. The first film of his trilogy of films on the Mahabharata traditions, *Kelai Draupadai*, was the official selection at the prestigious BlowUp Chicago International Arthouse Film Festival in 2016. At the DIY Film Festival of Los Angeles, it received the Best Foreign Film award. The other films of the trilogy are *Ninaivin Nagaram* (Landscape and Memory) and *Kalpavaasi* (Textures of Time) on the centrality of Vanavaasam in Indian Traditions. The two books are *Mahabharata of the Mind* and *Kaleidoscope: The Idea of Four*. Currently, V.R. Devika, Raghu Ananthanarayanan and Sashikanth are working with the Tamil Nadu government in getting UNESCO recognition for the Mahabharata Traditions of Tamil Nadu as 'Intangible Cultural Heritage'.

Why and How the Mahabharata Was Written

After the sage Vyasa had composed the four Vedas, Brahma felt that one required tremendous scholarship to understand them. It was not possible for an ordinary person to comprehend them. He felt the need for a text, which would distil the essence of the four Vedas and present it for everyone. Thus, he requested Vyasa to compose the fifth Veda: the Mahabharata.

When Vyasa demurred, Brahma reiterated the need for a story reflecting the Vedic truths but with added emotional intensity. It was essential for the progress of mankind in general and the householder – who remained the key to social cohesion and wellness in society – in particular.

It is said that the Mahabharata should not be read, but heard. 'However, it is impossible to listen to the entire text in one sitting and comprehend its meaning. Therefore, the epic is narrated in fragments, which allows the listeners to comprehend its deeper layers. The epic holds multiple layers of meaning and it is through listening that one can uncover each layer and reach its core. However, this uncovering cannot happen overnight. It is a lifelong process. The Mahabharata is not the story of just any war, but THE war happening inside each of us. It is the story of the war of the mind.'[2]

Background

The war in the Mahabharata is fought between cousins of the Kuru dynasty. It begins on an introspective note. 'The principal question the epic poses is this: What determines an ethically correct action? At one level, it is a compendium of multiple stories of people addressing various ethical dilemmas in their own lives, set against the framework of the fatal war, in which there are no winners in the end.

---

2 Sashikanth Ananthachari, *Mahabharata of the Mind*, a first-person narrative of participating in an amazing Mahabharata festival [Work in progress].

The epic travels back and forth in time, narrating many mirror stories, which add several nuances to the ethical dilemmas the protagonists face.'[3] On several occasions, a heroic and *dharmic* action by one of the key Kaurava characters could have avoided the war.

The Vow of Bhishma

King Bharata of the Puru dynasty is considered the first great monarch of the Indian subcontinent, and the title of the epic is derived from his name. His descendant Shantanu has three sons: Devarata, from his first wife, Ganga; Chitrangada and Vichitravirya, from his second wife, Satyavati.

Before marrying Shantanu, Satyavati made him promise that only her children would rule the kingdom. To appease his father, Devarata renounces his right to rule and takes a vow of celibacy so that he would have no children to contest the kingdom with his half-brothers from Satyavati.

He is thus called Bhishma – the one who has taken a terrible vow. To die without any progeny is considered a terrible misfortune in Indic traditions. When Bhishma voluntarily takes this upon himself, it becomes the framing narrative of the story.

Vyasa's Role in the Birth of the Pandavas and Kauravas

After his father's death, Chitrangada becomes king. His rule is short and uneventful, and he dies soon after. Vichitravirya then takes the throne under the guardianship of Bhishma, and marries two sisters by the names of Ambika and Ambalika. However, he too dies young, leaving no heirs behind.

Satyavati then begs Bhishma to give up his terrible vow and take the young widows as his wives. Even though the Kuru dynasty needs Bhishma to continue the lineage, Bhishma chooses to stick to his vow and remain celibate.

---

3 *Mahabharata of the Mind.*

It is here that Vyasa enters his own narrative. He is the first-born son of Satyavati, fathered by the sage Parashara. Though Vyasa chooses the life of an ascetic, his mother asks him to ensure that the Kuru dynasty does not end with the death of Vichitravirya.

The storyteller Vyasa obliges and fathers three children with Ambika, Ambalika and their maid. The three children are named Dhritarashtra, Pandu and Vidura, respectively. As Dhritarashtra is born blind, his younger brother Pandu becomes king, with Bhishma continuing as the guardian of the throne. The third half-brother, Vidura, stakes no claim to the throne, being the son of the maid to the queens.

'Thus, a distinctive feature of the Mahabharata is the participation of the author in the story he has written. Vyasa is both the author and the progenitor of the principal characters of the story. This makes the text self-reflexive, and this quality is scrupulously maintained in all narrative and performative traditions of the text.'[4] As renowned poet and scholar A.K. Ramanujan succinctly puts it, when these stories are recounted, 'Even a fool cannot resist it; he is entranced and caught up in the action. The listener can no longer bear to be a bystander but feels compelled to enter the world of the epic: the line between fiction and reality is erased.'

'As a listener, you are simultaneously both within and outside the epic. Thanks to this unique approach to writing, listening to this epic is like listening to one's own story.'[5]

'What unites [the] Mahabharata with the grand old epic traditions is that they are narratives of exile and return. To be a good king and a

4 Sashikanth Ananthachari, *Kaleidoscope: The Idea of Four*, on the aesthetics of the Mahabharata traditions [Work in progress].

5 A.K. Ramanujan, 'Three Hundred Rāmāyanas: Five Examples and Three Thoughts on Translation', in *Collected Essays of A.K. Ramanujan*, ed. Vinay Dharwadker, Oxford India Paperbacks, 1999. 'Three Hundred Rāmāyanas' is an essay Ramanujan wrote for a Conference on Comparison of Civilizations at the University of Pittsburgh, February 1987.

good human being, one first has to suffer and kill the demons inside and outside.'[6]

The story of the Mahabharata starts with the conflict between the sons of Dhritarashtra and Pandu for the right to the throne.

The Curse of Pandu

One day, when Pandu is out on a hunt, he sees a deer couple making love. Impulsively, he shoots them down. The deer couple turns out to be a great sage and his wife. As he dies, the sage curses Pandu that he too would die during the act of making love.

A repentant Pandu abdicates the throne to Dhritarashtra and leaves with his wives Kunti and Madri to live the life of an ascetic in the forest. But Pandu does not want to die without leaving an heir. Kunti tells him of the wondrous boon she was bestowed upon by the sage Durvasa.

Kunti's Boon and the Birth of Karna

Durvasa is an ascetic famous for his quick temper. One fine day, when Kunti is a young girl, her father asks her to ensure that Durvasa is comfortable during his stay in their palace. Durvasa is pleased by how well he is taken care of by Kunti. He teaches her a mantra through which she can invoke any celestial being and give birth to a child who will eventually incarnate the invoked deity.

Kunti becomes curious and invokes the Sun God, Surya. She immediately gives birth to a child, born with golden armour and earrings. Still unmarried, Kunti is alarmed by this turn of events and abandons her son by the river. The child is found, adopted and raised by a childless charioteer couple as their own son. He grows up to be Karna.

Pandu asks his wives Kunti and Madri to chant this mantra, and five children are born to them. These five children, known as the Pandavas,

---

6 From 'Vanavaasam', a presentation by Sashikanth Ananthachari with Richard Schechener on the Mahabharata Traditions of Tamil Nadu, New York University, 30 October 2020; curated by Arvind Rajagopal.

are incarnate celestial beings. From Kunti are born Yudhishthira, son of Dharma, the god of justice; Bhima, son of Vayu, the god of wind; Arjuna, son of Indra, the king of the *devas*. From Madri are born the twins Nakula and Sahadeva, sons of Ashwini, the god of healing.

Birth of the Kauravas

Meanwhile, Dhritarashtra marries Gandhari. Gandhari does not know she is marrying a blind man till the day of her marriage. When she finds out, she is beset by despair. She feels betrayed by her father.

Gandhari decides that to spite her father, she will spend the rest of her life blindfolded. Her brother, Shakuni, decides to stay back with her sister to support her. She gives birth to a hundred children, known as the Kauravas. The eldest, Duryodhana, stakes a claim to the throne.

Return of the Pandavas

One day, Pandu gives in to his desire for Madri and succumbs to the curse during the act of making love. After their father's death, the Pandavas return from the forest to Hastinapura with their mother Kunti. They start living with their cousins, the Kauravas, under the guardianship of their grand-uncle, Bhishma.

Yudhishthira, the first son of Pandu, is the eldest among all the cousins and has the strongest claim to the throne. With this, the seeds of conflict are sown.

Karna, the eldest son of Kunti, and thus the rightful heir, is raised to be the son of a charioteer and grows up not knowing his right to the kingdom. He learns the art of warfare and becomes a skilful warrior. However, his skills remain unrecognized, as he is constantly taunted for being the son of a charioteer. Karna continues to look for legitimacy.

Duryodhana recognizes Karna's skills, befriends him and makes him the king of Angada, a minor kingdom. Karna remains indebted to Duryodhana and chooses to fight for him, although he knows that Duryodhana is not following the *dharmic* path.

The House of Wax and Second Exile

With two known strong claimants to the throne, a decision is taken to divide the kingdom and let Duryodhana and Yudhishthira each rule half the kingdom. However, Duryodhana has no intention of sharing the kingdom. He orders a palace made of wax to be built for the Pandavas and deceitfully requests them to stay there till the kingdom can be properly divided.

Duryodhana schemes to burn the palace when they are asleep. While the Pandavas somehow escape the burning palace with their mother, another woman and her five sons spending the night there die. When their remains are found, everyone takes them to be of the Pandavas and their mother; they believe it is they who have died in the fire.

The burning of the wax palace is the crucial moment when the die is cast and war becomes inevitable. The Pandavas are forced to live incognito, resuming life in exile. Their lives are still under threat if they are discovered by Duryodhana.

Their fortunes change when Arjuna, in disguise as a poor Brahmin, wins a contest. The prize is Draupadi, a Panchala princess. Taking her home, Arjuna tells his mother that he has won a prize in a competition. Without asking to see what the prize is, Kunti tells him to share it equally with his brothers. Thus, Draupadi is wed to all five brothers.

Through this newly forged relationship with the kingdom of Panchala, the Pandavas find their first strong ally. Krishna, who is Kunti's nephew, is also a close friend and an ally of Drupada, the Panchala king. He is also very fond of Draupadi, whom he considers a sister.

The Pandavas now return to Hastinapura to demand their share of the kingdom. As the prospect of a fratricidal war becomes a reality, Duryodhana is forced to concede land to the Pandavas. Reluctantly, he gives them an inhospitable forest, the Khandava, as their share of the kingdom.

Indraprastha

The Pandavas build their kingdom on this reclaimed forest land and declare Indraprastha as its capital. Yudhishthira's palace is built by the divine architect Mayan. The palace of illusions he builds becomes the next narrative element, propelling the story to the fateful war.

After establishing his kingdom at Indraprastha, Yudhishthira becomes a powerful monarch. Local kings declare their allegiance to him. Krishna advises him to consolidate his power by performing the Ashwamedha Yagna and declaring himself the Chakravarti, or emperor, of all the lands in his region.

Yudhishthira sends his brothers to win the allegiance of all kingdoms. Once that is done, all the kings of the land are invited to the Rajasuya ceremony. The pride of place is given to the Kauravas, as they are, after all, part of the family.

The Humiliation of Duryodhana

When Yudhishthira courteously offers to show Duryodhana around the palace, he refuses the offer, preferring to explore the palace of illusions on his own. However, in Mayan's palace of illusions, nothing is what it seems. During his walk through this magical palace, Duryodhana confronts his own jealousy and anger in seeing the prosperity of his cousins.

Befuddled by the labyrinthine palace, Duryodhana trips and falls. He feels deeply humiliated as he sees Draupadi, the wife of the Pandavas, witnessing his fall. He seethes in anger when he hears her laughing merrily at the sight. From that moment on, Duryodhana becomes obsessed with revenge and wants to shame the Pandavas and Draupadi.

The Game of Dice

Duryodhana conspires with his principal advisor, his maternal uncle Shakuni, to plot the downfall of the Pandavas. An open war is not an option as the Pandavas are far stronger than the Kauravas. Duryodhana decides that deceit is the only way to achieve his ambition.

Since Yudhishthira is known to have a weakness for gambling, Shakuni advises Duryodhana to invite Yudhishthira for a game of dice. Shakuni possesses magical dice that fall on whatever number he desires. The plotters build a palace and invite their cousins in a reciprocal gesture to stay at Duryodhana's new palace. A friendly game of dice is also included in this invitation.

Yudhishthira, against the advice of Draupadi and his brothers, accepts this invitation. Incited by Shakuni, he first gambles and loses his kingdom; then he loses his brothers and himself. Finally, when he has nothing left, he pledges and loses their wife, Draupadi, to the invincible gambler.

Duryodhana decides to savour his victory by demanding that Draupadi arrive at the royal assembly, in order to be the slave of the Kauravas. Draupadi refuses, stating that Yudhishthira had no right to wager her in his gambling. A furious Duryodhana sends his brother Dushasana to forcibly drag Draupadi to his court.

Draupadi, exploding with anger, confronts the court. She demands justice and fairness. However, the elders remain frozen and indecisive, watching the violation of *dharma* as mute spectators. In his desperate bid to further humiliate her, Duryodhana asks Dushasana to publicly disrobe her in the open court. This is the most important episode in all performative traditions of the epic, exhibiting the display of power at its worst.

However, Dushasana is foiled by the magical intervention of Draupadi's godbrother, Krishna. Draupadi takes a vow that she will not be satisfied until the entire Kaurava clan is decimated. The elders of the warring cousins intervene at this point in an attempt to resolve the conflict. Dhritarashtra feels repentant and decides to restore the freedom, lost wealth and kingdom to the Pandavas. Duryodhana is very unhappy.

Shakuni and Karna convince Duryodhana, and through him, Dhritarashtra, to challenge Yudhishthira to a last game of dice. If Yudhishthira loses this game, the Pandavas and their wife Draupadi have to live in exile for twelve years and another year incognito. If their whereabouts are discovered in the one-year period of living incognito, then the Pandavas have to live in exile for another thirteen years.

Yudhishthira plays the game of dice and loses again. Though the Pandavas could have easily defeated their cousins in a battle and reclaimed their kingdom, Yudhishthira feels bound by his code of ethics, and the Pandavas begin their exile. It is agreed that should they successfully complete their period of exile, Duryodhana will return their kingdom to Yudhishthira.

The Twelve-year Exile

During the period of exile, the Pandavas listen to the stories of their ancestors and mirror the stories of kings who found themselves in similar predicaments. The stories are narrated by the many sages who visit the Pandavas in this period, and teach them the philosophy of yoga and inner transformation. Through these stories, the Pandavas confront the dilemmas in their own lives. Each of the Pandava brothers also undertakes intense spiritual practices to acquire celestial weapons.

This is also the period when they address their inner demons and confront their shadow selves. Each of them undertakes *tapas* (self-transforming austerities) to cleanse themselves of their shadow energies. It is only through *tapas* that they gain mastery over their minds. This allows them to embrace the full power of their gifts and wage a just war.

Agnyaatavaasa, Staying Incognito

After twelve years, Sahadeva is sent to look for the place in which they could live during the final year, when they have to be undiscoverable. He identifies the Virata kingdom as the perfect place to go incognito.

Yudhishthira becomes an advisor and gambling companion to the king; Bhima becomes a cook; Arjuna uses a boon given by his father Indra to change into a woman and becomes a dance teacher; Nakula becomes a stable hand; and Sahadeva, a cowherd. Draupadi becomes one of the queen's maids.

A year passes and the Pandavas and Draupadi successfully complete their thirteen years of exile. However, when they return to Hastinapura, Duryodhana goes back on his word and refuses to return their kingdom. A war becomes inevitable.

The War

The famous exposition of the Bhagavad Gita is placed at this juncture. Before the war begins, Arjuna tells Krishna to drive to the centre of the battlefield, and there, he puts down his weapons. Seeing his relatives, friends and teachers on the other side, Arjuna asks the fundamental question: what is right and what is wrong?

The dialogue explores many philosophical and pragmatic aspects of life. Krishna walks Arjuna through the meaning of life, our place in the universe, and the meaning of *dharma*. It is no longer a war for the kingdom, but a righteous one in which *dharma* prevails over *adharma*. Finally, Arjuna is asked to find his conviction and act for *dharma*.

A terrible war is fought, and good people from both sides lose their lives.

The war goes through many twists and tragic turns. The Pandavas discover too late that Karna was their eldest brother, and he dies a meaningless death. After the tragedy of Karna's death, Duryodhana remains the last warrior standing.

Finally, Duryodhana too is killed, by his arch-enemy, Bhima. Yudhishthira is crowned the king of the combined empire.

'The stories of Mahabharata have been the source of many myths in the subcontinent, and are used to understand war, peace and justice. The plurality in the storytelling and performative traditions of the epic provides a great insight into the layers of meaning the epic contains. It highlights the personal and humane aspects of the war for *dharma*, where each character struggles with their personal dilemmas and nuances of the social context that constrain them.

War then becomes an act of reinventing oneself, an act of creation rather than destruction. The concept of war in this sense does not simply manifest itself on the battlefield of Kurukshetra. It manifests in every character, and the conflict in each of their stories reshapes the entire narrative. Peace here holds a different meaning altogether, where it is not just the absence of armed conflict, but also a sense of equilibrium and self-realization.'[7]

The Mahabharata in Society

'We human beings are defined by stories. What are the narratives that define us, determine how we relate to the world and help us understand how we relate to others and finally to ourselves?'[8]

A.K. Ramanujan said, 'No Hindu ever reads the Mahabharata for the first time. And when he does get to read it, he doesn't usually read it in Sanskrit. As one such native, I know the Hindu epics, not as a Sanskritist (which I am not), but through Kannada and Tamil, mostly through the oral traditions. I've heard bits and pieces of it in a tailor's shop where a pundit used to regale us with Mahabharata stories and large sections of a sixteenth-century Kannada text; from brahman cooks in the house; from an older boy who loved to keep us spellbound with it (and the Kannada Arabian Nights which he was reading in the Oriental Library) after cricket, in the evenings, under a large neem tree in a wealthy engineer's compound; from a somewhat bored algebra teacher who switched from the binomial theorem to the problems of Draupadi and her five husbands.'[9]

The stories are already there in common knowledge. The stories of the epics are often alluded to in the local idioms and most people are familiar with them even without ever having read them. The Mahabharata has stories set in different parts of the Indian subcontinent, and local storytellers make it a point to refer to the tales

---

7 *Mahabharata of the Mind.*

8 Ibid.

9 Ramanujan, 'Repetition in the Mahabharata', in *Collected Essays of A.K. Ramanujan.*

set in their respective regions. Thus, the Mahabharata belongs to every part of the land.

The imagery and narratives of the Mahabharata have been retold in many forms over the years to reflect on the socio-political context at hand. The tradition continues through the storytelling traditions in various parts of India. For example, in Tamil Nadu, over 300 villages hold a Mahabharata festival every year during the winter months. The epic is performed as village rituals, narrated as a story and enacted as a theatre in the traditional Koothu form. 'It is fascinating to observe how an epic about a catastrophic fratricidal war could become the glue holding together communities with a sense of belonging over the ages.

These performances include multiple layers: the political, the social and the personal. As we listen to the epic, we reflect on who we actually are and embark on a journey of self-discovery.'[10]

---

10 *Mahabharata of the Mind.*

PART 1
Tales of Power from the Mahabharata

Overview

Peter Drucker, whose writings contributed to the philosophical and practical foundations of the modern business corporation has said, 'Culture eats strategy for breakfast.' But what is 'culture' and how do we shape it?

Let's try understanding culture using the analogy of a petri dish. When we give a blood sample to the lab for testing, a tiny sample is placed in a petri dish to do a culture test. The petri dish has a specific gel that allows only certain bacterial or viral cells to grow and kills the rest. Through this method, the lab can check if there is evidence of the proliferation of the intended organisms.

Every organization's culture is like a petri dish, and allows only particular behaviours to grow. Observing the culture closely, we can identify which behaviours it energizes and enlivens, and which it dampens.

A key aspect of organizational culture is the kind of heroism it nourishes. Every culture has an implicit and explicit idea of what heroism would mean in their context. Does your organization encourage heroism, or is such risk-taking not seen as a positive? Are employees encouraged to be heroes and bring about change?

As we have seen, the Pandavas are the archetypes of five seats of power that underpin leadership. Each leadership style evokes and empowers a particular psyche and nurtures a particular culture both unconsciously and consciously. Organizations grow and evolve when they learn to deploy appropriate types of power. Though an organization needs all five types of leadership, based on contextual challenges, it may need to emphasize a particular type of leadership.

For example, the power and passion of a Bhima archetype are very important in the start-up phase. As the organization matures, a Yudhishthira is needed to create order and scalability. It is not that a start-up has no structure or system, only that the Bhima spirit of adventure is the key to success at that stage. An organization that does not change its leadership based on its changing context will get thrown into the dustbin of history, no matter how successful they are currently.

The Pandava archetypes can help to understand the psychic energy and heroic potential of an individual. They also help to create an enabling culture in the organization. Although it may not be apparent, the five Pandavas work together as a team. They bring forth different skills and propensities. They argue, disagree and dissent, but ultimately act together for a common cause.

Are the Pandavas examples of perfection? Yes and no. The persona and behaviour of these heroes are not only human but also exemplary. You can see the whole unfolding of each their characters, from the seed to its manifestations: the patterns which get entrenched, the sorrow it creates and how they transform themselves through exile. However, they could overcome their shadow sides and discovered ways to transform themselves, while their counterpoints the Kauravas succumbed to the internal contradictions and vicious processes generated by a psyche ensconced in unexamined and inappropriate mindsets.

There are many stories with Yudhishthira, Bhima and Arjuna as the chief protagonists, where Nakula and Sahadeva are mostly supporting characters. Many folk stories on these two princes try to make up this lacuna. However, being prominently visible is not the only type of heroism that is critical for building organizations and institutions. In my study of human behaviour, I have found that not only do people create their own narratives, but these narratives also often reflect their own dilemmas and inner processes.

Krishna: Our Deepest Intelligence

The most famous episode in the Mahabharata – the Bhagavad Gita – shows Arjuna recounting his *dharma sankata* – the struggle to choose between alternatives that seem equally valid. Even after having been cheated of his rightful heritage and having suffered exile, Arjuna questions if the war is truly *dharmic*. Just before the start of the war, he places his chariot between the two armies – which symbolizes the pivot of balance between the two sides of his mind – and has an intense and deep dialogue with Krishna, the Divine Intelligence. It is here that Arjuna asks: 'In doing what I am doing, what am I really doing?'

Krishna helps Arjuna look closely at reality and his personal biases and, in doing so, clears his mind. He decides that he is indeed on the right path. This ability to introspect about the paradoxes of life and deeply examine the polarities, the pulls and the pushes of one's context, is an essential ability of a great hero.

Here, I consider Lord Krishna as one's deepest intelligence, which one can access through contemplative conversations and meditative self-reflection. This idea of God has been emphasized in the Upanishads through *mahaavakya*s (the great sayings). Thus, we are looking at Krishna not as a god but as Intelligence.

Can you access this deep reservoir of intelligence in your consciousness? One's ability to access this deep consciousness is the most prized capability in Indic thought. This is especially important to consider in a leadership context, where the responsibility for making meaning out of reality and taking decisions falls on the leader.

Contrasting the Pandavas and Kauravas

During the war, the Kauravas set up a fairly hierarchical structure, with Bhishma at the helm. Karna is never given a chance to fight beside him, and enters the battlefield only when Bhishma falls. This Kauravic approach to enforce clannish bonds and respect obligations can be clearly contrasted with the way of the Pandavas, where the will to act from *dharma* dictates one's participation.

During each day of the war, the Pandava army is headed by the person who has the right knowledge and capabilities for the given situation. The Mahabharata relates the discussions that are held among the Pandavas' council of elders before these choices are made.

The ways of the Pandavas reflect mutual respect and dignity, while the Kaurava way is about hierarchical structures, status-bound behaviours and rigidity. The Pandavas exemplify the importance of contextual intelligence, while the Kauravas get caught in their internal tensions and personal entrenchments.

We, too, can make *dharmic* and *adharmic* choices. No individual is just one Pandava type. Each of us is a unique combination of these five archetypes. Our particular life trajectory shapes us in specific ways. To make transformative changes in our lives, we must start by observing our behaviours, and then use our relationships, responses and habits as a mirror to ourselves. We must take a step backwards and inwards.

As we do this, the seeds in us unfold and manifest as we understand who we are. In this mindful and attentive observation of the whole inner process, a deeper Intelligence acts. We become what we were meant to be, and the best that we can be.

The Quick and Easy Pandava Profile

Let us now understand the regular practice that will help you deploy power during critical encounters at work. You must have a good idea of your propensity and its enablers and derailers to start with. We'll start with a thought experiment using a short tale. As you read the story, note down your responses on a piece of paper.

There is a young person who is very talented and leads a fairly successful life. As this person grows, he realizes that mere acquisition of skills is not enough without an insightful understanding of oneself. At a point like this in one's life, it is important to review one's narrative, reflect upon one's propensities and prepare for the journey ahead.

For the purpose of this story, we will assume that this person is you, and you have started the journey to discover yourself. As you start your journey, a gatekeeper to the new road pops up and asks you what you value most.

1. Structure, stability and predictability
2. Adventure and sensitivity
3. Service to others
4. Pursuit of knowledge
5. Deep enquiry into the way a system works

Think about the question and list the answers in order of preference.

As you walk further, you reach a crossroad. An old man sitting by the road asks, 'What excites you the most?'

1. Setting up procedures and rules for the efficient and predictable functioning of a system.
2. The excitement of a challenge and a strong desire to win.
3. Working with others, providing infrastructure to make them succeed in their work.
4. Delving into the unknown, acquiring skills and knowledge, engaging in intellectual conversations.
5. Making myself and those around me reflect and ask deep questions about themselves and about the system.

Think about the question and list the answers in order of preference.

Next, you meet a friend on the road. Your friend asks, 'How do you relate with power?' Do you believe in …

1. power and authority given by the system, which must be exercised in a responsible manner;
2. your own power and conviction;
3. the power of teams;
4. the power of knowledge;
5. power that lies in being able to remain centred, listen to the pulls and pushes of the situation and take balanced decisions?

Think about the question and list the answers in order of preference.

As you walk further, you ask yourself, 'What makes me dysfunctional?'

1. Without structure, I feel lost, so I compulsively impose structure.
2. I can become ruthless and create fear in others.
3. I find it very difficult to seek help for myself, and end up sacrificing much.
4. I suffer from analysis-paralysis.
5. I often get caught up with the difficulty of resolving the dilemmas and polarities that I see and get stuck with self-doubt.

Think about the question and list the answers in order of preference.

Now, ask yourself: 'What trips up my actions and distorts my intentions?'

1. I get frozen when emotions get triggered, and blindly follow precedence and what the rule book says.
2. I cover up my lack of foresight with an urgency for action and end up becoming reactive.
3. I hide my feeling of inadequacy to take charge and end up vanishing into the background.
4. I love abstraction and end up showing off my knowledge and complicating the issue.
5. I seek external anchors to take care of my inability to deal with self-doubt, without being discriminating about the real motives of the anchor.

Think about the question and list the answers in order of preference.

Now look at your answers.

You have by now figured that the answers represent the Five Seats of Power that we have discussed so far: Answer 1 is the propensity of Yudhishthira, or the Power of Order and Stability; 2 is Bhima, or Passion and Action; 3 is Nakula, or Compassion and Service; 4 is Sahadeva, or Curiosity and Knowledge; and 5 is Arjuna, or *Dharma Sankata* and Integration. (*Writing down your scores on a piece of paper will help you as you go forward).*

If you assign points to your answers – 5 points for first choice, 4 for second choice and so on – and add up the points, you will see a pattern. For example, you can get a 25-point score for answer 1 if that is your first preference in all the five questions. The lowest you will get is 5 points when a preference is the last in every case. Normally, one would assign varying preferences, but, on adding up the totals there will be a highest, a lowest and numbers in-between. Maybe answer 2 totals up to the highest, answer 1 is the next lower, answer 4 the next, and 3 and 5 bring up the tail end. Your profile suggests that you tend to respond with the Bhima in you, temper it with Yudhishthira's wisdom. Your lowest preference is for the Arjuna type of questioning. Having this profile with you will help you as you read through the book and use it as a way of reflecting on your own behavioural patterns. There is no right or wrong pattern, no ideal one either.

You would have chosen different responses as you encountered each situation. This is natural, as each of us is a unique combination of the five propensities.

You probably find that you favoured one of the five more than the others. This, too, is natural, as we tend to develop along one of several possibilities. This preference comes from a combination of our gifts as well as our life experiences.

Now, reflect on the critical events in your life and try to discern the pattern. Which is your most preferred power, and which is the one you like least? Which of these seems to flow authentically and powerfully and which ones make you feel blocked?

These thought experiments give you an idea of the configuration of heroic propensities unique to you. Respect this and nurture it.[1] You would have realized as you made the choices given in the story that all of us have all these propensities in us, albeit in varying and unique combinations.

The Pandavas and the Five Seats of Power

The Pandavas illustrate the great difficulty in making *dharmic* choices and how to resolve the dilemma between one's natural propensity and one's commitment to *dharmic* conduct. Each of them adopts a different way to make their choices and deploy their energy.

Yudhishthira: The Power of Order and Stability

When an individual acts out the Yudhishthira archetype, he experiences the tension between intuition and action. He has deep knowledge, is wise and has a comprehensive perspective based on tradition. He determines what is right and wrong based on what is laid down as law. But in relying on precedent and socially prescribed norms, a Yudhishthira archetype tends to suppress his own feelings and intuition. However wise he may be, in his actions, he will strive to go by the book.

When the Yudhishthira type masters his inner tensions and contradictions, the heroic potential of this archetype is unleashed. In this form, Yudhishthira becomes capable of entering spaces that are chaotic and lawless, displays tremendous self-discipline, and ushers in stability and safety.

Bhishma represents the counterpoint of this archetype. The Bhishma archetype tends to get entrenched in a rigid form of this power in a manner that lacks contextual intelligence. In making a choice in the

---

1 For a more accurate reading of your pattern, visit our website www.quinnergy.com and take the questionnaire called the Pandava Profile. To know more about the questionnaire, see 'Pandava Mandala' at https://taoleadershipacademy.com/program.php?p=pm, accessed on 14 February 2022.

current moment of truth, he does not make an active choice but falls back on a programmed set of choices, confined by the tasks that had been conceived in a different context.

Bhishma aims to be a model of perfection and is coached and trained to behave in appropriate, prescribed ways. In his aim to be beyond reproach in his actions, he does not break prescriptive boundaries, even in the face of adversities. He prefers to be respected rather than be seen as the one who breaks tradition.

Bhima: The Power of Passion and Action

When the tension between the inner evocation and the search for appropriate action is resolved in *dharmic* ways, the true warrior emerges. Bhima epitomizes passionate and energetic action. He is the Pandava who embodies this archetype.

The Bhima archetype is a person of great strength and lives passionately. He loves deeply and expresses himself without inhibition. When provoked into action in the face of a crisis, he can respond with extraordinary strength. He can be relentless and completely focused on overcoming danger.

However, the Bhima archetype has to resolve the tension between his passion and forethought. Strategizing and planning are not his strong points, and this could make a Bhima archetype very emotional, easily provoked, reactive and impulsive. When a Bhima archetype learns to temper his passion and energy with forethought, he can be successful.

Bhima's counterpoint is Duryodhana. He disowns reasoning when he is consumed by his passions. He does not have the ability to set goals and direct himself purposefully, unless triggered by his antagonism. He is ruled by impulses and reacts with rebellion when he is thwarted.

Nakula: The Power of Compassion and Service

When an individual resolves the tension between his deep compassion for his community and the unrelenting demands of the context, the Healer archetype emerges. Nakula epitomizes the attitude of sacrifice and service to the system.

The Nakula archetype acts on the premise that the system he belongs to is far more important than himself. He does what is required in a necessary situation, not because he is invited to do so but because of an inner drive to uphold the system. The keyword for the Nakula propensity is facilitation. His focus on serving the system causes him to sacrifice himself for the system, and he ignores his individual feelings in the process.

In this sense, he is selfless. He becomes the invisible infrastructure builder for the system, but is not recognized for his contribution. He is the much-desired team player who is ready to supplement and complement others.

To be successful, a Nakula archetype has to anchor himself in his compassion without becoming self-effacing. He can then live for the system instead of sacrificing himself and burning out like the proverbial candle. He does not shy away from confrontation and also does not absorb the pain of others in a dysfunctional way.

Gandhari is the counterpoint of Nakula. The Gandhari archetype fragments herself from her feelings of betrayal and devotes herself to the task of being an obedient wife. In action, she is superb, very efficient and totally in command. Her own aspirations are never apparent. She does what is required in the situation. Though she does not seek benefit for the self, she hopes that the family she sacrifices so much for will recognize her contribution. She holds her martyrdom stoically.

Sahadeva: The Power of Curiosity and Knowledge

When the tension between one's need for certainty and the demand for action is resolved, the Hermit archetype emerges. Sahadeva epitomizes this archetype. He limits his interaction with the environment to the minimum. He is a keen observer and the theoretician of the system.

The Sahadeva archetype is committed to observation and insight. He is acutely aware of reality and is a databank of knowledge. He can intuitively understand how the future might unfold. However, he does not impact the world using these resources, unless invited. He does not come alive in the situation and is content to remain a spectator.

If a Sahadeva archetype can find a way to harmonize his intuitive insights with his keen observation and analysis, he can become a great strategist and a seeker who enquires deeply and comes up with innovative ways of engaging with the world.

Shakuni is the counterpoint of this identity. He nurses a deep grouse and fulfils his own agenda by becoming the most trusted confidant of Duryodhana. He uses his insight and acuity of understanding to manipulate the situation for the benefit of himself and the Kauravas.

Arjuna: The Power of *Dharma Sankata* and Integration

The four archetypes we have explored so far represent the four pillars on which the social system[2] depends in order to flourish, but it perpetuates status quo. Yudhishthira represents the power of order; Bhima, the power of passion; Nakula, the power of service; and Sahadeva, the power of knowledge. They represent internal adjustments that the system makes constantly to ensure that it functions efficiently and effectively every day.

They continuously monitor the organizational functioning and act to maintain the systemic continuity. While these four propensities are essential for proper functioning, they can only uphold the present, not the future.

Arjuna represents the archetype of the questioner-integrator. He stands between his inner evocations and the emerging context, and between compassion and curiosity, and balances the four. He is the one who faces the *dharma sankata*.

The Arjuna archetype has to find the fine balance between the choice for the self or the system he belongs to. Arjuna also has to decide which

2 The word 'system' is used to refer to any organized group of people; it could be a family, a small firm, a large organization, or a community. These systems will have their own purpose, ways of communicating and structuring themselves. However, the archetypes we are examining are found in all successful societies across the world. They have also been valorized in world mythology.

system he belongs to: the affiliative or the rational, the given or the emerging. When he resolves this tension, the Arjuna archetype becomes the invincible warrior who acts from deep conviction and contextual awareness guided by Divine Intelligence.

Arjuna's counterpoint is Karna, who is the mightiest of the sons of Kunti. He displays courage and integrity, despite being shamed by the system for his low birth. His relentless search is for legitimacy, for belonging to his true family. He struggles to express his true self and resolves his ambivalence through complete surrender to the one who offers compensation for this painful inner search.

In the process, he gives up his ability to use his vast resources to confront the system and transform it. He becomes a pawn in the hands of the person who affirms him. Karna's actions and choices then become inappropriate and destructive, both to the self and to the system. His enormous generosity and devotion get misplaced.

Join the Discussions

I will now share some discussions I had with some business leaders. We took up stories from the Mahabharata that resonated with us, and reflected upon them from our own perspectives. We went into what the stories mean to us, what they remind us of and some examples of managers who, in our experience, reflect these propensities.

The three individuals who joined me in these discussions are:

Shruti Goswami[3]: A much sought-after leadership coach, psychotherapist and organizational consultant with decades of experience.

Samir Raman: An entrepreneur who founded a start-up in the Silicon Valley after a very successful career in IT and is now in the agricultural sector.

Randhir Kumar: One of the pioneers of the IT industry in India, he was part of the top management of a very successful IT company; he is presently an angel investor mentoring start-ups.

---

3 The names mentioned here are all fictional.

Each one of us relates to the Mahabharata differently, and it is therefore natural that as you read our discussions, you will have differing points of view. I request you to join the conversation by making your notes.

At the end of the discussion for each Pandava, I encourage you to write your own version of the Pandava. To get the most out of it, this must be seen as an opportunity to discover the hero within and not as an external 'objective' debate that serves no real purpose in self-discovery.

SECTION 1: Yudhishthira, the King

Yudhishthira represents the King archetype. He is the judge and the administrator. A Yudhishthira archetype anchors stability and certainty and provides the foundation and solidity essential to building an organization and administering it efficiently. Yudhishthira's motto is Order and Predictability. He tends to downplay and hold back his own feelings and intuitions. This tendency to value stability over dynamism limits the organization's risk-taking ability.

Story 1: The Patient and Practical Yudhishthira

More than a year has passed since the Pandavas began their exile.

One day, Draupadi confronts Yudhishthira and complains about the kind of life they are leading when compared to Duryodhana, who is enjoying not only his own privileges but also their share of the kingdom.

'Oh, just look at the way your brothers are living,' she laments. 'Bhima is in a pitiable condition, Arjuna has now lost his beauty, Nakula and Sahadeva are so dull. Aren't you angry, seeing this unfairness?'

Yudhishthira makes no response.

Looking into Yudhishthira's eyes, she continues, 'We are all kings, and I am a queen, but how we have been cheated! What is rightfully ours has been snatched away through deceit. Doesn't anger rise in you when you think of this? The mere thought of Duryodhana should make your blood boil.'

Yudhishthira remains silent.

She sighs, 'What is the point in reminding you about our situation when you give no response? Much like forgiveness, kings should also feel angry at the right time and place. If we do not do that, forgiveness is taken as a weakness. People do not respect their kings for not showing anger and forgiveness at the right hour. Where is the anger that will fuel you to go and face Duryodhana?'

Finally, Yudhishthira responds.

'Anger destroys mankind and does not lead to prosperity,' he says. 'It is only when we conquer anger that we can be prosperous. Do you mean to say that everyone who is angry at someone should go about killing? If this is how one releases anger, then what is to become of the world? Our elders and texts have advised against reacting in anger.'

He quotes from Kashyapa: '"Forgiveness is dharma, *forgiveness is sacrifice, forgiveness is the Vedas, forgiveness is* shruthi, *forgiveness is the truth and forgiveness is the ultimate".'*

'I must act once I harmonize anger through forgiveness, which is the dharmic way,' Yudhishthira says. 'As a king, I must not react in anger and that is why I am not going after Duryodhana. Even though we are in terrible misery and trouble, continuing to walk on the path of dharma *is the only way out.'*

An agitated Bhima speaks up.

'You talk of so many ideals and virtues,' he argues, 'but I say we should go and sort this out once and for all. After all, we are Kshatriya warriors, ready for a battle any time. It is strange that you talk like a Brahmin, conjuring up theories of forgiveness. You forget that we have Kshatriya blood running through our veins. Your Kshatriya dharma *should push you to go and fight to retrieve what is rightfully ours.'*

Yudhishthira calmly replies, 'As a Kshatriya, I understand my dharma. *I stand by my word and promise. I stood in the durbar and decided to play the game of dice knowing fully well that we could lose. Yes, that is destiny, but having made my promise I must honour it.'*

Bhima counters, 'It was an unfair game.'

Yudhishthira responds, 'Well, if you feel that it was unfair, why did you not speak up during the game? None of you protested. Do you think that I would not have listened to you if you spoke up? Of course I would have. Bhima, today there are many kings who swear by Duryodhana's power and will fight against us. We are outnumbered. We are sure to get killed, and I, as a king, cannot allow us to be foolish. People like Drona, Bhishma and others are enjoying their status and luxury because of Duryodhana. I know we will have to fight them one day, but not today. With our limited support and resources, it is foolish to fight them now.'

Reflections on Yudhishthira

RANDHIR: I found that Yudhishthira talks sense when he admits that they are outnumbered with no allies and resources to fight. To expand on this point a bit more: if Yudhishthira decides to fight the Kauravas immediately, they would not garner any support as that would break the promise of exile. To not keep a promise is *adharmic*. After twelve years and *agnyaatavaasa*, there is a better chance for them to gather support. It is very practical at one level.

RAGHU: I will go a bit further and say that, usually, the biggest mistake one makes is to think that strategy means to act. In the story, Yudhishthira clearly interprets strategy to imply that it is the time to wait and not act. Timing is key.

SAMIR: A sales head usually goes excitedly to the CEO, saying that the market is booming, competitors are aggressive and are closing deals, and so it is imperative to move forward. But a strategic CEO questions this: 'We can jump into the game too. But do we have the right infrastructure? Do we have the right technology to deliver? If we are incapable of delivering on our promises, then our reputation goes for a toss. That is worse for us.'

RANDHIR: I have an example of the benefits of waiting. One of the companies I am advising is consulting in the social sector. When the CSR law was passed in India, a whole new set of opportunities opened up. Many start-ups came up to cater to this sudden demand. There was huge pressure on the CEO from investors as well as employees to move quickly.

But the CEO advised caution and abstained from venturing into this new territory. He felt it was too soon, since the clarifications on the law were just coming up. If they got it wrong, it would be a huge loss to their reputation. They decided to move into the space three years later. They spent one year building the offering and are now winning clients quite rapidly.

Patience does have a virtue. The concept of first-mover advantage makes many organizations rush into new areas without assessing their contexts and internal capabilities. Companies that wait patiently can at times create long-lasting impact and steady growth.

SAMIR: I had a similar experience with a client who was looking to acquire a certain new technology. Our competitors were offering a price 40 per cent lower than ours, which was quite surprising. There was a lot of pressure to clinch the deal. During the discussion, we realized that it would be suicidal if we matched the price. We also understood that it would be suicidal for the other vendor as well. We decided to let go of the deal at that time. But we did strengthen our capability and waited for the customer to come back to us. Even though the entire implementation team was quite relieved, I did get a lot of flak from sales for not clinching the deal. In a few months, not only did we get the order from the customer, but we also got many more orders from this customer later.

RAGHU: In a long war, there are two strategies, either to lay siege on the enemy and wear them down, or to build clear defences that cannot be breached. A true Yudhishthira capability is drawing a clear boundary and then sticking to it while strengthening the forces behind those boundaries. The examples shared are cases of clear boundaries being drawn and held.

Yudhishthira cautions against anger, but also against reactionary and bravado behaviour. This marks a critical difference between a powerful Yudhishthira and someone hiding behind laws and books without being aware of himself or the context.

SHRUTI: A powerful Yudhishthira is not devoid of feelings or cut off from the context. He or she knows how to hold feelings in check and be patient, even if it means waiting for thirteen years.

RAGHU: Yes, I agree. However, one must not confuse the heroic holding of one's anger or impulsivity with the cowardice shown when one uses lofty statements as a proxy for inaction. These stories bring out a powerful Yudhishthira in action with an anchorage in the current context.

RANDHIR: True. If one can hold these propensities in a certain balance, one is creating a space for a voice of wisdom to speak rather than simply being an emotionless judge.

SHRUTI: A person who does not have the emotional maturity or patience would use these arguments. It just seems that Yudhishthira was in touch with the wise voice within, and didn't let his shadow take over. Waiting for the right time to act does not equal inaction.

RAGHU: Exactly. One must remember that while we talk about archetypes, each of them has dysfunctional aspects when they let their fears speak through the victim. A Yudhishthira who cannot get in touch with the danger of a situation will simply become a hollow vessel with no wisdom. He will keep quoting precedence without any sensitivity to understand the situation.

SAMIR: People think Yudhishthira was just a righteous king who followed the rules. He understood that it was his righteousness that helped gather support. He understood the power of structure and legitimacy clearly. He understood *dharma* not only as a concept but also contextually.

There was an incident during the war when the Pandavas were not able to deal with Drona. Knowing how much Drona loved his son, Ashwathama, they gave an elephant the same name, and then killed the elephant. Krishna convinced Yudhishthira to tell Drona that Ashwathama had died.

Yudhishthira understood why he had to do it and did not hold on to his righteousness. He told Drona that Ashwathama had died, softly muttering *the elephant*. Holding on to an absolute frame of truth devoid of contextual intelligence is counterproductive.

RAGHU: Let me give you another example. I worked with a foreman who was very firm with his role boundaries. The sales team would continuously put pressure on him to deliver products either immediately or before the agreed schedule. He would always refuse, saying, 'Once a timeline has been agreed on, I won't deliver before it's due. But if there is a delay of even a minute after that, I am answerable.'

Although the products were ready much before the due date, he would tell me, 'If you keep agreeing to the salespeople's demands, your boundaries are violated, and later, they can even put pressure on you to give up quality requirements just because the customer needs it urgently. So, one should be very careful.'

RAGHU: The dialogue between Bhima, Draupadi and Yudhishthira is very critical. Bhima is impulsive and passionate about getting into action, and Draupadi is casting doubts over Yudhishthira's manhood and capabilities as a king. But Yudhishthira is completely anchored, not giving way to guilt or shame. The dysfunctional side of a Yudhishthira plays out only when he is unable to be in touch with his emotional sensitivity. The ability to play the role with full sensitivity is the real power of a Yudhishthira.

RANDHIR: Yudhishthira roles are complex because they must go by the book and, at one level, have to be very impersonal. It is not so easy because they hold a lot of tension and emotions inside. As they are acting on behalf of the system, Yudhishthiras have to go beyond their emotional pulls, and be dispassionate and fair.

SAMIR: It seems that a Yudhishthira imperative is essential for change management and to help organizations navigate through the changing context with steadiness and grace. The right balance between taking a risky step, and building stability and certainty is essential for progress. This calls for sagacity and wisdom.

SHRUTI: Strong organizations built with a view of long-term sustainability are created by Yudhishthiras. Unfortunately, this often goes unrecognized, whereas the aggressive entrepreneurial style is often recognized. However, the latter style may or may not be able to help build a powerful, long-lasting organization.

RAGHU: Yudhishthira builds the capacity for predictable and concerted action. Institutions are built by making people feel valued, and by making sure they remain committed all the way. Capacity means to create policies and operating procedures, and ensure that every process is done smoothly.

SHRUTI: In the story, Yudhishthira was very much in touch with his Nakula side in terms of the feelings expressed by the other Pandavas, his Arjuna side in seeing the entire context and their position rather than acting impulsively, and his Bhima side, which is expressed in the war later.

RAGHU: You are bringing in a very interesting point for us to keep in mind as we reflect on the Pandava propensities. It's that we have all the five propensities in us, albeit in different proportions. We have to be alive to them and deploy them appropriately. There is a dominant propensity, but one has to be aware of the others as well. For a theatre performance to have integrity and vibrancy, everyone involved must be attentive to each other. Not just the players on the stage, but the people operating the lights, the helpers backstage, the make-up persons and so on, have to be in complete harmony.

SHRUTI: If Yudhishthiras are not alive to other propensities, they can also easily hide behind the veil of rules and policies as justification for inaction.

RAGHU: Also, one will be in trouble if one holds other propensities in contempt. When this happens, one struggles to engage with a person who has a different dominant propensity.

RANDHIR: I have faced situations in which, despite having a dominant Yudhishthira propensity, I must act and be a go-getter like Bhima. What do I do when I realize that I am not in touch with my Bhima propensity? Here, I can get someone to do the job instead. When I am self-aware about my propensities and the level of excellence that I am not capable of, I get someone else to do the job instead.

RAGHU: That's right. Everyone has all five propensities. Some are more dominant than others. You need to value the configuration of propensities and once you recognize it, you must nurture it. At the same time, if a Yudhishthira always keeps himself under control and doesn't give in to temptation, he will die of boredom.

It was important in the story for Yudhishthira to give in to the temptation of gambling. Else, he would have never known this ability to break boundaries and discover new possibilities. Of course, you must also be careful to not gamble like a madman without being able to consolidate or pull back! The balance between a strict and uptight streak and an extreme bravado streak is important and is the source of power.

RANDHIR: Allow me to narrate the story of a company; let's call it 'Mobile Unlimited'. This company had a near-monopoly domination in its market space, a sector that was growing at 100 per cent annually. The company was led by its brilliant and very aggressive co-founder and CEO, Arun Kumar.

As the company was growing, they hired someone called Rakshit as a COO to help streamline operations. Rakshit came in to find an energetic company, but where most of the employees did not even know to whom they reported. New products and ideas were bubbling everywhere, but there was a crisis every other day due to the instability of newer products being delivered to the market.

Many other competitors had started coming in and taking market share from the company. This was leading to constant fights between the technology and sales teams. After one of the crises – in which a newly released product was failing in the field – Arun, along with the sales head, put the blame on Rakshit. The customer was ready to shift to a competitor who was ready with a replacement.

Rakshit listened quietly. He then pointed out that the competitor had twenty people working on that one product, whereas Mobile Unlimited could spare only half a person. Their CTO was totally dedicated to that one product, whereas Arun's CTO had to look after twenty products. Rakshit insisted that they could not let competitors define their strategy. Though Arun was not very happy about it, some key people agreed with Rakshit and decided to focus only on five key products that were getting them 90 per cent of the revenues.

In the next six months, there was a turnaround, and no competitor could come even close to Mobile Unlimited in terms of scale and performance. The company was generating so much cash that after one year, they could break into international markets.

RAGHU: In this case, the organization was able to listen to the importance of the Yudhishthira propensity and realize that this was an important power to internalize without losing the Bhima energy.

Story 2: Who Should Lead?

The great war of Mahabharata was to last only for eighteen days, and by the end of it, the victor had to be ascertained. Till the last day, however, Duryodhana's side wasn't defeated.

Yudhishthira and Bhima engage in a conversation to decide who should be the leader of the army on the eighteenth day. Bhima nominates himself, citing his need for revenge on Duryodhana, and that he should be the one who defeats him.

Both go to Krishna and explain their decision to him. Krishna remains silent all along and thinks deeply. After much thought, Krishna disagrees with their decision and suggests that Yudhishthira be the leader. Yudhishthira and Bhima are confused. Yudhishthira asks Krishna, 'Why me? I am not even a great fighter like Bhima. Why not make Arjuna the leader? Isn't he better than me?'

Krishna answers, 'Ending a war is not the same as escalating it. To end a war, one needs a clear understanding of the boundaries that must not be crossed. This kind of understanding of assertion is there only in you, Yudhishthira. Thus, I ask you to lead the war.'

RANDHIR: What a beautiful story! If my understanding is correct, what Krishna is saying is that Bhima can win battles, but only Yudhishthira can end the war – and they are not the same thing, is that correct?

RAGHU: Yes, Bhima can only keep fighting and escalating it without knowing how to end it. Here, 'end' also means winning decisively for peace. One has to build a future after a war.

SAMIR: So, that is the tough part because the enemies who fought you have to accept your leadership after they have been defeated.

RAGHU: Yes, you must be respectful towards them, help them heal and move on.

SHRUTI: These are very critical qualities, especially during mergers and acquisitions or during significant change.

RANDHIR: This reminds me of an incident from my past. There was a company called Technosys that had ambitious plans to grow and go global. The company was growing at a breakneck speed. Many companies had started implementing the Capability Maturity Model (CMM) for software development designed by Carnegie Mellon to establish credibility. The Technosys CEO, Naveen, believed that they should do it too.

In his monthly meeting with senior management, Naveen recommended that they go for the highest level of CMM. There was quite an uproar. Everyone pushed back, saying that they are already stretched managing the fast growth and that there is absolutely no bandwidth to do something as significant as implementing CMM.

Naveen asked Patrick, the head of sales, what he was seeing in the market. Patrick mentioned that some customers had told him that most of Technosys's closest competitors were going in for CMM certification, and might already have a head start.

Sanjay, the head of corporate strategy, offered to take on the responsibility, as he also felt that there was no other option. Since he had a cross-sectional view across all the functions, he was in a good position to define what needed to be done. Naveen thanked Samir for his offer but asked him to work under another person for this initiative.

It was Deepak, an old-timer heading one of the smaller business units, who was asked to lead the initiative. Everyone was surprised, because while Deepak was considered a hardworking manager, he was not necessarily one of the brightest. However, Naveen realized that this initiative would need Deepak's resilience, his ability to stand his ground and insist on conformance without offending people.

Sanjay was aghast at having to work under someone who he felt was significantly inferior to him intellectually. Naveen explained his logic to him, saying that what was required was an unflagging focus on execution to run this initiative. At the same time the initiative needed intelligence, spark and energy, which Sanjay could bring. Naveen stressed that all these qualities are required if they want to not only catch up with competitors but also go ahead of them. Sanjay reluctantly bought into the logic and agreed to work under Deepak.

When they faced huge resistance across the organization, Sanjay saw how Deepak could overcome the resistance through his sheer doggedness. He started respecting Deepak's different style of leadership and its relevance in the current context.

It was mainly due to Deepak's unwavering focus that Technosys became the first company among its peers to achieve CMM certification, despite starting late.

RAGHU: This story highlights how important it is for organizations to recognize situations that require order. People dislike such processes, thus making the job very difficult for people who are entrusted with this job. And that is why you need Yudhishthira, to respect boundaries and create an order even while ending the war.

SHRUTI: I think one of the greatest qualities of Yudhishthira is that he understands what needs to be done and then sticks to it without wavering. To remove the uncertainties, putting things in order is Yudhishthira's forte, and he keeps persisting with that.

SAMIR: Once, Company X was getting acquired by a much larger company, Company Y. The business head of the acquirer was thrilled at the acquisition, as it meant that he would have a much larger team. He was told by his boss to sit with the CEO of Company X and come up with a post-acquisition organizational structure. If the structure could not be decided upon within forty-eight hours, the acquisition would not take place.

It was quite a bold stand. Most acquisitions fail as talent from the acquired company is treated shabbily and they leave, taking the customers with them. In this case, after exhaustive discussions, the organizational structure was decided upon, and the merger process was smooth.

RANDHIR: This is like Krishna advising that it needed Yudhishthira to end the war. The leader realized that the acquisition process, which often goes through acrimonious exchanges and turf battles, is not a win–lose situation. It is the beginning of a new phase of collaboration. Unless this post-acquisition team was in place, the acquisition was bound to fail.

RAGHU: Many times, organizations sadly do not understand the criticality of creating order once the battle is over. I was once invited to consult for an organization that had been created through a merger. Years after the merger, I could walk into the manager's room and guess quite accurately which part of the former entity he had come from!

The two sides of the new partnership never gave up their old identities. Instead of a dialogue that would enable the emergence of a new way, the company became a battleground with each side trying to prove that their methods were better.

SHRUTI: This is a very important aspect that needs to be understood by entrepreneurs who usually do not value the gifts of a Yudhishthira propensity during organization building. 'Yudhishthiras are boring and dull while Bhimas and Sahadevas are creative and innovative' is not the narrative that will help companies go far.

Story 3: Yudhishthira and Gambling

'I do covet the prosperity and the wealth of the Pandavas,' laments Duryodhana in the court. 'Yet such wealth is not mine, and I doubt if I could ever possess them. Every day I see their wealth grow and our prosperity diminishing; so how shall I be happy, my father, my king?'

'I shall play with my dice and win for you the prosperity of the Pandavas that you so seek,' Shakuni proclaims proudly.

'Father, let Shakuni win it for me. He is an expert at rolling dice,' urges Duryodhana.

'O Prince, your way is fraught with dire consequences and sure to bring ruin,' cautions Dhritarashtra.

'Dice has been in use since ancient times. Without weapons and destruction, without any loss of life, it will open the gates of heaven and bring us the prosperity that will make us equal to the Pandavas,' beams Duryodhana.

'Your words will not do us good; your actions will bring us destruction. You shall repent in future, but do what is agreeable to you,my son. Vidura, please go to Indraprastha and invite the Pandavas to a game of dice,' says the king.

Vidura meets Yudhishthira in Indraprastha, and after exchanging pleasantries, says, 'It is the king's wish that you come and play a friendly game of dice.'

'Gambling will lead to quarrel, and knowing this, none may play it. What is your advice?' asks Yudhishthira.

'It will indeed bring harm. I tried to dissuade the king but failed. Do what you think is good, O King!' responds a dejected Vidura.

'Who apart from the deceitful sons of Dhritarashtra would be present to gamble?'

'There would be many, and the chief among them will be Shakuni.'

'From what you say, some of the most deceitful gamblers will be present along with Shakuni. I am unwilling to gamble, unless I am challenged and invited to do so by Shakuni himself. If challenged, I shall gamble and that's my vow. Fate is the master of the universe. It will show the path eventually.'

Saying this to Vidura, Yudhishthira goes ahead to make arrangements for departure the very next day.

The next morning, Yudhishthira enters the magnificent hall with his brothers. After greetings and salutations, the Pandavas take their seats.

Shakuni approaches them.

'Welcome, Yudhishthira. The assembly is packed, and we have been waiting for you. Roll the dice and play with us.'

'Deceitful gambling is a sin. Do not defeat by deceit like a cruel man, for it is best to win by righteous means,' warns Yudhishthira.

'It is with victory in mind that an educated man approaches the ignorant,' Shakuni replies. 'A man skilled in weaponry approaches one who is not, so also a man who is skilled in the art of dice approaches one who is not. I approach you the same way. If for the fear of losing, you call me deceitful, then you may desist from playing.'

Challenged thus, Yudhishthira says, 'I shall not withdraw, for fate is all powerful.'

Yoked by the power of fate, Yudhishthira lays out his first stake. 'Here is my beautiful necklace of fine pearls, threaded with gold, churned from the depths of the ocean.'

Duryodhana matches the stake and Shakuni plays. The chain is lost.

'I have beautiful jars, each filled with a thousand gold coins. My treasury is filled with many such jars and many more filled with silver and gems. I stake my treasury thus,' says Yudhishthira.

Duryodhana matches the stake, and Yudhishthira loses the treasury.

'My royal chariot, by which I arrived, is equal to a thousand chariots,' says Yudhishthira. 'It is decorated with tiger skin, adorned with precious gems and drawn by eight steeds that are as white as moonbeams. I stake it.'

The chariot is lost to Shakuni's throw of dice.

A thousand elephants, chariots with steeds and charioteers are pledged and lost; 10,000 dragons with draught animals are lost; 60,000 of his select best warriors are pledged and they too are lost.

Yudhishthira pledges 400 of the most precious jewels encased in sheets of iron and copper, and loses them too. Innumerable cows, sheep and goats that graze across the kingdom are staked, and Yudhishthira loses them all.

'I bet cities, towns, villages and all the houses in them that belong to me,' says Yudhishthira. He loses to Shakuni again.

'This fair-coloured Nakula, with mighty arms and broad shoulders, the one who is dear to me, I stake,' proclaims Yudhishthira.

'Consider him won,' says Shakuni. He rolls the dice to claim the stake.

'My dear Sahadeva, who administers justice and has a reputation for learning, I stake him.' The evil Shakuni rolls the dice and wins the other twin.

'I know the two sons of Madri are dear to you. Are your other two brothers even dearer? Is that why you have not staked them?' jeers Duryodhana.

'Do not try to cause disunion among us,' Yudhishthira says, glaring at his cousin. 'Like a boat he will take us to the shore of victory in the sea of battle: this Arjuna I stake, though he does not deserve to be staked.'

'The foremost wielder of the bow is now ours,' says Shakuni, winning again. 'You now have only Bhima, the last of your wealth. Stake him too!'

'I shall play with Bhimasena, our leader in battles, my illustrious brother, matchless in prowess, foremost wielder of mace in the world and the crusher of foes.'

'He is now ours, just as all your wealth is ours now. Is there anything else that you could wager?'

'I alone am left, and I wager myself too,' says a defeated Yudhishthira. 'If I lose, I shall do all that one is bound to.'

'I have won. You have lost yourself like a sinful man. How could you wager yourself when you still possess wealth that belongs to you? Stake that which is dear to you – the princess of Panchala – and win yourself back, O King!' sneers Shakuni.

'I shall play with you,' complies Yudhishthira, 'staking Draupadi of slender waist, beautiful and fragrant as a lily. One who is soft at heart and

possesses a wealth of beauty and virtue, one who is compassionate and of sweet speech. I stake her.'

The assembly is agitated, and tears roll down the eyes of many. Bhishma, Drona and Kripa sit tight, perspiring. Vidura sits with his head in his hands. Karna, Dushasana and others laugh aloud. Dhritarashtra, unable to contain his excitement, keeps asking, 'Is the stake won? Is the stake won?'

Shakuni rolls the dice.

Draupadi is lost.

SAMIR: This scene is key to the entire epic. Yudhishthira, the king, loses his composure and keeps on increasing the stakes in the hope of winning everything back. I always wondered, what happened to Yudhishthira – couldn't he see the trap he was walking into repeatedly?

RAGHU: These are the shadow sides of the Yudhishthira propensity. A leader who believes in order and the rule of law gets pulled into gambling, where the outcome is defined by chance. It is at the other end of predictability. He is unable to respond adequately to unexpected outcomes and gets caught in the vortex.

The biggest difference between heroic action and *asuric* action – when one is caught in the shadow of one's propensity – is the state of emotion one operates from. Here we see Yudhishthira getting caught up in fear, rather than operating from the state of equanimity (*shaantham*). We see this behaviour in ourselves when we become rigid, holding ourselves to strict discipline. A part of us yearns to break the shackles and be uninhibited.

It is important to act from a space of *shaantham*. Once one loses equanimity, one will simply act in ways that are self-destructive. In the story, we see Yudhishthira losing a sense of perspective and thus failing to act from his highest heroic potential. Losing one's mind under stress and allowing the propensities or the shadow archetypal energies to take over one's life is disastrous. A leader who believes in order and predictability can freeze when faced with severely unexpected situations.

Why would someone with the Yudhishthira archetype agree to gamble in the first place? It is because no person is entirely one archetype.

The Yudhishthira archetype may have the propensity for predictability; however, he also has some amount of spontaneity inside him. The role he has to play does not allow for this spontaneity to be fulfilled. As a release, it can lead to the leader taking sudden high risks, which if not operated from a place of *shaantham* can lead to ruinous results. History is replete with leaders whose one such action has led to their downfall and negated all that they have achieved.

The Yudhishthira archetype has to accept that, as a leader, he is more than his image. His accepting the invite is symbolic of capitulating to his disowned side. In the epic, Yudhishthira agreeing to the terms of exile was his way of accepting that retreat, reflection and deep inner work was required at that stage of his life.

It was no coincidence that in the one year of living incognito, Yudhishthira's primary role was to play dice with a king – but this time as a servant, without the power he otherwise was blessed with due to his birth. This was required for him to accept his compulsion but indulge in it in a manner in which he is able to exert control on the choices he makes.

A journey of transformation can start only when we get in touch with our subconscious needs, stop living in denial and accept our vulnerabilities. *Agnyaatavaasa* is a metaphor for getting completely lost in your shadow side such that you are unrecognizable even to yourself, because you are exploring spaces you were living in denial of – the spaces that may not be rational or legitimate, but have a compulsive energy locked up in them. And from that, you emerge knowing yourself and your shadows, and in control of the choices you make.

RANDHIR: One can argue that Yudhishthira could have walked out once he realized he was being trapped.

RAGHU: Walking out would have been smart, and the Pandavas would still have half the kingdom. But when will they confront the inner demon that showed up? How will they dissolve the shadow energy and transform it? They will know this only when they can confront a life-and-death situation, and they act with pure, undiluted, undistorted power. In the intensity of the challenge, no compulsive energies rise up unbidden.

SHRUTI: Why did the other Pandavas and Draupadi stay silent and not question Yudhishthira when he accepted the challenge?

RAGHU: All brothers have explicitly accepted the leadership of Yudhishthira. They are in it together. They accept Yudhishthira's judgement. We ought to look at this episode as a beautiful drama where, in spite of one's better judgement or better sense, the compulsive energies that lie unexamined take over.

SHRUTI: I still do not understand why the brothers remained quiet.

RAGHU: In my experience, when I had accepted the authority of a senior and trusted him fully after they had been fairly consistent in making good decisions over time, I found myself surprised and almost paralysed when they acted in irrational ways. I had become dependent on my chosen leader and suddenly had to find my feet!

In the story, each of them accepts Yudhishthira as their leader and follows him implicitly. In a way, they disowned their decision-making capability and delegated it upwards to Yudhishthira. And thus, they were caught in a double bind. If the structure requires me to accept someone as a leader, then his decisions must be respected. What do I do when the leader takes a decision that is not correct, as per my understanding? If I act from my own sense of indignation or doubt, I disrespect the system. But if I don't, I disregard my own intuition. It is a double bind – I am damned if I do and damned if I don't.

Organizations do not want any surprises, only excellent implementation. However, when one gets into leadership positions, the behaviours that had yielded success for a decade or more become one's limitations. What does the manager do? If he tries something new, he will have to abandon his formula for success. If he does not, his latent capabilities will never unfold.

At these thresholds, you have to discover willpower. Only then will you find the courage to give up old habits, step into the new, and learn. Adults find this unlearning very difficult because their identity is largely linked to being competent and capable. Unlearning is easier said than done, and cognitive understanding of what needs to be done is not enough. A deep reorienting of the psyche is essential to unleashing hidden talents and act with power.

Dear Reader, let's pause a bit and review: Were there any 'Yudhishthira moments' in your life? How did you respond? What insights do they offer you about your ways of using power and your leadership style?

SECTION 2: Bhima, the Warrior

Bhima is the Warrior archetype. He brings a leadership style that is assertive, challenging and adventurous. Bhimas are empire-builders who seek ways to grow the organization's boundaries and engage the competition in win–lose battles. Bhima's motto is passion, expansion and impact. Forethought could be overridden by the excitement of adventure.

For a Bhima, everyone else is either an ally in one's journey or a challenge to be overcome. He is ruled by a need to possess the other. This is also the energy of self-expression and dynamism. Systems that nurture this energy resemble an arena. Competition and challenges fuel the system, and individual victories characterize the dynamics of the system.

Story 1: Bhima and Hanuman

From the northeast comes the enchanting fragrance of the celestial lotus, Sauganthika. Charmed and delighted by it, Panchali speaks to Bhimasena: 'My heart is gladdened by this beautiful flower of heavenly fragrance. I shall give this to Yudhishthira. Get me some so that I may take them to our hermitage.'

With his bow and arrow, Bhima races to do as he is bid. Animals and birds run away in confusion. Nothing can stop Bhima in his desire to please Draupadi. Hearing the commotion, Hanuman recognizes his brother Bhimasena from afar. He desires to do him good and secure his safety.

Hanuman lies across the narrow path to the heavenly lake, as if overcome by drowsiness. He yawns loudly, lashes his long tail and roars like thunder. The sounds of the lashing tail rises above all and reaches Bhima. He roams about and searches for the source of the sound.

He sees Hanuman lying on an elevated rocky base. Seeing him lying alone in the forest, Bhima quickly comes to him and utters a loud roar. Hanuman opens his eyes partially, looks at him with utter disregard and addresses him: 'Why have you woken me up, ill as I am? Born a man, knowing dharma *and reason, you should show kindness to all creatures. You have not taken advice from wise men. You destroy lower animals with little sense and childishness. Why have you come to the forest, devoid of humanity and humanness?'*

Bhima replies, 'Who are you, sir? I am a descendant of Kuru, born to Kunti, begotten by Vayu, known by the name Bhimasena.'

Hanuman smiles. One son of Vayu speaks to the other: 'I am a monkey and I am unable to grant you passage.'

'O monkey, make way. Get up, do not meet grief at my hand.'

'I am ill. I have no strength to rise. If you are resolved to go, then leap across me.'

'I cannot disregard the Paramatma *that pervades all bodies. Therefore, I cannot jump over you. If I had attained ultimate realization, I would have leapt across you and this mountain as Hanuman did the ocean.'*

'Who is this Hanuman you speak of?'

'He is my brother, excellent and accomplished, intelligent and strong, celebrated in the Ramayana. He leapt across the ocean and went to Sri Lanka to search for Rama's wife. I am equal to him in might and strength. Give me way, or I will send you to the abode of Yama.'

Knowing Bhima's pride, Hanuman decides to have some fun. 'Be kind to me as I am old and have no strength. With pity, go ahead and move my tail.'

Proud of his own strength, Bhima carelessly takes hold of the tail with his left hand, but cannot move it. He then pulls the tail with both his arms and fails. He exerts with all his might and even then, fails to raise the tail.

When he fails after many attempts, Bhima comes to Hanuman's side and stands with great shame. He bows his head and speaks with folded hands, 'O great monkey, be kind to me and forgive my harsh words. Who are you? I am

Vayuputra and thus the younger brother of Hanuman; yet, I am unable to move your tail. Please pardon me and reveal your identity.'

'I am Hanuman, the one who leapt across the ocean for Lord Rama. I am very happy to see you here. O Bhima, this passage is impassable for mortals and out of concern for your safety and well-being, I have obstructed your passage. But the lake you have come in search of lies in that direction.'

Overjoyed, Bhima bows his head and addresses his brother, 'I am fortunate to have seen you. Please fulfil my wish to see your matchless form when you crossed the ocean. I shall be satisfied.'

Hanuman assumes his full, gigantic size. Bhima is astonished when he sees the huge frame blazing as bright as the sun. He closes his eyes, joins his hands and speaks, 'O Lord, I am unable to look at you, shining like a rising sun. You are immeasurable and irrepressible. I have seen your great form. Now please do decrease it. But I have a question to ask. With you by his side, why did Rama have to fight Ravana himself? He and his raakshasas *would have been no match for you. You could have killed them all.'*

Hanuman speaks solemnly, with great affection: 'Yes, Bhima. That Ravana was no match for me. Had I killed him, the glory of Rama would have been obscured. He won everlasting fame by killing Ravana and bringing Sita back to his own city.'

Hanuman makes Bhima an offer of friendship. 'When you rush upon your enemies, I shall add my roars to yours. From the flagstaff upon Arjuna's chariot, I shall send forth great shouts that will dampen the courage of your enemies as you destroy them.'

Bhima bows down to him in respect and Hanuman shows him the way to the Sauganthika flowers.

SAMIR: Draupadi told Bhima that she wanted Sauganthika flowers to give to Yudhishthira, and he did not feel any envy! This is the part of the story that stood out for me. It is incredible! Apart from this, when Bhima confronts Hanuman with all his powers and yet is unable to move his tail, Bhima quickly realizes that he is dealing with someone more powerful than himself. He does not let the ego or bravado cloud his thinking, and he immediately moves into a space of humility and bows to Hanuman.

RAGHU: Yes, he stopped using brute force and stepped back to gauge reality, to understand what he was facing. He steps back into a state of equanimity and listens to his clear inner voice to understand what is going on.

SHRUTI: The deep love and devotion Bhima has for Draupadi is unquestionable. He leaves everything and goes to find the flowers. It strikes a chord with me because if you really love someone deeply, you would drop everything to do something for them. No other archetype really understands this intuitively as much as a Bhima.

RANDHIR: I was struck by the importance Bhima gives to relationships. He really wanted to connect with and know more about his brother Hanuman. Once he recognized whom he was talking to, there was a childlike curiosity in wanting to see Hanuman in his mighty form. That touched me.

SAMIR: The incident where Bhima meets Hanuman is very common in people with this propensity who take the problem head on, without really understanding the context. Hanuman asked him who he is, but Bhima did not ask who he is initially. It seemed Bhima was not putting in any effort to understand who he was facing. He was focused on overcoming the challenge single-mindedly to win at any cost.

RAGHU: Here, Bhima is seen as someone who can set aside envy and bravado. He quickly understands that the challenger is mightier than himself. He accepts his limitations and becomes humble. When the opportunity arises, he moves in to make Hanuman his ally rather than antagonize him. This kind of understanding and humility is possible only when the heroic potentials of the Bhima propensity is evoked.

An immature Bhima would show bravado and bluster. Here is a big lesson about making someone your ally instead of treating them as your enemy. People with the Bhima tendency can get into one-upmanship all the time when they do not operate from *shaantham*.

SHRUTI: I would also like to add how Draupadi invites or recognizes the softer side of Bhima by invoking feelings of love and devotion apart from his great physical strength and machismo.

RAGHU: To add to that, Bhima archetypes who get caught in their shadow sides never face their fears. They continuously create fear among others to hide their own fears. So, they would never know when to stop and create collaborations instead of conflict.

The stereotypical stories of the Bhima being a superhero to conquer and defeat all enemies keep on doing the rounds, without showing the vulnerabilities or fears that he must acknowledge. Vulnerability is seen as a weakness and limitations are seen as lacunae to be kept hidden from everyone, including from oneself.

Sadly, the fighter persona is the popular version. The behaviour of people in leadership positions is seen through a one-dimensional lens of the stereotypical Bhima – the Rambo type of lone hero with no weakness, who single-mindedly does what his commander wants him to do.

SAMIR: Let me share a contemporary example to probe this a little more. I know of a person I'll call Sudarshan, who was brought in to ACE Corporation to start a new line of business. He was a master storyteller and wore his passion on his sleeve. He was also extremely aggressive in what he promised to the client, both in terms of low cost and high throughput. He rarely sat with the delivery teams to understand what their work entailed. Soon, there were heated conversations between the delivery and sales teams.

The delivery team worked long hours to meet targets. Each client requirement became a project by itself. It did not scale as there was no time for thinking. Simple, repeatable tasks were manually done each time as resources were not allocated towards automation. Standardization was never Sudharshan's concern. Soon, the delivery team was on the verge of burnout, but the top bosses were happy to see the top line grow and thought Sudharshan was a hero.

Inevitably, problems started and customer dissatisfaction grew. As the situation got worse, the CEO insisted on a process for the sales team to assess capabilities before making customer commitments. Sudharshan and his team were neither geared nor willing to provide that. But they were forced to do it. Sudarshan used to get very angry when asked to submit a feasibility report.

Though the quality of delivery improved, the clients no longer saw ACE as responsive. Sudarshan started losing clients, and the rift between the delivery and sales teams grew. The revenues fell as fast as they had grown. The new line of business came to a standstill.

Instead of learning how to create a harmonious team, Sudarshan became increasingly aggressive. He felt that others were getting in the way of his victorious march. Ultimately, the division was handed over to a new business head.

Sudarshan would continuously attack others for the smallest reason. The aggression that gave the initial impetus to expand the business soon became a liability when Sudarshan showed an inability to consolidate his gains, create capability and plan the next phase of growth. His restlessness and love to engage in battle became compulsive. It was sad to see the teams disintegrate.

RAGHU: Bhimas must value their unique capabilities. However, in the context of an organization, it would prove detrimental if the shadow side takes over. We must understand our shadow sides, fears and vulnerabilities to be a true hero. Today, the dominant narrative subtly encourages everyone to be a Bhima, even if they don't have a dominant Bhima propensity. The volatility of the context does demand boldness and courage from a leader, but it also asks that this propensity be anchored in insightfulness and contextual intelligence.

RANDHIR: I can relate to that. In many companies, people believe that they have to act aggressively to be visible. The system also, at times, tends to recognize and reward aggression. Even if the person by nature is not aggressive, they have to act aggressive. It creates tremendous inner tension.

I had a colleague who joined us from an organization where one had to be aggressive to feel like they belonged there. However, this person was actually very compassionate. He had probably spent a year with us when one day he came to me after meeting an ex-colleague of his.

He said, 'My former colleague kept using swear words in every sentence. As I hadn't noticed it when I was working there, I too must have been doing the same.' He paused and added, 'It is not in my nature to be aggressive. I am so glad I left. I feel like a better human being today.'

RAGHU: It's a very good example of having to conform to a norm, even if that's not you. Let's not forget that Bhima went looking for the flowers not for himself but for his loved one. None of the actions taken by a heroic Bhima is motivated by 'what is in it for me?'. His passion is placed in the context of his belonging. The shadow side of Bhima would simply care about personal glory. Duryodhana displays this side clearly. He is unable to share any part of the kingdom with the Pandavas, and is driven by envy of their achievements and the love and recognition that they are showered with.

SHRUTI: So, there should ideally be no conflict between the softer and the aggressive side for a Bhima, right?

RAGHU: At an archetypal level, if I am a strong Bhima archetype and I do not understand or appreciate the softer side – in myself, or others – I will not have respect for people who are kind and supportive. What makes Bhima complete is that there is awareness of both sides, and they are each respected.

The Saugandhika flower is a symbol of the many parts inside us, to help us recognize the negatives along with the positives that give rise to a beautiful flower. After all, the lotus grows out of the muck that lies at the base of a pond. So, if you look at it from the archetypal lens, Bhima is converting a potentially negative context into something very beautiful and positive by being alive to his softer, more invisible propensities. The challenging context does not trigger envy or bravado.

SHRUTI: To be a true warrior, we also need to explore the other four archetypes, am I correct?

RAGHU: Yes, but not with the aim to be someone you are not. You need to explore within your own authentic and natural propensities – the gifts and talents that you are endowed with – and be aware of their limitations.

Story 2: Duryodhana's Humiliation

Duryodhana is the counterpoint of Bhima's propensity. He has similar capabilities but is unable to get in touch with his vulnerabilities and overcome the envy he feels. Here, we look at a story of Duryodhana to highlight the *adharmic* side of the Bhima propensity.

Karna and Shakuni speak to Duryodhana: 'O great Prince, your joy and happiness would be complete when you enjoy your own prosperity and watch your enemy in adversity, much like looking down from the hilltop to see others crawl on the ground below. The Pandavas are living by the lake in the Dwaitavana forest, clothed in the barks of trees and skins of hunted animals. They live upon fruits, seeds and grains they have scrounged for and subsist on the meat of animals that they hunt for themselves and their retinue of followers. Let us, clad resplendent, go watch them as they trudge through their day.'

A beaming Duryodhana replies, 'I have carried such thoughts in my mind, my dear friend and uncle. However, I am afraid we will never get the permission of our king, my father, as he is always grieving for the Pandavas. Do find a plan to convince King Dhritarashtra so that we may all go.'

The next morning, Karna comes up to Duryodhana with the plan. 'O dear king, our herds of cattle are in Dwaitavana, and we can visit the forest on the pretext of ensuring that our cattle are safe. This is a good reason that should convince your father.'

Though Dhritarashtra is not convinced, he is unable to refuse and reluctantly gives them his permission to go.

Duryodhana, Karna, Shakuni, Dushasana and their brothers reach the lake in Dwaitavana with their retinue of thousands of chariots, horses, elephants and men. They set camp not far from the lake shore. Duryodhana orders his men to build a pleasure house for him, and then goes to the shores of the lake.

As the soldiers try to enter the forest for wood to build the house, the Gandharvas emerge from behind the trees and stop them from entering. The king of the Gandharvas, Chitrasena, was visiting with his apsaras *and had closed the forest to all mortals. The soldiers go back and report the closure of the woods to Duryodhana.*

Angered, Duryodhana sends a large army of soldiers and some of his great warriors to enter and possess the forest. The Gandharvas report these developments to their king.

'Punish the wicked men of the foolish Prince Duryodhana,' orders Chitrasena.

Seeing the Gandharvas showering arrows upon them, the mortal soldiers of Duryodhana take flight. Despite all his warriors having fled, Duryodhana stands his ground. He is surrounded by the Gandharvas, who break apart his chariot and cut down his horses and charioteer. As Duryodhana falls to the ground, the Gandharvas close in on him with the intent to kill.

Chitrasena himself arrives and seizes Duryodhana, taking him prisoner. Dushasana and the other brothers and sons of Duryodhana are also captured, along with the ladies of the royal household.

Duryodhana's soldiers rush to Yudhishthira, seeking his protection.

'The wretched Duryodhana had come to see us deprived of luxury and suffering under the heat, cold, wind and rain,' rages Bhima. 'Someone in this world has taught him a lesson. Let them suffer!'

'Hush! This is not the time for cruel words,' says Yudhishthira. 'Differences and dissension in a family are common, but one should not let the honour of one's family be stained. We cannot let our family be captured. Even an ordinary Kshatriya will help one who has come to him seeking help. Gather our men now, go forth with Arjuna and the twins. Talk to the Gandharvas. If they do not agree to release everyone, do fight them lightly. And if that does not make them see sense, crush them with your mighty arms. Great joy shall be yours in rescuing Duryodhana, a miserable prisoner of the Gandharvas, would it not?'

Delighted with the thought, Bhima, Arjuna and the twins go into the forest to meet the Gandharvas.

'Stop!' cries Arjuna, seeing the Gandharvas. 'Free my brother Prince Duryodhana and go back your way in peace.' The Gandharvas laugh at him and launch their arrows at the Pandavas.

Chitrasena comes after Arjuna with various weapons, tactics and illusions, all of which are deflected by Arjuna. As Chitrasena realizes his weakening position, he cries, 'Behold Arjuna, this is your friend that you are fighting.' Arjuna and the Pandavas lower their weapons and calm their horses. The Gandharvas and the Pandavas all step down from their chariots and embrace each other.

'Chitrasena, why have you kept our brother Duryodhana in chains?' says Arjuna. 'Do free him and his family, as commanded by our brother Yudhisthira. They are our family too.'

'Arjuna, my dear friend, this wretch came here to watch your brothers, Draupadi and you in misery. Knowing this, the lord of the celestials commanded me to bring Duryodhana and others in chains to teach them a lesson. Yudhishthira does not know these thoughts and actions of Duryodhana.'

'Chitrasena, he does know about this. If you are my friend, let us go meet Yudhishthira and hear it from him.'

They go to Yudhishthira and tell him all that has happened.

'It is our great fortune that celestials such as yourself have shown such care for us,' says Yudhishthira. 'It is your kindness that you have shown in not killing our brothers. You have accomplished what your lord has commanded. Do free our wicked brother and re-establish our family honour. Having accomplished all that you had set out to do, do return the way you came.'

Hearing such soothing words, the Gandharvas free all their prisoners and go back to the heavens.

Then Yudhishthira speaks to the humiliated Duryodhana, who is surrounded by his brothers and wives. 'Child, descendant of Bharata, be not rash again. Rashness leads to destruction. Go back to Hastinapura and live well without despondency or joylessness.'

RAGHU: This story brings out the most magnanimous side of the Bhima archetype as well as its darkest side. What is the larger purpose for which one uses one's gifts? What happens when one becomes egotistical and self-centred in the use of power?

SAMIR: Despite the strong urge to take revenge, if one can step back and see the broader picture beyond the hurts or victimhood, then there is a huge scope for *dharma* to prevail.

RANDHIR: I remember a situation from the mid-'90s, when the Indian IT industry was trying to establish itself. The incoming business was still a mere trickle. There were two young executives, Rahul and Rohit, who were working with two rival IT companies. Both had the same client and operated out of adjacent buildings in Bangalore. Rahul won a large order after fierce competition from Rohit, which drained both of them emotionally, especially Rohit, as he lost the deal.

A few weeks later, Rahul was having problems as the connectivity to the client site was very unstable. He knew Rohit's company had set up a tall tower that provided very stable connectivity. Rahul approached Rohit to see if they could share the tower space for their connectivity. Despite having lost a hard-fought deal, Rohit immediately agreed to help Rahul. Rohit knew that getting client orders, which could be done out of India, was far more important in the long term than gloating over a competitor's misery in the present.

There was fierce opposition to this in Rohit's company. Rohit called all the key decision-makers and requested them to keep the larger picture in mind. He pointed out that it would create far more opportunities not only for their own company, but also for all of them.

Now, over twenty years later, both the companies have grown a thousand times bigger even as they continue to be fiercely competitive.

RAGHU: True, it is important to put aside one's own greed and excessive competitiveness to step back and see the larger picture. I know many examples in the IT sector in which a top firm would refer a potential client to a competitor. After all, that is how the entire IT industry in India was built: through understanding when to collaborate and when to compete.

SHRUTI: I can think of the example of Steve Jobs, who was thrown out of the company he founded, before returning after having learnt his lesson. Walter Isaacson's biography describes this phase of Jobs's life as one where he had to experience humiliation to rediscover his self-confidence.

RANDHIR: Yes, one of the first things Jobs did after returning was to get his fiercest competitor, Microsoft, to invest 150 million dollars in Apple. I remember seeing the television broadcast in which it was announced. Apple employees and fans booed. For them, Microsoft was a dirty word. I remember Steve Jobs raising his hand and shaking his finger and the auditorium going quiet.

Not only did this move help Apple come out of potential insolvency, but it also made them spend their resources in areas beyond computers. Microsoft divested a few years later after making a tidy profit. Steve Jobs turned a potential Duryodhana moment into a Bhima moment!

SAMIR: This is one of the greatest examples of knowing when to collaborate and when to compete. For those of us who were young in the 1980s, the Apple and Microsoft rivalry was not just fierce, it was personal. But after they smoked the peace pipe, both were better off for it.

RAGHU: If one loses sight of the larger picture, there comes a time when the writing on the wall becomes clear. Driven by egotism and blinded by the idea of glory, we don't think of withdrawing, or at least pausing to regroup before renewing the attack.

SAMIR: Duryodhana had an opportunity to reflect after this incident with the Gandharvas, yet he did not.

SHRUTI: A Bhima archetype reflects not only strength but also a tactical orientation. In the Mahabharata, we also have the description of a dialogue the Pandava brothers have before the war, in which Bhima is willing to give up his need for revenge. He is very concerned about avoiding a war that would be destructive for the whole kingdom. He was very keen for the peace mission to be successful.

RAGHU: Impulses like vengefulness and lust only strengthen the false, fleeting sense of self. It is important for the leader to introspect whether he is motivated by a sense of compassion and equanimity, or if he is being egoistic. If one is calm and balanced while studying the context and making a choice, then one has gone beyond the egotistic gratification to a holistic sense of self. It is this, and not fighting or killing, that is true heroism.

SAMIR: I have another start-up crisis story from my days in California. In 2001, my business literally went to zero in no time. I tried hard to meet the payroll demands of the forty employees. In fact, I even put in my personal cash to wade out of this problem.

An investor in my company was keen to have my company merge with another company in which he had invested. We had multiple rounds of talks, but I resisted because the other company was simply a body shop, a software organization that just provides the manpower for a foreign organization to use and direct, whereas we had significant, real and strategic projects in hand. I was at that time a Duryodhana, completely blind to the context and wanted to save the company by myself. I could not accept someone else helping me out.

The deal fell through, and I was preparing to go into Chapter 11 bankruptcy. One of my employees approached me and said, 'Sir, why don't you make peace with the other party and let's just get out of the jam? We need to survive too.' I was still not convinced though.

To my good fortune, the deal was initiated again. But this time, I realized that it's just not about me and my pride – there were employees who were on work permits; they had family responsibilities. I finally swallowed my pride and said okay to the deal.

In hindsight, it was the right thing to do, but I was blinded by my ego. I did not want to accept defeat and was ignoring the larger reality and responsibility facing me, so caught up was I in wanting that company to be my success story.

RAGHU: One of the key aspects of the Bhima archetype is that they need a challenge, or an opposition to provoke them. This leads them to build up a counter-dependency, in which they cannot identify their role and identity without any enemy. It becomes an all-consuming tension.

If an enemy turns into a friend, then the anchor to their identity is gone. This is another shadow side of the Bhima archetype: creating an identity based completely on this counter-dependence of a burning need to have an enemy at all times.

SAMIR: Such a person is his own worst enemy. If he finds no enemy to battle, then he takes out his vengefulness and anger on himself.

SHRUTI: Yes, I think so too. During one of my coaching experiences, the top leader of a bank said to me: 'I am the only hero here. I come alive when I can douse fires.' It was not easy for him to see that he was often escalating issues that did not pose a serious threat. He would set up people as his antagonists in meetings, and then would wonder why there was so much resistance to his ideas. It was very difficult for him to understand that the hypervigilant stance with which he went into any situation not only made him see opposition where there was none, but it also provoked people. It created a crisis where there was none. He couldn't be a hero if there were no fires to be doused.

RANDHIR: Oh yes! I joined a company that was doing brilliantly but had a crisis every other day, and there were too many heroes dousing fires. The next day, emails would go around thanking the hero of the previous day, and he would be feted all around! As this was getting out of hand, it was decided to break the cycle.

We announced a new reward and recognition scheme every month – those teams whose releases had zero field issues would be recognized. Nobody could argue with the logic of that decision, and it was interesting how, within a few weeks, the concept of heroism changed in the organization. It led to stronger teamwork and defect-free releases.

RAGHU: That's a good example. That is why revolutionaries or oppositional individuals do not necessarily make leaders who can build and nurture. I have seen many turnaround experts who feel restless once the job is done. They go searching for problems they can solve or something they can fight.

Let me give you my personal example. After graduating from IIT Madras, I did a couple of years of apprenticeship before joining the family business. I would take up anything I did with a lot of passion and devote a lot of time and energy to hone my skills. I saw myself as an adventurous go-getter – a Bhima, in a sense.

Being an engineer, I gravitated to managing the shop floor. I had to work really hard and make a lot of changes. The challenge of the situation was exciting. As I was streamlining the operations, it became clear that marketing was a huge issue. As long as the shop floor was struggling, the marketing department kept putting the blame for all problems on the manufacturing head.

However, it soon became clear that there was no sales pipeline! As I delved deeper into the problem, I discovered a mess in the way that the finances were being operated. Money was being borrowed from loan sharks because bank dues were delayed. In short, the company was sick and going down a bad spiral.

The Bhima in me geared up for battle. I dropped everything and focused on setting the mess right before the whole edifice crashed. I was newly married and had just become a father. However, there was no time for family, hobbies, friends, or anything other than the job at hand. Everything just fell away in the face of this grave problem.

The adrenaline rush was something I relished. My engagement with the family members who were running the show often became tense and heated. But they gave me space because my vitality and warrior orientation were essential to turn things around. It took a few years to bring things to an even keel, and eventually, the family decided to sell the company.

I was still running on adrenaline until the day the sale was finalized. After the brief celebration, I went back home and realized that my life had been so consumed by my work that I was now staring into a vacuum. The excitement and the adrenaline rush had become a very powerful affirmation of myself as a warrior. Now that the war was over and the battlefield was empty, I was lost. Inside me, there was this enormous restless energy, but nowhere to direct it.

Luckily for me, I found a guru and began learning yoga from him. This became the anchor I needed to reshape myself. The guru was able to help me through this very difficult and delicate phase, and the practice of yoga helped to calm my nerves and re-anchor myself in *shaantham* whenever I caught myself becoming stressed out. It took me a while to recalibrate myself and reorient my life.

Story 3: Bhima and the House of Wax – Hidimba *Vadha*

Since there are two claimants to the kingdom, it is decided that the Pandavas and the Kauravas will share the kingdom. However, before the Pandavas can build their new capital, Duryodhana wants to destroy them. He presents the Pandavas with a beautiful palace made of wax, and plots with his friend Purochana to burn it down with the Pandavas inside.

The Pandavas are forewarned by the gentle Vidura as they are leaving Hastinapura. They begin living in the palace of wax, giving gifts and alms to the people of Varnavata. One day, the Pandavas receive a warning signal from Vidura. On a night of celebration, the Pandavas set the palace on fire and escape through a tunnel. Destiny has brought another woman with her five sons to that palace. All of them are killed in the fire.

The Pandavas escape to a nearby forest and keep on walking for a long time.

Yudhisthira says, 'We are tired and stranded in the dark forest without knowing our way. We do not know if Purochana is dead or if he has sent his men to look for us. Our mother is thirsty and so are we. Bhima, my strong brother, take us upon yourself and carry us like a swift wind out of this dark night.'

Bhima carries them with a smile, clearing a path for himself through the dense, dark forest. Fatigue has enveloped them all. Kunti says in a tired voice, 'I am the mother of five sons and in their midst, yet I burn with thirst.'

Struck by those words, Bhima finds a giant banyan tree and sets his family down.

Turning to Yudhisthira, he says, 'I can hear the call of Saurus cranes and sweet sounds of other waterfowl. I will go and fetch some water while you all rest here.'

Bhima soon comes upon a lake, drinks, bathes and re-energizes himself. Carrying some water for his family, he speeds back the way he came. He finds his brothers and mother asleep on the ground, overcome with tiredness.

Not far from there lived a fearful and powerful raakshasa *by the name of Hidimba. He was fond of eating human flesh. Drawn by the smell, he spots the sleeping Pandavas from a distance. He calls out to his sister, Hidimbi: 'My favourite food is here. Have no fear, go and tear into them. We shall eat their flesh, drink their blood, and full with their meat inside us, we shall dance with joy.'*

As commanded by her brother, the raakshasi *goes towards the banyan tree. However, as she approaches the Pandavas, she is smitten by the handsome Bhima. His broad shoulders, mighty arms and glowing beauty makes her fall in love with him. She decides that he will be her husband. Urged by her desire, she disregards her brother's instructions and takes on a beautiful human form.*

Bedecked with divinely beautiful ornaments, Hidimbi approaches Bhima. Bashful, and with a smile upon her lips, she says, 'Who are you, handsome, and who are these heavenly-looking beings asleep upon the earth? And who is this beautiful lady? This forest is fierce, and my brother Hidimba rules this place. He loves human flesh and, desiring yours, he has sent me to kill you all and fetch meat for him to enjoy. Having seen your handsome form, and with my heart and body pierced by the arrows of Kama, I have fallen in love with you. I desire to have you as my husband. Marry me, come with me, I shall carry you and fly up in the sky, far from my brother.'

'What kind of brother and son do you take me to be, to forsake them to a flesh-eating raakshasi *for the sake of lust?' retorts Bhima.*

'Awaken them all, and I shall rescue you all from my cannibal brother,' says Hidimbi.

'Oh, beautiful and delicate lady, I would not wake my family up when they are so tired. There is no raakshasa *that I fear. Go, my shy one, and bring your brother to me.'*

Impatient at the delay, Hidimba walks towards the Pandavas himself. Alarmed, his sister offers again to carry the family through the sky, safe and away from her giant brother.

'Oh, I do not consider you weak, but I have seen what my brother can do to human beings. Come with me,' she implores.

Seeing his sister in a beautiful human form, Hidimba understands her intentions.

'You lustful woman! You bring dishonour to all our ancestors. Ignoring my hunger and smitten with love, you are spending time with this weak human. I shall kill you along with these humans,' bellows the raakshasa. *He rushes at his sister, gnashing his teeth and his eyes red with anger.*

'Stop,' Bhima says. 'My brothers are asleep. Fight me first, so that they may not wake up. Do not hurt this woman in my presence. She has been overcome by the god of love, who pervades all beings. Do not harm her, but fight me. You will be dead soon, and the forest will be safe for all.'

Hidimba charges at Bhima, who catches him by his arms and drags him away from the banyan tree. A fierce fight takes place between the two. They fight like two powerful elephants, yelling, roaring and pounding at each other. The commotion wakes all the brothers and their mother. They get up to see the beautiful Hidimbi in place of Bhima.

'Who are you and why are you here alone?' Kunti asks.

Hidimbi explains who she is, how she was sent by her brother and how she fell in love with Bhima. 'I chose your handsome son to be my husband, and though I tried to suppress my passion, I could not. My brother came looking for me. Now your son has dragged him away and is fighting over there so as to not awaken you all.'

The four brothers hasten to the place where the two giants have been fighting. They were tearing into each other, beating each other with fists and rolling on the ground.

At one point, when Bhima is held to the ground by Hidimba, Arjuna says with a smile, 'Bhima, you must be tired fighting this raakshasa. *Leave him to me, and I'll finish him. You go and rest.'*

'This is neither your fight nor your business,' growls Bhima. 'This raakshasa *has no escape from my clutches!'*

'Dawn is breaking and the raakshasas *grow more powerful at this hour. If you cannot finish him, then let me do it.'*

Inflamed by these words of Arjuna, the enraged Bhima lifts Hidimba and flings him like a doll upon the ground, killing him. He then sends forth a roar that fills the whole forest.

The Pandavas are filled with joy and decide to go towards the nearby town. As Hidimbi tries to follow them, Bhima turns to her and says, 'Revenge is the way of the raakshasas, *and you too will seek to avenge the death of your brother. Go back to where you came from, else I shall send you to your brother.'*

Yudhishthira intervenes. 'Even in anger, you shall not kill a woman,' he declares.

Hidimbi turns to Kunti and pleads, 'You know the pangs of love that possess me. I have forsaken my friends, family and way of life to be with your son as my husband. If he were not to accept me, I shall end my life. Permit him to marry me. I will forever be at your service. With my powers, I can carry all of you anywhere you wish and rescue you from any danger that may befall you. O graceful lady, make your son my husband.'

Kunti finally relents and Yudhishthira gives them his blessings, telling Hidimbi that she can be with Bhima until they have a son together. Hidimbi agrees and carries Bhima away to spend time together. Eventually, a son, Ghatotakacha, is born to them.

SAMIR: A perfect Bhima story that related to so many aspects of myself as the story went along. Bhima has the ability to love deeply and go to any lengths for the person he loves. Amidst the rawness and strength, there is a beautiful, softer and compassionate side, seen in simple activities like bringing water and keeping vigil. I see a great mix of softness and power.

SHRUTI: Arjuna's constant provocation to Bhima to finish the fight led me to think: haven't we all fallen to similar provocations?

RAGHU: There are many Bhima archetypal leaders who are aggressive and yet take good care of their teams with emotional balance. It is interesting how this story shows both the aggressive and the softer sides of the archetype as well the counterpoint by juxtaposing Bhima, Hidimbi and Hidimba. Bhima expresses courage, anger and affection. When these feelings are not bound within *dharmic* limits, they become cruelty, greed and lust.

Hidimba does not know how to limit his impulses and appetites. Thus, he is portrayed as a flesh-consuming *raakshasa*. Hidimbi is able to listen to her more refined and noble *daivic* self, and these propensities are expressed aesthetically. She transforms from a grotesque creature into a beautiful woman who is both attractive and persuasive. This is a wonderful example of how getting in touch with your true inner feelings can transform even a so-called monstrous person into someone admirable.

SAMIR: A Bhima is willing to be bound by a *dharmic* leader and his love for significant people in his life. The reason I say this is because in many organizations, I find a lot of go-getting leaders who are also very caring. These Bhima leaders are in touch with their emotional sides and are willing to be vulnerable without seeing it as a weakness.

RANDHIR: True. I know of a very aggressive person who became the CFO of a cash-rich listed company. He saw the company cash earning measly interest in bank fixed deposits and identified it as a problem. He convinced the CEO that the shareholders deserved better returns. He invested a small part of the cash in the stock market.

Unfortunately, the market turned bearish, and the investments made losses. Though the company could have easily hidden these losses, the CEO and CFO decided to be transparent about it. They admitted their mistakes in a letter to the shareholders. It was a courageous act that had many in the company worried. It could have led to a loss of trust in the company. However, what happened was the opposite: trust went up as the market felt that the company is transparent.

RAGHU: Two things come to light about the Bhima archetype: one is the ability to act on behalf of someone you love, and the other is the ability to act out of your own passion, which includes your trusted team. The shadow side is the Hidimba character, who needs to satiate his hunger by consuming human flesh. Metaphorically, it means that when our appetite takes over, we tend to consume mindlessly as it gives us a lot of meaning and joy. So, it would just be a self-aggrandizing kind of behaviour.

SAMIR: We make heroes out of those who show Bhima's capabilities. Steve Jobs was very insightful and yet brash. They see the brash part without seeing how caring he was. This latter quality allowed him to get the best out of his teams.

RAGHU: This is a very important point. As you know, we are a composite of the five archetypes. In a story like the Mahabharata, these are exemplified and the characters made more linear than they really are. We do the same today when journalists report about iconic figures.

For example, Steve Jobs had the ability to understand design, see the future of technological innovation and be a paradigm shifter. He showed many Arjuna and Sahadeva propensities. However, his Bhima-like qualities are more sensational. After all, romantic heroes are more attractive as protagonists.

Dear Reader, let's pause a bit and review: Were there any 'Bhima moments' in your life? How did you respond? What insights did they offer you about the ways you use power and your leadership style?

SECTION 3: Nakula, the Healer

Nakula can experience the essential humanness in every person and is capable of profound empathy. He is a nurturer and a friend. He provides leadership in the form of institution-building, and believes in serving others before himself.

A leader with Nakula propensities builds trust and evokes a sense of belonging to the organization. However, he can get lost in his deep empathy, internalize the pain and angst of the organization, and get weighed down.

Nakula in the Mahabharata

The handsome twins Nakula and Sahadeva are born to Madri, who invoked the Ashwani Kumaras using Kunti's boon. The Ashwinis are extraordinary healers, and thereby Nakula grows to be a healer who was skilled in Ayurveda. The word 'nakula' means 'full of love'.

In the Mahabharata, there are very few stories that highlight the actions of Nakula and Sahadeva as the prime protagonists. Nakula is considered to be the most handsome of all the Pandavas, but little else is known and written about him. Yet, the twins are always present and often consulted by Yudhishthira. There are often references that point to the vital roles they played while remaining in the background.

We have to rely on well-known folk tales to get insights into their differential capabilities, and extrapolate our interpretation of the Nakula propensity from these.

After the death of Madri, her brother Shalya, the ruler of the kingdom of Madra, brings his nephews Nakula and Sahadeva to Madra each year. When they come of age, Shalya reveals his desire to make the twins his heirs. He invites Nakula to be a king instead of remaining a mere prince in the house of Hastinapura.

However, Nakula refuses. His devotion to his stepbrothers and stepmother, Kunti, is very strong, and he is happy to be of service to them. Instead, Nakula travels far and wide to ensure the acceptance of Yudhishthira's pre-eminence through negotiation and friendship instead of war. Skilled in diplomacy, he is able to secure the alliance of many kingdoms by offering affection and inclusion.

During *agnyaatavaasa*, Nakula approaches King Virata, saying he is a skilled keeper of horses who can cure their illnesses. King Virata has the best horses in Bharat Varsha and is happy to have a skilled person to tend to them.

Duryodhana comes to hear about this skilled horse-keeper in Virata's kingdom. Knowing Nakula's skill with and love for horses, Duryodhana sends some spies to find the Pandavas' hiding spot. The Pandavas discover the spies, but are in a dilemma. If they kill them, they might inadvertently reveal themselves. But they cannot risk doing nothing.

Nakula comes up with an ingenious plan. He suggests killing the spies using methods that can pass as accidents, such as dropping rocks or drowning. The Pandavas carry out this plan, and the spies' deaths are written off as to have happened from natural causes. No foul play is suspected. This tactic came to be called 'Nakula Dharma'.

After the Mahabharata war, King Shalya once again offers his kingdom of Madra to the twins. He is convinced that Nakula can be a great king. It is a great opportunity for Nakula to establish his own kingdom, and he accepts the offer this time. However, due to his love for his brothers, he remains in Hastinapura and hands over the administration of Madra to Shalya's sons.

One of the well-known episodes of the Mahabharata is the final journey to the Himalayas undertaken by the brothers and Draupadi. They each fall and die before they reach the final destination because of a flaw they had. When Nakula passes away, Yudhishthira remarks that Nakula was secretly proud of his appearance, and that was his undoing. This could be the secret narcissistic side of a self-effacing and self-sacrificing Nakula.

Story 1: An Abridged Story from the Uddhava Gita in Srimad Bhagavatam

Once when four of the Pandavas are with Krishna, Nakula asks Krishna, 'What is Kaliyuga? What will happen during Kaliyuga?'

Krishna smiles. 'Let me demonstrate it to you.' He picks up a bow and four arrows and shoots each of the arrows in different directions. Then, he orders the four Pandavas[4] *to go and bring them back. The Pandavas go off in different directions in search of the arrows.*

Nakula finds the arrow he is looking for and is on his way back when he witnesses something odd. Passing a cow that has just given birth, he sees that the cow starts licking the calf to clean it. However, she continues to lick it even after the calf is clean. With great difficulty, people are able to separate them, but the calf is already injured. Nakula is puzzled by this behaviour of a normally calm animal.

When Nakula returns, he asks Krishna the meaning of what he saw.

Krishna explains: 'In Kaliyuga, parents will love their children so much – similar to the love shown by that cow to her new-born calf – that it will actually spoil them and will destroy their lives.'

4 Four, because Yudhishthira was absent; he was off on a journey.

There are some small references in the Mahabharata that speak about Nakula's commitment to serve his brothers. An example is when Nakula defeated Dushasana during the war. Even as Nakula was about to kill his enemy, he remembered Bhima's vow of killing Dushasana himself. It was more important for Nakula to enable his brother to fulfil his vow than to prove his own prowess, and left Dushasana for Bhima to finish.

This allows us to advance the idea that acting from compassion and being committed to selfless service are the distinguishing characteristics of Nakula. He was a nurturer and offered all his energies to serve his brothers selflessly. However, he could also become a smothering and possessive individual who could even hurt the one he is supposed to nurture.

SAMIR: So little has been written about Nakula. It is sort of similar to how everyone knows the actors, directors and producers of famous films. But the names of hundreds of people who worked tirelessly behind the scenes are mostly not well-known.

SHRUTI: Since Yudhishthira gave Nakula the responsibility of handling army operations, we can say that it was Nakula holding up the infrastructure, ensuring that all the preparations were made and the supplies were plentiful. It was Nakula who ensured that horses and weapons were kept in good condition and ready for use.

RANDHIR: Unsung Nakulas are remembered only when things go wrong. The providers of the tools who are necessary for action are never remembered. In that sense, the Mahabharata is no different, as the heroism of infrastructure providers is hardly talked about.

RAGHU: This reflects how little we value the idea of infrastructure, especially in an organizational setting. Organizations are structured in ways that devalues this role. Maintenance departments are vital to production and productivity, but seldom given prominence. We all know the criticality of those who provide service to the front-end employees, the 'heroes' of the story.

SHRUTI: When there are bright Arjunas and Bhimas around, where does a Nakula go?

RAGHU: Nakula had many unique qualities that made him a great hero in his own right.

SAMIR: Though we cannot generalize, I can certainly think that Nakulas are found more in back-end support functions.

RANDHIR: Not necessarily back-end functions. There is a good friend of mine who is a very successful salesperson but has a strong Nakula propensity. Let's call him Anil. Anil was so successful because his way of selling was to understand and take away the customer's pain. He will never sell just to meet his targets.

Recently, I met a retired ex-CEO of one of Anil's clients. He told me that Anil still stays in touch with him, even though he has no influence over securing any orders for Anil!

Nakulas can make great salespeople. They need to overcome their shyness though.

SHRUTI: The story where Nakula suggested how to deal with the spies is a good example of addressing a problem without being directly aggressive. And yes, Nakula did actually fight brilliantly in the war. He does have that capability.

RAGHU: That's a good example, but I will say it's a rarity. I am reminded of an experience I had when I was doing a study for an organization. I talked to many people in various departments. The administration head broke down as soon as he started talking to me. His words were very hard-hitting: 'This is the first time someone has asked my views about the organization. I have been in this company for the past twenty-five years, and I have a good idea about how things work around here. But people talk to me only when something is not working.'

SHRUTI: They are called invisible people because you do not see them in action. They quietly do their job in the background and leave.

SAMIR: In the software industry, the software maintenance team often ends up being the under-recognized Nakula. Once, a top IT company was partnering with a staff augmentation company for software-related services. In one of the monthly calls with their delivery lead, the customer representative was very happy with the software team that was put in place. He mentioned a team member who was doing the maintenance functions and insisted that this person start working with the product feature enhancement team. He didn't want this person to be 'wasted' just doing maintenance.

It took a bit of time for the customer to understand the importance of the contribution of the person looking at maintenance. It was interesting to see that unless one is a part of the development team, one's contribution tends to get undervalued. All the software professionals will know that the most difficult job is trying to find bugs in someone else's code!

RANDHIR: I wonder whether this habit of not valuing the enablers starts from home. Don't we see women helplessly saying that they are 'only' housewives? It's not as if one can add value only by earning money.

SHRUTI: Organizations are trying to address this through what they call issues of diversity at the superficial gender stereotype level. I see a lot of women struggling with issues of assertiveness, and they accept supportive roles while feeling resentful and underappreciated. The real issue is the propensities of a Nakula – to put others first and serve others with compassion – are not always recognized.

RAGHU: We also see this depicted in movies about warrior heroes. Any show of emotion or seeking of help is seen as a chink in the armour. There is shame in feeling vulnerable. However, if one is in a battle, there is a high probability of getting hurt, whether physically or psychologically. Therefore, one needs help to heal. This is the nurturing space that is portrayed as shameful in these depictions.

RANDHIR: Why is it shameful?

RAGHU: It is not considered acceptable for great warriors to say that they would not be able to fight for some time in order to recuperate. This basic need for nurturance and replenishment is seen as a weakness.

RANDHIR: Can it also be considered a loss of independence when you depend on someone to help you recuperate?

RAGHU: Absolutely! There are many who feel that if they acknowledged the fact that someone helped them, it would make them look small. Many times, they totally ignore and undermine the service a Nakula is providing. However, it is a myth that one acts independently of infrastructure, of nourishment, of a whole deeply interconnected network of roles.

A colleague of mine was going through a rough patch. I used to listen to his stories regularly. After about six months, he stopped talking to me completely. He wouldn't even acknowledge me. I was very puzzled. I told one of my mentors in the same company about this situation. He simply said, 'Well, he was talking to you to heal himself, and now that he has healed, he has disowned you because you remind him of that part of him that was hurting and vulnerable, a space which is something shameful.' It was quite an eye-opener for me.

SAMIR: I have witnessed similar incidents. I was often called the 'agony aunt' in my organization because a lot of people found in me a good listener. Once their issue for which they were lamenting was over, I rarely saw them again!

RAGHU: Great generals like Field Marshal Montgomery, fondly referred to as the 'Spartan General' (a senior British Army officer who served in both World Wars and the Irish War of Independence and who is famous for having defeated Rommel in World War II), spent a lot of time in the trenches with their soldiers. Every single soldier was made to feel important. It is a great general that acknowledges the importance of soldiers. They are people who recognized the importance of the Nakula propensity in creating a sense of belonging and kinship among the soldiers.

In fact, most people do not realize that the leadership in the armed forces spends a lot of effort to create camaraderie among its members. Many business organizations expect teamwork and belonging from their members without displaying concern for their well-being.

RANDHIR: One thing I understood about people with this archetype is that they are often unwilling to bask in the limelight and claim credit.

In my previous organization, the person leading IT operations would always say it was a team effort whenever we praised her for great work. When she was announced as the employee of the quarter, I could see some people asking each other, 'Who is she?'

RAGHU: I'd like to share an experience I had in a large family group company that had been in business for many years. They decided to modernize their operations, and consultants were appointed to bring about the desired changes. One of the changes suggested by the consultants was to introduce a new incentive policy across the group.

The senior managers saw the dangers of this policy as inequalities in pay would increase. The policy had an inbuilt bias towards the more glamorous roles like marketing. One of the general managers went to the top management and told them that he did not want the new pay hike. He suggested that the hike be distributed to his team in the fairest way possible.

The leadership readily agreed. This process of distributing the hike worked very well. Despite the managers not being recognized for their sacrifice, the business went on to excel as a team and exceed their strategic goals.

RANDHIR: In one of my previous companies, the CEO decided to give stock options to employees as a reward. One of the senior leaders strongly suggested that such rewards be given based on seniority and length of time at the company. However, the CEO wanted to base rewards on merit. Ultimately, both schools of thought prevailed: half the quota was given based on seniority and the other half based on merit.

A manager heading the most successful business unit received the merit quota in the first year and then again in the second year. He felt uneasy and sensed some tension in the team because of this selective reward scheme. He told the CEO that the performance of his unit was not only his success, but also of his team. He wanted to distribute his reward among them.

The CEO agreed and asked all unit heads to identify high performers in their respective teams, all of whom would be awarded merit-based stock options. The reward list expanded, and the scheme became very popular because it recognized not only the more visible performers, but also people in back-end functions.

SAMIR: This is in contrast with a 'fast-track promotion' policy that was adopted for a year in our company. The top 2 per cent of high-performing employees would be rewarded with out-of-turn promotions. On paper, this sounded good. But in reality, it led to attrition, even among the high performers who could not make the cut. The ones who were promoted were also not happy as they saw their friends suddenly becoming distant and cold. The initiative was quickly done away with, but it took some time to recover from the damage done.

RANDHIR: There was a time when my team at work had gone for an offsite team-building event, which included rappelling. Even those among us who were normally confident people became nervous, but we could all successfully complete the course. We were excited with what we had accomplished and were busy congratulating each other for showing courage.

After the excitement had died down, the facilitator asked us if any of us could recollect the face or name of the person on top of the rock face who was holding the safety rope for each of us. None of us could.

'The person on top was slowly giving you the rope based on your progress; neither too much nor too little,' said the facilitator. 'He was encouraging and not holding you back, knowing when to let go, when to control, when to encourage. He protected you but did not overprotect, allowing each of you to go through the grind, overcome your fears and respond to the challenge. Do you consider this as a form of leadership? Or is this just a support that you take for granted?'

This question got us thinking about all that is invisible in good leadership.

RAGHU: That is a great example of servant leadership, and it highlights the importance of teamwork and interdependence. Often people who are highly self-reliant find it tough to trust others. These kinds of team-building activities help us recognize support we receive that may be invisible, but is vital.

SHRUTI: I, too, have found that during such challenges, many self-assured employees who always feel that they don't need anyone's help are made to face the realities of interdependency. Such people tend to take for granted people who help them.

RAGHU: In my experience with building teams, I have discovered that having safe and trustworthy emotional infrastructure is very important. That happens when every member of the team knows that while his strengths and success will be appreciated, his vulnerabilities and failures will be understood and accepted with grace. This is the Nakula propensity to understand and empathize with people when they are down and help them regain their strength.

Knowing that others will provide support allows each individual to bring their best and not be concerned about failure. Risk-taking, experimentation and learning from failure become easy. In the Volatile Uncertain Complex Ambiguous (VUCA) world, it is critical to have leaders who can build the right organizational capabilities and infrastructure for action. The team members have to value the Nakula role and actively include everyone in tactical and strategic decision-making.

There are two areas that are not often in the limelight when one is considering strategy, but in which a Nakula could help: one is the preparation that goes before a fight, and the other is the replenishment and recouping after the fight.

RANDHIR: I can vouch for the preparation part. In my previous job, we were doing a big project with a company called H-phone. Our engineering team had come up with a new technology that excited the marketing department. They decided to make a big splash with billboards across the country and ads on TV and in newspapers. They worked with media agencies and the launch date was finalized. Everyone in the marketing team was quite excited.

The launch would have resulted in a large call surge to our system. Two days before the launch, we were told about the campaign and given the data on the expected call surge. The operations team was taken aback at the short notice, but as we were the vendors, we started working frantically to set up the infrastructure. However, we were dependent on a key IT infrastructure person from H-phone who had to provide us with additional bandwidth and additional space in the server room. He refused to do it at such a short notice and advised us to not go ahead with it.

The marketing team was aghast! They threatened and then pleaded with him to get it done as soon as possible because they had already booked all the advertising slots and spaces. He refused and went home. The marketing team went running to the CEO. However, instead of calling the IT person, the CEO blasted the marketing department for not involving the others from the beginning.

RAGHU: Unfortunately, Nakulas like this IT guy are forced to assert their power by withholding infrastructure. It is a tough lesson to get others to understand the importance of their role in smooth organizational operations.

RANDHIR: That's right. When the infrastructure holder's power is not acknowledged, then yes, they can resort to holding back support. This hurts the organization and creates not only delays but also conflict. It is an unhealthy show of power.

Nakulas are usually invisible. To become visible, they do drastic things. In the case we just discussed, if the IT team had been brought into the process much earlier, they could have planned the launch better and provided critical inputs to refine the marketing message. Had the IT guy succumbed to pressure and agreed to do as he was asked, he would have been blamed if something went wrong!

SHRUTI: In many of my coaching conversations, I see people offer their skills and talents unconditionally. Not explicitly expecting anything in return is typical of a Nakula archetype. But that does not mean that they don't have implicit expectations, and one of them is recognition.

RAGHU: Unfortunately, this widely prevalent inability to value the power of Nakula gets internalized among the leadership of most companies. There was a very successful leader with a strong Nakula propensity. He was an excellent strategist and an analytical thinker, apart from having a deeply compassionate nature.

However, in a leadership profiling exercise, his company asked him to improve his assertiveness and be more like a Bhima. Seeing how Bhimas are feted, he tried to be like one. However, he began to feel tremendous stress in trying to be what was not his natural dominant propensity.

When I talked to him about the five Pandava propensities and told him about the strengths of a Nakula, he was relieved and delighted. He could accept who he is and build on his strengths, which included an ability to build very loyal and high-performing teams. He began helping his teams by mentoring each person on how to improve his or her capabilities.

SHRUTI: That is a good example of how a Nakula can be a good CEO. If a Nakula can work on his shadow side, there is no stopping him. We also saw how his uncle, King Shalya, felt that Nakula was fit to be a king.

RAGHU: Nakula was capable of going to war and was a good swordsman. He did not become a prisoner of his propensity and feel that he is incapable of fighting.

SAMIR: Satish Dhawan, the third chairman of the Indian Space Research Organization (ISRO), when one of their launches failed, attended the press conference and admitted the failure. However, when the next rocket launch succeeded, Dhawan allowed Abdul Kalam, the head of the project, to attend the celebratory press conference along with other key team members. That was a true Nakula propensity displayed by Dhawan.

RAGHU: In his pathbreaking paper titled 'The Servant as Leader', Robert K. Greenleaf (the founder of the modern Servant leadership movement and the Greenleaf Center for Servant Leadership) extols the virtues of a Nakula style of leadership. He writes that the natural feeling of wanting to serve others also functions as a very powerful motivator for this type of leader. These are people who make sure that other people's aspirations and needs are being served. They ask themselves: do those served grow as persons? Do they, while being served, become healthier, wiser, freer and more autonomous?

SHRUTI: What is the future of a Nakula type of leader?

RANDHIR: In his initial communication to employees, Satya Nadella of Microsoft made many statements that reflected the Nakula archetype. In an article extolling the virtues of Nadella, some of his Nakula leadership styles are highlighted:

> Nadella is a contemporary CEO able to emphasize the kinds of soft skills that are often derided in the cutthroat world of corporate politics but are, in today's fast-moving marketplace, increasingly essential to outsized performance...
>
> Nadella's approach is gentler. He believes human beings are wired to have empathy, and that's essential not only for creating harmony at work but also for making products that will resonate.
>
> 'You have to be able to say, "Where is this person coming from?"' he says. 'What makes them tick? Why are they excited or frustrated by something that is happening, whether it's about computing or beyond computing?'
>
> His philosophy stems from one of the principal events of his personal life. In 1996, his first child, Zain, was born with severe cerebral palsy, permanently altering what had been a pretty carefree lifestyle for him and his wife, Anu. For two or three years, Nadella felt sorry for himself. And then – nudged along by Anu, who had given up her career as an architect to care for Zain – his perspective changed.
>
> 'If anything,' he remembers thinking, 'I should be doing everything to put myself in [Zain's] shoes, given the privilege I have to be able to help him.' Nadella says that this empathy – though he

cautions that the word is sometimes overused – 'is a massive part of who I am today.'[5]

RANDHIR: Microsoft has truly gone through an unexpected transformation under Satya Nadella. There were some surprises when he was chosen as CEO, but clearly, he was the need of the hour for Microsoft. More than business strategy, he took on the massive challenge of transforming the culture of such a large company. It couldn't have been done without the strong compassion and empathy of a Nakula.

SAMIR: As the business context becomes more unpredictable, innovation will become the key to success. If a leader is expected to be quick at introducing products, the infrastructure has to support him. When we read public documents about Apple, we can surmise that Steve Jobs used to drive the product and innovation side, while Tim Cook managed the infrastructure.

All the Apple products were released on the designated dates in multiple locations, despite the numerous last-minute design changes mandated by Steve Jobs. Tim Cook and his team had built the infrastructure to handle such volatility. Obviously, the Nakula role of creating the capacity to deliver was respected by the company, but Steve Jobs was the primary hero.

RAGHU: I have come across many successful leadership teams that are tandem teams. There is one person who plays the more visible role, but he actively collaborates with and values the colleague who plays a supportive role. Both recognize and respect the fact that it is the combination that works. In organizations where different aspects of power and the relationships between them are not understood, power games get played out.

---

5 Harry McCracken, 'Transforming Culture at Microsoft: Satya Nadella Sets a New Tone', INTHEBLACK, 1 June 2018, https://www.intheblack.com/articles/2018/06/01/satya-nadella-transforming-culture-microsoft, accessed on 5 November 2021.

Often, founders of successful organizations have well-knit teams with diverse capabilities that work together seamlessly. After the founders hand over control to the next generation, the new leadership has to appreciate this invisible strength and glue or risk losing the emotional infrastructure that engenders trust and coherence.

Dear Reader, let us take a moment to review. What were some 'Nakula moments' that you have experienced? How did you respond? What insights did they offer you about your ways of using power and your leadership style?

SECTION 4: Sahadeva, the Hermit

Sahadeva is the epitome of the seeker and the hermit. He is a knowledge creator. He stands for discovery and innovation. Sahadevas need to know before acting, and often valuable time is lost in this desire to be completely sure. Sahadeva likes to work in the background and does not want to stand out, much like his twin, Nakula.

As there are only a few episodes in the Mahabharata where Sahadeva is seen independently, I have relied on many folk stories to create a picture of this archetype. Here are a few snippets.

Of the five Pandavas, Sahadeva is the youngest and Kunti's favourite child, though he is born to Madri. He is given the least responsibility. This makes him a keen observer. Draupadi describes him as thus: 'Sahadeva, formidable in war and observant of morality, master of the swords, heroic, intelligent, wise and never wrathful. There is no other man equal to him in intelligence and eloquence amid assemblies of the wise. He could answer any question on moral values and the Vedas.'

Sahadeva is portrayed as the best astrologer in the land, who can predict the war but cannot act to change its course. He cannot reveal his knowledge to anyone because of a promise he has made to Krishna: to speak only if invited and stick to what is asked of him. This perhaps explains his relatively silent role in the epic, when compared to his brothers.

Krishna makes Sahadeva take that vow, as knowledge, if not used wisely, can be quite dangerous. Sahadeva has to carry the burden of knowing without being able to tell anyone. Even when he foresees ominous events, he has to accept that he cannot stop them from happening.

Sahadeva is considered a great spy, as he can easily blend in and become inconspicuous in a variety of situations. Folk storytellers reveal how Sahadeva spies on the spies of Duryodhana during the exile. When Yudhishthira asks him to take responsibility for finding Duryodhana's spies, or for finding the right place for *agnyaatavaasa*, Sahadeva needs encouragement to acknowledge his unique gifts.

Sahadeva feels proud that, for a change, it is he who would be responsible for the safety of all the brothers. He steps up to take on the leadership challenge thrown to him by Yudhishthira and, through his success, justifies the trust placed in him. After the war, Yudhishthira officially appoints Sahadeva as his personal advisor. Yudhishthira speaks of him as wiser than Brihaspati, the divine teacher of the Devas.

Sahadeva is a great devotee of Lord Krishna and is believed to be the first one to recognize Krishna as a divine being. When the Rajasuya Yagna is conducted by Yudhishthira for his appointment as *chakravarti samraat* (benevolent universal ruler), there is a discussion about whom Yudhishthira should pay his first respects to.

There are many elders such as Bhishma, Drona and Dhritarashtra in the room. However, Sahadeva, in a rare moment of courage, stands up and says, 'It should be Krishna.' It leads to a commotion as Krishna is the king of a minor kingdom and only a distant relative of Kunti. But in the end, Sahadeva's advice prevails.

Krishna once asks Sahadeva, 'What should be done to stop the war?' Sahadeva replies that Krishna must be tied down and imprisoned, all the Pandavas along with Duryodhana must be sent away in exile and Karna must be made the king. Krishna challenges Sahadeva to tie him down. Sahadeva starts to meditate and envisions Krishna as a baby. He then ties Krishna down with his love and affection, and Krishna is unable to free himself. Suitably impressed, Krishna blesses Sahadeva with divine vision.

When the war is imminent, Yudhishthira wants to make one last effort for peace. He asks Krishna to go to the Kauravas with a *sandhiprastav*, a proposal for peace. Krishna asks Sahadeva what he wants.

'Whatever you want is my wish too,' Sahadeva replies.

Krishna smiles and tells Sahadeva that Yudhishthira will be satisfied with just five villages, and asks him which five villages they should ask for.

Sahadeva knows that Krishna wants war in order to demonstrate the difference between *dharma* and *adharma*, so he chooses five villages in the heart of Hastinapura. Since there is no way that Duryodhana will allow the Pandavas to reign in villages inside Hastinapura, the peace proposal is bound to be rejected.

Sahadeva is respected for his knowledge by the Kauravas as well. On the advice of Shakuni, Duryodhana once approaches Sahadeva to ask for the auspicious time (*muhurutam*) to conduct the prayers before the war in order to ensure that the Kauravas emerge victorious. Despite the Kauravas being their enemy, Sahadeva feels that it is his *dharma* to be truthful when asked for information. After considering various star alignments, Sahadeva advises Duryodhana on the most auspicious time for the Kauravas.

However, when Krishna hears about what Sahadeva has done, he uses his own divine powers to realign the stars and create the right *muhurutam* for the Pandavas instead. The Kauravas end up praying when the stars are not aligned for them.

One year before the *agnyaatavaasa,* Yudhishthira asks each of the brothers for their views on the ideal place to hide during the exile. He asks Sahadeva to find the best place where they can hide incognito. Using his brilliant spying skills, Sahadeva disguises himself as a commoner and visits many places, eventually deciding that the Virata kingdom would be the best choice for *agnyaatavaasa.*

Sahadeva advises everyone to enter from different directions at different times, so as not to arouse suspicion. He has found out about jobs available in the kingdom, and based on each brother's strength, he suggests the role each should pick. With this knowledge, Sahadeva helps his brothers work out a clear strategy. It is a very critical role because if the brothers are seen and identified before the end of the *agnyaatavaasa* year, they will be exiled for another thirteen years.

During the *agnyaatavaasa,* Sahadeva becomes a cowherd and wanders off into the forest. He is in his own isolated space, more distant and unreachable than any of his brothers. He has plenty of time to think while the cows graze.

SHRUTI: I used to wonder why we know hardly anything about Sahadeva. The promise he makes to Krishna explains why. He is always there, observing deeply. He gives his advice only when asked.

RANDHIR: Sahadeva recognizing Krishna as a deity intrigues me. We always associated Krishna more with Arjuna than with anyone else. If we are saying Krishna represents our innermost intelligence, then are we saying that it was Sahadeva who first understood the importance of being in touch with your inner self?

RAGHU: That's a great observation! Only when it comes from one's innermost intelligence does knowledge become timeless wisdom. Curiosity and enquiry into the phenomenon outside of the self is devoid of an introspective quality and often becomes dry and utilitarian.

SHRUTI: I found the story about Sahadeva binding Krishna with love and affection quite touching. What is the significance of that?

RAGHU: My interpretation is that we are capable of learning and being insightful only when we have the mind of a child – full of curiosity and wonder, always fresh and open. This would also imply that, like a child, Sahadeva did not take himself seriously. Sahadeva focused on philosophy and the study of the Vedas. The path to the inner realms is open only to those who have an innocent mind that is free of ego. Sahadeva's ability to blend in could also be attributed to this lack of ego, which gave him the ability to observe carefully and imitate others like only a child can.

SHRUTI: Then why, despite being the key knowledge holder, one who knew all rituals and processes, was Sahadeva so much in the background?

RAGHU: Gathering of knowledge and its deployment are two separate things. The former takes time. Research, study and experimentation are needed in order to verify that a hypothesis or an idea is robust and can be used. These processes have to happen in protected spaces. The knowledge used in rituals is called *guptam* (secret) because it requires extraordinary sensitivity and insight to truly comprehend them. These activities are, in essence, required to be done in the background.

SAMIR: If I extend it to organizations, there are so many occasions when the R&D teams are never part of strategic or problem-solving meetings. Their contribution or presence is always in the background.

RANDHIR: In the last two decades, the knowledge industry has become more important, and this has led to persons with the Sahadeva propensity being more valued. Many of them have become entrepreneurs themselves. Twenty-five years ago, a person from R&D would rarely be involved in strategic discussions, especially in non-tech companies. I remember one of the biggest concerns of CIOs of non-tech companies in the 1980s and 1990s was about how to get the CEO's attention! It changed dramatically with the advent of the internet.

SAMIR: I agree. Operations people used to be scared of R&D guys trying anything new. Also, those scientists were considered to be socially awkward geeks!

RANDHIR: However, their role as spies was always valued. The sales team would procure a competitor's products, and R&D team would reverse-engineer them in no time! I knew a chemical engineer who was working in a company manufacturing a new kind of alloy. He used to get excited whenever the sales team brought him a competitor's newly launched product. He had to figure out what the others had done and how they could do something better. In that sense, war, or getting the better of competition, excites them.

SHRUTI: One thing that stood out from the stories was how reluctant Sahadeva was to take on responsibility. We have also seen how learned people are sometimes very hesitant to take ownership for an action.

They would instead see it from multiple sides, and to a question on what should be done, their favourite response would be 'It depends'! In fact, they can frustrate others through this refusal to make a commitment.

RAGHU: Yes, a Sahadeva would often rather let a Bhima or an Arjuna act, and let a Yudhishthira provide his judgement. However, once they realize that the system is critically dependent upon them, they will step up, as we saw in these stories. They know the power of knowledge, but for that very reason, they tend to be very cautious in offering it. They are aware of the dangers of incomplete knowledge and improper use of knowledge.

Sahadeva relied on his intellectual capabilities to express himself. During the war, he battled Shakuni. He had taken an oath after the game of dice to kill him. Shakuni is the counterpoint of Sahadeva, the manipulative strategist and mastermind of the Kauravas. A heroic Sahadeva is a canny strategist and focuses his power by being dispassionate and incisive.

SAMIR: In technology teams, I have seen that those who are able to visualize the business from all aspects are the ones that can see the need for innovation. Many CEOs keep such people as advisors as a part of the core decision-making team. This enables the company to be data-driven with up-to-date knowledge.

SHRUTI: The pull towards clairvoyance and knowledge was unique to Sahadeva. The idea of consensus-building between the Pandavas that we often see in the epic goes against the idea of having one boss who is all-knowing. The Mahabharata clearly gives space and leadership to each of the brothers appropriately.

RAGHU: Let me expand on this. In Indic thought, there are three kinds of *balam,* or external powers: *kaala balam,* the power of right timing; *yoga balam,* the power of right allies; and *aasana balam,* the power of right hierarchies.

These are distinct from the idea of *shakti,* which is an inner capability. The three forms of shakti are *iccha shakti,* the intensity of intent; *kriyaa shakti,* the depth of capacity; and *jnaana shakti,* the acuity of knowledge.

There is a need to be in touch with all of these to really know what needs to be done. Sahadeva was a master strategist because he had the subtle observational skills to understand things in depth. This unique capability of Sahadeva is an example of *jnaana shakti*. He exemplified this when he took responsibility for how they would spend the *agnyaatavaasa*.

SAMIR: I remember that in the journey to their end, as each brother falls and Yudhishthira mentions the not-so-*dharmic* side that they held closely guarded, he says of Sahadeva upon his death that 'he was too proud about his knowledge'.

RAGHU: I think the trouble is that such people prefer to be in the background. I remember a knowledgeable R&D person who was shunted around, until the Total Quality Management (TQM) movement started. He was finally recognized and made part of the core TQM group as a clever engineer who could solve problems. TQM essentially requires a solid understanding of statistics and math. The vital part played by Sahadevas in the growth and evolution of organizations is becoming apparent now.

SHRUTI: Manufacturing was always about doing rather than thinking. The bulk of the thinking was outsourced to experts at universities or research institutions, and organizations simply tried to become proficient in the delivery process. This is changing now.

RANDHIR: That could be the reason many people with Sahadeva capabilities had been inclined to join academia or research organizations. You could say that they were invisible to the average manager in most organizations. Therefore, I am pleasantly surprised that these days, many start-ups are recognizing the research innovation aspect as being the key differentiator.

RAGHU: I think the surprise is also because having a Sahadeva propensity makes one very cautious, wanting to ensure that the knowledge one professes is robust. A Sahadeva's power comes from the careful and systematic definition of the problem and solutions. If their solution is seen as ineffective, they will lose their power. No scientist worth his or her salt will make definitive statements until they verify and test their hypothesis many times.

Many young people now are far more daring with their innovations as the context is more welcoming. The start-up culture is one of high risks matched with incessant innovation. Naturally, there is limited time for R&D. Learning and improving on the fly will be key. How the Sahadeva archetype steps up to this need will be interesting to see.

RANDHIR: As a start-up investor, I am seeing how the funding for R&D and innovation in India is increasing significantly.

RAGHU: Apart from the ability to innovate, Sahadeva can see emerging patterns and, therefore, has an insight into what the future would look like. Many of the early IT leaders were Sahadevas who used their insight to create a whole new industry in India. Mr F.C. Kohli, the founder and first CEO of TCS, and one who is credited to be the thought leader behind the IT revolution in India, had the ability to understand technology. His encouragement to educational institutions like the IITs to invest in R&D in computer sciences was key to building Indian expertise.

SAMIR: These days, countries such as China and the US are fighting intensely to be the next knowledge hub. As technology keeps driving change, Sahadevas become more sought after.

RAGHU: The trend started two centuries ago, when science started playing a prominent role in our lives. Europe was able to dominate the world because of the way it converted scientific discovery into usable technology. One of the most interesting books written about the power of the Sahadeva propensity and the price an organization pays for not knowing how to value it is *The Secret Life of Information* by John Seely Brown. He writes with great insight about the achievements of Xerox's Palo Alto Research Centre (PARC), which he headed.

In those labs were made the first concepts of a desktop PC, graphical operating system and mouse, among several other innovations. But

Xerox was not able to understand the value of this knowledge, and other entrepreneurs monetized the innovations! There is a famous story about Steve Jobs visiting PARC, seeing the prototype of a mouse, windows icons, etc., and realizing its immense potential, which PARC did not.

SHRUTI: What has changed in the last few decades is that the appetite for risk of Sahadevas around the world has increased.

RANDHIR: From my experience of working with start-ups, what I can say is that a founder who is tech-savvy and also has marketing knowhow is still rare. The best combination would be to have two co-founders, one good at tech and the other at marketing. This combination of a Sahadeva and a Bhima could work well.

RAGHU: But can Sahadevas in the knowledge-based economy handle the sudden power, glamour and money that comes with success? As they scale globally, remaining rooted in *dharma* and listening to their inner voice, always asking that question, 'In doing what I am doing, what am I really doing?', will be so critical. Otherwise, they will end up being Shakunis, using the tools they have for personal benefit at the expense of the well-being of society in general.

SHRUTI: Can we look at the *adharmic* counterpoint and see if we can get a clearer idea of the core capabilities of this propensity?

RAGHU: The Mahabharata clearly says that Sahadeva fought Shakuni in the war. Shakuni is the strategist but lacks the capability for action that Duryodhana has. Shakuni is always behind the scenes and provokes others to play, never having accountability himself.

RANDHIR: Shakuni was a trickster, someone who uses the tools or knowledge that he has but others don't, to just further his own interests rather than the cause of *dharma*. He gets so carried away by his smartness that he forgets where *dharma* ends and *adharma* begins.

I am reminded of a case I heard recently, about a personal advisor to an extremely wealthy business tycoon by the name of Balu. The advisor, Shrikant, was working on managing Balu's personal finances. He was quite brilliant and also showed great judgement when it came to investing. Shrikant never showed any personal aspirations, and Balu had tremendous confidence in him.

One day, Balu received a message from his bank , questioning some transactions, and became suspicious. Shrikant said there must be some mistake, but Balu had an independent agency audit his bank accounts. They discovered that Shrikant had been smartly siphoning money out of Balu's accounts for many years. He had already managed to steal a very large amount.

It is interesting to note that when Shrikant was confronted with the findings, he just grinned and said, 'It took you so long to catch me!' He was getting a kick out of being just one step ahead of a shrewd business tycoon!

RAGHU: That's a good example of the shadow side of a Sahadeva. In the 1980s, Peter Drucker had predicted that knowledge workers would become more important as technological innovation becomes the key to competitiveness. We are seeing his prediction come true. Let us hope that these knowledge workers will be like Sahadeva, who discovered the strength of Krishna – the voice of consciousness – and not turn into tricksters like Shakuni after being dazzled by the amount of money pouring into these new sectors.

Dear Reader, let's take a moment to recall some 'Sahadeva moments' in your life. How did you respond? What insights did they offer you about your ways of using power and your leadership style?

SECTION 5: Arjuna, the Paradigm Shifter

Arjuna is the questioner archetype. He is the one who understands paradoxes and polarities. This is paradigm-shifting energy. The motto of an Arjuna is 'creative destruction'.

Arjuna is insightful, and this enables him to see systemic ills, imperfections and vulnerabilities. He engages in deep reflection and questioning until he touches the wellspring of inner inspiration.

However, until he reaches that point, he could come across as hesitant and doubting.

Story 1: Kirata and Arjuna

During the exile at Dvaiytavana, Yudhishthira spends sleepless nights worrying about the prowess of Karna and the might of warriors such as Bhishma, Drona and Kripa. 'Will I ever get back my kingdom or will I keep wandering from one forest to another with my brothers and Draupadi?' he thinks anxiously.

One day, Vyasa appears. He urges Yudhishthira to ask Arjuna to go on a tapas *and seek weapons of power from Rudra and the lords of the four directions: Indra, Yama, Varuna and Kubera.*

Delighted by Vyasa's words, Yudhishthira speaks to Arjuna.

'Upon you rests a great burden, Arjuna! Commit yourself to austere ascetic practices and meditate deeply. Go north and seek Indra. The celestials have collected and given all their great weapons to him. Do pray and seek him, and he will give you the weapons. He is your father.'

Arjuna picks up his great bow, Gandiva, and its inexhaustible quiver, casts his eyes to the heavens and sets out towards the north.

Soon, he reaches the Himalayas and walks over the mountain ranges day and night until he arrives at Indralok. There, he hears a voice commanding him to stop. He looks around and sees an effulgent ascetic, lean and with matted locks.

'O child, this is a land of peaceful ascetics,' cries the ascetic. 'There is no fight here and nor any use for your great bow or arrow.'

The ascetic tries to persuade Arjuna to drop his weapons, but the Pandava remains steadfast in his purpose and refuses. The ascetic then reveals that he is Indra himself. 'I am pleased,' declares Indra. 'I grant you a boon, anything you desire.'

'I seek to learn from you how to use all your weapons,' Arjuna replies. 'Grant me this.'

'You have already reached a great place where there is no need for weapons. Ask for any other bliss.'

'I do not desire any other bliss nor seek celestial prosperity. I have left my brothers and wife behind in the forest. If I were not to return to them to avenge our enemies with the weapons I seek, I shall bring everlasting shame upon myself.'

Indra says kindly, 'When you meet the three-eyed Shiva, the lord of all beings, and obtain his blessings, then I shall give you my weapons.' After that, he disappears.

Firm in his purpose, Arjuna enters a forest abounding with a variety of fruits and flowers. Here, Arjuna immerses himself in his ascetic practice.

Shiva, the destroyer of sins, is pleased with the intensity of Arjuna's austerities. He takes the form of Kirata, the hunter, and goes to the forest with his great bow and snake-like arrows. He is accompanied by his wife, Uma.

As Shiva comes upon Arjuna, he spots an asura *named Muka, who has taken the form of a boar. He intends to kill Arjuna. Arjuna also sees the boar charging him. Stringing his Gandiva at lightning speed, he roars, 'I have done you no harm, yet you seek to kill me. I shall send you to your death today.'*

Kirata asks Arjuna to stop. 'The boar was first aimed at by me,' he declares. 'It's my hunt.' Ignoring him, Arjuna shoots his arrow. At the same time, Kirata shoots a flaming thunderbolt. Struck by the thunder and lightning of the two arrows, Muka, the demon, is killed.

With the danger gone, Arjuna looks upon Kirata and with a smile asks 'Why are you wandering these forests? Are you not afraid? You have shot at the boar who had come intending to kill me. This is contrary to the rules of the hunt.'

Smiling, Kirata replies, 'We dwell in these forests. It is our abode. You seem delicate and brought up in luxury. Why do you wander these forests full of danger and difficulties?'

'I have my bow and arrows. Did you not see how this demon who came as a boar was killed by me?'

Kirata responds, 'I aimed at this asura *first, and I shot and killed it first. You are proud of your strength, but today you will not escape from me. I shall shoot my arrows at you and you may shoot at me with yours.'*

Accepting the challenge, Arjuna showers a volley of arrows. Kirata shoots back. A fearful fight ensues between the two. Kirata receives the arrows of Arjuna with cheer, and stands unmoved and unscratched. Wondering at the sight of his arrows not harming his rival, Arjuna firms up his resolve to send him to his death. He fires more powerfully but Kirata remains untouched. Soon, Arjuna's quiver is empty. Shiva's power has overshadowed the magic of the quiver.

Seeing his quiver empty, Arjuna is seized with fear. He tries to strike Kirata with his bowstring, but Kirata snatches the bow away with impunity. With no choice left, Arjuna takes out his sword. With all his strength, he lands a blow upon Kirata's head with his sword. It's like one that can smash rocks. However, it is the sword that breaks into pieces. Undeterred, Arjuna continues to fight with trees and stones until Kirata knocks him unconscious.

When Arjuna regains consciousness, his body is covered in blood and his heart overwhelmed with sorrow. In his mind, he prays to Lord Shiva and showers his image with flowers. He is amazed to see the same flowers fall upon the head of Kirata.

Arjuna's eyes widen and his heart fills with joy. He prostrates at the feet of Kirata, understanding that he is none other than Shiva. Shiva blesses Arjuna even as he begs forgiveness for his rashness borne of ignorance, which made him fight Shiva.

Embracing Arjuna cheerfully, Shiva consoles him. 'I have pardoned you. Your bow will once again be powerful and your quivers, inexhaustible. I am pleased with your prowess and your tapas. *Ask from me what you desire.'*

'O Lord, I seek the fearful weapon Brahmashira and to learn how to use it in my fight against Karna, Bhishma, Drona and Kripa.'

'I shall give you this weapon, which can be discharged by the mind, the eyes or by words,' says Shiva. 'But it must not be shot without proper reason, or at a weak enemy.' He then imparts to Arjuna the knowledge of the weapon and bestows it upon him.

As Arjuna stands there, Varuna, the Lord of Water and the West, appears before him. He is joined by Kubera, the Lord of Wealth and the North; Yama, the Lord of Death and the South; and the great Indra, the Lord of the East.

Yama speaks with great love to Arjuna and blesses him with his mace. Varuna blesses him with his noose that when used cannot be resisted by enemies. Kubera blesses him with a mighty weapon called Antardhana, which is capable of putting the enemy to sleep. Indra blesses him with a chariot.

Having blessed him with all the weapons, the great celestials vanish.

RAGHU: In the Koothu version of the Mahabharata from Tamil Nadu, there is an additional subplot in the story. In that version, Arjuna encounters two other obstacles before he reaches Indralok. Let me narrate those extra scenes.

Soon after Arjuna starts his journey, he meets Perundi, a *raakshasi.* She is totally smitten with Arjuna and tries to make advances. Arjuna ignores her and continues his journey.

After a while, he meets Mohini, a great *apsara*. Mohini is also very attracted to Arjuna. Though Arjuna too is attracted to her, he is able to control his passion and rejects her advances. Arjuna resists both desire and aversion before he can meet Shiva.

RANDHIR: Interestingly, in the Saugandhika story, Bhima soon understood that the monkey in his path was a force much more powerful than himself. But, in this story, Arjuna does not realize who he is dealing with until he is knocked out by his challenger.

RAGHU: That is an interesting observation. What does it really mean? Arjuna is also called *vibhuti purusha* – an extraordinary person. Is it possible that such an unquestioned champion could have internalized the awe people held him in and become blind to his own limitations?

We must also look at internal and external reinforcements about his greatness. He has performed extremely tough austerities to achieve this greatness. This may lead to an ego-based sense of achievement, when one thinks that one has accomplished something that no one else could. All of us have these moments. We feel boosted by the praise from others and lose sight of our real capabilities and limitations.

A true hero needs to be deeply in touch with the nature and measure of his or her capabilities. He should know how to engage with external challenges appropriately, based on internal foundations and not an artificial image of one's own self. I think this is a key learning Arjuna gains in this encounter.

RANDHIR: One of the conditions Shiva puts on the usage of the weapon he bestows upon Arjuna is that it must only be used against those more powerful than himself. I find this so relevant in a corporate context. There are times where a junior employee stands up for a certain issue and sticks to their guns because of their values or beliefs. It takes huge courage and power to stand up to your seniors, especially in group settings. And it takes humility and self-confidence for a senior employee to treat such courageous juniors with respect.

RAGHU: It is also about testing whether the person has the strength to stick to his values or not. To be able to stand in front of everyone and stick to your core values, to not turn a discussion into a debate, to not turn a negotiation into a process of extraction by greater authority or privilege: these are all core capabilities of a respected leader.

SAMIR: There were two things from the story that made me think. One is that it is not enough to be simply be aware of our personal powers and limitations. We must also understand the systemic view. The other is the scene when Arjuna's most powerful weapon failed. Could he still stand up and fight? If the powerful external tools are taken away from you, can you still find the strength to battle on? That is something worth thinking about.

RAGHU: These two points tell an important difference between Yudhishthira and Arjuna. Yudhishthira's power stems from his positional authority and how he uses it effectively. Even when Arjuna is stripped off external sources of power, he can still fight. He is able to do so on the basis of overwhelming *dharmic* insight, which he is able to articulate in clear terms.

SHRUTI: When Shiva teaches Arjuna about his weapon, he tells him that he can use it with his mind, eyes and words. It is not a typical external weapon such as a gun or a bow, and seems to say that the most powerful weapon is actually inside ourselves. Its power can be unleashed through how we think, see and speak.

But what made Arjuna so special that he was showered with these powers?

RAGHU: Arjuna first came to terms with his aversions when he encountered Perundi and his desires when he met Mohini. Those were the early steps in his commitment to a purpose much bigger than himself. He learnt not to get caught up with personal pulls or pushes. Thus, he learnt how one can be dispassionate in a situation.

Then comes the *tapas*, or austerities, to develop the stamina to weather challenges and stay firmly grounded in one's purpose. This preparation is very important before starting any venture. The idea of tapas in a modern context refers to the process of gaining maturity by anchoring deep within. The weapons are a symbolic realization of the rewards gained in the process.

The next step is to confront the ideas of the self that one has internalized through external affirmations. Can we look at those ideas honestly and determine what is reality? When Arjuna fought Shiva in the form of Kirata, he was faced with the next step in his learning. He had to understand his limitations and internalize humility.

Many times, personal humility tends to be lost by those who have achieved a lot with single-minded purpose and hard work. In those cases, one has to face a struggle, symbolized by fighting Shiva, to realize one's limitations. Only when this is understood and humility is found is one bestowed with rewards, symbolized by the weapons.

Let me give as an example a pharma company that was making a niche drug. They were uncompromising in quality and went quickly from being a start-up to being a multinational. Soon, they had become a giant among dwarfs in the Indian market. The media raved about them, they were stock-market darlings and case studies were written about their success. Their international growth was boosted by epidemics and disease outbreaks that happened just when they had accumulated huge stocks.

The founding team had described themselves as learners at the outset, but soon, they started to believe their own hype. They felt that they had built a good base and started to look beyond without understanding the new trends and markets well, thinking that a simple replication of the pattern they had followed so far would ensure success.

However, despite realizing that they didn't have a good grip over the new market, they simply fought harder without stepping back to analyse. The harder they fought, the deeper they sank into trouble! This simply bewildered them. It took some hard knocks before they realized that they were still a dwarf among global giants.

SAMIR: Yes, it is easy to get blinded by success. The organizations that understand their powers and yet remain sincere and humble enough to listen to counsel are the ones that can build on early successes. They do not look for affirmations and are ready to listen to a different point of view. This ability to be a little sceptical of their own ways helps them to evolve. Their leaders usually act from conviction and insight, and not from the power of the chair they sit on.

RAGHU: Humility is an ability to value self-doubt and to know when to re-examine the assumptions and conclusions on which one's understanding of the organization and the context is based.

RANDHIR: Many times, a misstep will fill us with doubts and make us lose self-conviction. Other times, success makes us overconfident, and we stop listening to others. There needs to be a fine balance between the two.

RAGHU: In my view, timeless leadership is anchored on four capabilities:

- *Awareness*: Arjuna possesses deep sensitivity and extraordinary intelligence. He is portrayed as one who has conquered sleep, and thus, he is aware and awake at all times. That is why he was chosen as the one to do the *tapas* necessary to obtain the special gifts from Indra
- *Balance*: Any difficult situation is a space of high intensity. *Tapas* can burn away compulsive energies such as craving and aversion. This inner cleansing creates the ability to be in such situations without getting perturbed or swayed.
- *Contextual Intelligence*: A balance between self-conviction and open-mindedness is essential to understanding oneself with respect to context. Strategizing lacks depth without an insight

into the context and an ability to gauge one's capacity to respond to the emerging context.

- *Dharma sankata:* To discover a *dharmic* response, we have to delve within and understand the whole system and different opposing solutions to a situation.

Any imbalance in these four would prevent a leader to see the multiple possibilities, and the pulls and pushes of a situation. He would not be able to manage the anxieties of others, nor exercise wise judgement.

RANDHIR: How did Arjuna display all this in the context of this story? Didn't he keep on fighting with Shiva?

RAGHU: Let us see how the fight fits into the context. Firstly, Arjuna removes the inner imbalances that can become a source of distraction by not engaging with Mohini and Perundi. He then invites Shiva to engage with him. In this encounter, he discovers both his strengths and his limitations. So focused is he on getting the weapons that he just wants to get the obstacle out of his way.

However, he does not step back and ask himself what the obstacle means in that context. Only when he discovers his humility and regains his understanding of the context can he evaluate the challenge with intelligence. It is only then that he is able to take the appropriate action.

The gifts Arjuna then receives from the gods are metaphors for the capacities he discovers within himself: integrity, intensity and insight.

SHRUTI: Where is the *dharma sankata* for Arjuna in this story?

RAGHU: Arjuna has to introspect in the face of opposing pulls, discover conviction and commit to action.

SHRUTI: Were the weapons given by Indra and others used to solve the *dharma sankata*s?

RAGHU: If you look at the weapons not in a literal sense but as being symbolic of inner resources. This ability of Arjuna is amply demonstrated in his dialogue with Krishna.

SHRUTI: What is the significance of each of these weapons given to him by the gods?

RAGHU: That's a very good question. Yama gives him a mace to use against *raakshasa*s who were born among human beings. This weapon symbolizes control of the *asuric* side, which could be uncontrolled passions within and brute forces outside. Let's place this in a contemporary context. Looking back at some of the unsuccessful business cases we examined, we could say that the *asuric* tendencies of the leaders had come to the fore in most of those cases. They were unwilling to be humble and instead used what they thought was their strength to fight more intensely, but not more wisely.

Varuna gives him a noose, or *pasham,* as it is called in Sanskrit. It symbolizes control and restraint: our ability to stay aware and balanced in contexts that become very intense. Indra gives him a chariot, which symbolizes traversing and exploring unknown territories. The best leaders are always looking at expanding their business to new markets to stay ahead of competition.

Kubera's weapon puts one's enemies to sleep. This symbolizes advantage gained from being alert to things that your rivals may be blind to. As in an earlier example, large organizations such as Xerox 'went to sleep' and lost advantage gained in certain markets because their rivals were more alert. Another example is Apple taking over the personal music player market while Sony dozed off.

SHRUTI: When the world is full of multiple pulls and pushes, how does one know which weapon to use and when?

RAGHU: A deeper meaning of a *dharma sankata* is to understand the timing of a decision when there are multiple alternatives. It is often a lucid understanding of the context in which a system is situated that clearly brings out the *dharma sankata* and the consequences of a decision.

A *dharma sankata* is not a one-dimensional problem with a single permanent solution. It is a context that has many contrary pulls. The system exists in a context that not only changes, but also is beyond your control. Situations that have several alternatives crop up repeatedly, and we must decide the course of action that is most *dharmic* at that point of time.

When context changes with time, these pulls and pushes will throw up new challenges. The world we live in is dynamic, paradoxical, irrational, complex and inscrutable. Without inner resilience, integrity, wisdom and humility, we cannot succeed.

Story 2: Urvashi's Curse

Indra's chariot, pulled swiftly by golden horses, arrives at Arjuna's door. It is filled with powerful missiles, maces, thunderbolts and various other great weapons. It is visible only to those who have the ascetic merit to ride. Matali, Indra's sarathi, has brought with him an invitation from Indra for Arjuna to visit Indraloka.

Arjuna bathes in the Ganges, offers his prayers to the Mandara mountain and then climbs into the chariot. He then flies into the sky towards Indra's city of Amaravati. Arjuna wants to learn the science behind the weapons that the great gods have given him. In the great hall of Indra, he is welcomed by the celestials of Indraloka: the Gandharvas, siddhas *and* apsaras.

Arjuna walks up to Indra, his father, bends his head low and salutes him. Indra embraces Arjuna and, taking him by the hand, seats him on his lap. They are luminous, like the sun and the moon.

Indra gives Arjuna his favourite weapon: Vajra. Arjuna begins to learn how to deploy the weapon with his body, mind and eyes. One day, Indra calls him and says, 'I am happy with your progress. I would like you to spend some time with Chitrasena, the king of the Gandharvas. I would like you to learn from him the art of singing and dancing. It is very important and it will be very good for you.'

Arjuna goes to live with Chitrasena, and their friendship grows as time goes by. The great warrior learns various forms of vocal and instrumental music and various forms of dance.

One day, seeing the way Arjuna looks at Urvashi – the most beautiful of the apsaras *in Indra's court – when she dances in the great hall, Indra calls for Chitrasena and speaks privately.*

'Chitrasena, go to Urvashi today and let her know that she may wait upon Arjuna. Just as you helped him master the art of singing and dancing, you shall help him learn the art of being with women.'

Chitrasena goes to Urvashi and says, 'Arjuna is known for his grace, beauty and self-control. He is a genius who has great energy and intellect. He is a protector of heaven like Indra and a man of sweet speech. Our heroic Arjuna has cast his glance upon you. Indra has asked if you would let Arjuna be with you today.'

Urvashi replies with a cheerful smile. 'I have seen Arjuna and heard of his virtues. Upon the wishes of Indra and for the sake of our friendship, I will bestow my favours upon Arjuna. I am moved by his many qualities. Kama, the God of Love, has already filled my heart, and thus I shall go to him today.'

At the twilight hour, Urvashi approaches Arjuna's mansion. She is extremely beautiful and graceful, her long braids adorned with fragrant flowers. Stoked by her flaming desire, she moves with an abandon that makes her more beautiful.

Once she reaches the mansion, she sends word through the gatekeeper. Arjuna welcomes her with a fear-stricken heart. He closes his eyes out of modesty. He offers her worship, as one would to a superior.

'Foremost of the celestial apsaras, *I bow to you. I am your servant, what be your command?'*

Shocked by his words, Urvashi comes back to her senses and tells Arjuna all that she has been told by Chitrasena.

'O great lady, I consider you to be the wife of my superior,' says Arjuna. 'As gracious as Kunti, as motherly as Indra's wife, Shachi. I did gaze upon you with wonderment. I was thinking: here is the mother of the Puru dynasty, the progenitor of the Kuru dynasty, the mother of my race.'

'O son of Indra, we are free and unfettered to make our choice,' insists Urvashi. 'Do not send me away nor treat me as anything other than a lover. Take me to be yours now.'

'O celestial lady, I fall at your feet, please go away. I bow to you as your own son.'

Feeling insulted and trembling with anger, Urvashi curses Arjuna.

'You insult a lady who comes bearing a deep desire in her heart, upon the command of the celestial king and of her own accord. You have turned away a woman whose heart has been filled by Kama. For this, you shall live amidst women, bereft of manhood, losing respect. You shall live as a dancer among women.'

Urvashi turns and walks back to her mansion.

Hearing about the curse, Indra calls Arjuna to him.

'Today, Urvashi has become a true mother through you and this curse is a gift to you,' said Indra. 'In your thirteenth year of exile, this curse will prove to be of value. It will help you lead a covert life for a year. Once you have spent the year as a dancer without manhood, you will regain all that you would have lost, and the curse will hold you no more.'

SHRUTI: What does Indra teach Arjuna?

RAGHU: The story illustrates how Arjuna was taught how to master all the five elements. Indra also taught him about the sixth: *indriya*, the mind and its illusions when one is deeply challenged. It symbolizes a comprehensive understanding of all aspects of human capability.

SHRUTI: I found the emphasis on learning the fine arts most fascinating.

RAGHU: The fine arts awaken your senses and stimulate your sensitivity to the world around and within.

SAMIR: If we need to have control over the senses to progress, then we must learn how to use them in both masculine and feminine form. Feminine power is as important as the masculine. Heroism is not just about action but also nurturing.

SHRUTI: What is the significance of Urvashi's role in Arjuna's training?

RAGHU: It is all about inner balance, whether one uses one's capabilities for war or the arts. We need to have complete power over our decision-making. Arjuna is able to hold his balance with Urvashi, neither giving in to her nor exercising power over her. He places the present situation in the larger context to gain perspective and insight before acting.

This is very important in an organizational context. Only when a leader is completely anchored within oneself and doesn't need affirmation from others can he wield power with appropriateness and grace.

SAMIR: This is an important internal compass for any leader to develop, else one can easily get swayed away by external pulls and pushes.

Story 3: Arjuna and Krishna

As the war begins, Arjuna asks Krishna to drive his chariot to the middle of the battleground as he wants to see the faces of his enemies. As he looks at them, Arjuna realizes that he must fight and kill his family, teachers and friends. It makes him feel disgusted and sick. Arjuna drops his Gandiva and falls on his knees.

'I can't fight this battle at all,' he cries. 'The Gandiva is slipping out of my hands. I have no desire to fight any more. I am sickened by the thought of killing my relatives; thinking about it makes my mouth dry and my hair stand on end. Oh, what is the point of acquiring all this wealth and knowledge? What is the point of this solemnity and pleasures when you have no one to enjoy it with? I really do not desire this. Even if they kill me, it is fine because either way I lose. This war is a total waste and I cannot fight.'

Krishna asks Arjuna to reflect deeply on the meaning and purpose of life. His teachings explain the fundamental distinction between the transitory world and the eternal consciousness. An understanding of this distinction enables one to act with an attitude of selfless service that characterizes a self-realized person. One's actions can either bind one to this world or liberate one from it. Arjuna understands what it means to act with intense involvement and presence but with complete detachment from the fruits of one's actions.

Krishna talks to Arjuna about mundane levels of existence and the three fundamental aspects of prakriti *(nature):* sattva *(light, lucidity and joyousness),* rajas *(action, drive and dissatisfaction) and* tamas *(substantiveness, inertia and depression). He explains what these aspects are, how they act, how one creates a balance or imbalance in them through one's engagement with one's world, and how one transcends them.*

Lord Krishna grants Arjuna divine vision and reveals his cosmic form, his vishwaroopam. *All the possible ways in which nature can manifest herself, from the most sublime to the most grotesque, are revealed to Arjuna. Arjuna is overwhelmed and realizes that the Brahmin is imminent in every atom of manifestation.*

After taking Arjuna through this very profound enquiry into the nature of man and the nature of the world, Krishna asks him to ponder over what right action means to him. He tells Arjuna to follow his conviction.

The dialogue between Arjuna and Krishna delves into seminal ideas like *karma yoga* (the path of action), *bhakti yoga* (the path of devotion) and *jnaana yoga* (the path of insight). It is through these practices that a person performing actions in the outer world can discover how to renounce the fruits of those actions. The wise man, purified by the fire of contemplation, becomes capable of profound inner stillness while remaining powerfully present.

The dialogue examines what comprises *asuric* or demonic behaviour and what comprises *daivic* or divine behaviour. Finally, Lord Krishna explains the meaning of profound dispassion and renunciation, and how action that flows from this state of meditation reflects Intelligence.

RAGHU: Before we start the reflection, let us keep in mind our interpretation of Krishna as our innermost intelligence. Our Puranas speak about the presence of the divine in us. This divinity is accessed through pure intuition gained through meditation. This intuition throws up flashes of insight, visions and revelations.

Many people have spoken about their creative insights as the sudden luminous flash within them that changed their life completely. For example, saints and gurus such as Ramana Maharishi, Ramakrishna Paramahamsa, Vivekananda and Mahatma Gandhi have stated that they are manifesting a deeper Intelligence. With that in mind, let us reflect on what this story evokes in all of us.

SAMIR: Where Kurukshetra becomes a Dharmakshetra is a profound space. In the Mahabharata, the two pivots which stand out are Draupadi's disrobing and Arjuna's being consumed with doubts when he sees his elders on the other side. Draupadi's disrobing represented a society caught in its own greed, where the powerful failed to do anything, stuck as they were with the guidelines laid out by and the benefaction of those who ruled the kingdom.

We see an Arjuna who, after preparing for thirteen years, freezes at the start of the war. The conversation with Krishna reflects a mature Arjuna, who has gone through a deep *saadhana* and is able to question himself sincerely, bring to fore all his assumptions about human existence, its meaning and purpose before making a decision. And then comes the war, where the part of society that repeatedly refuses to change has to be destroyed.

SAMIR: To me the interesting part started when Arjuna said, 'Take me to the centre. I want to see the faces of those I have to fight and destroy.' There is something in him which is telling him, 'Are you seeing the other side as enemies?'

RAGHU: Duryodhana was very confident that victory would be theirs since Bhishma was on their side. He had the *neeti*, structural authority that rests on the letter of the law, on his side. But Arjuna says Krishna is on their side, which metaphorically represents the Divine Intelligence, an intelligence that goes beyond man-made structures and law. I am relating this situation to some of the prior discussions we have had on Yudhishthira, where he was continuously asked, 'What would ensure victory?' His answer always was, 'Only might and strength will not ensure victory; an ability to fight for *satyam* will.' Despite many provocations by his brothers, he stood by his belief. Let me use this point in the context of organizations where there is a difference between intent and goal. Goal is external, whereas intent is internal. It is this deep inner intent that is based on the conviction that one is acting for something meaningful that gives immense power to resist false pulls and pushes. A predatory manner of acquiring victory through muscle power, which is a goal-behaviour oriented externally will only get you pyrrhic victory at best.

RANDHIR: This brings me back to another question that Arjuna asked: 'What is it that we are fighting for?'

SAMIR: Arjuna had great confidence, but then showed his vulnerabilities when he put down his weapons. After visualizing the consequences of his actions, Arjuna was no longer sure whether victory was really a great prize.

RAGHU: In my own experience, whenever you are caught in a *dharma sankata*, your psychosomatic system gets disturbed. A modern physician will recognize all the symptoms that Arjuna describes as the symptoms of autonomic nervous system failure in the face of high stress! But not facing up to the various aspects of a challenge is not an option.

SHRUTI: Duryodhana was so confident of victory because Bhishma, the symbol of *dharma*, was on his side. However, we must emphasize that Bhishma was upholding an idea of *dharma* that was non-contextual. This was already evident when he didn't speak up in the court at the time Draupadi was being humiliated.

RANDHIR: Bhishma is held in such high esteem even today in Indian society. One day, someone introduced me as a 'Bhishma Pitaamah' and I was quite disturbed! Not only because I refuse to believe I am that old, but also because that probably is not me.

Yes, Bhishma is the epitome of discipline, but his commitment to a personal discipline is fragmented from the emerging context. He is oblivious of the consequences his choices have on others and the future. Bhishma is a good example of a person who has given up his inner self at the altar of his self-righteousness.

SHRUTI: Throughout his life, Bhishma is portrayed as the ultimate warrior, fiercely holding on to his vow. However, I can't think of a single instance where Bhishma talks about his own feelings.

RAGHU: Bhishma was given a boon to choose the time of his own death. It is a metaphor for allowing old ideas to fade out gracefully before making way for the new. But when old methods remain frozen in place, it does lead to a dilemma on how best to remove them while ensuring respect for what they have contributed. This is often the case in family businesses, where the founders or older management end up staying longer than they ought to.

SAMIR: I am reminded of a very powerful example of creative destruction at an extremely successful technology company I was working with. In the mid-1990s, they appointed a new CEO who had risen from within the ranks and had never worked at another company. Within three months of becoming the CEO, he called his leadership team and said that they are in the wrong business as the internet will completely disrupt what they were doing. His leadership did not share his paranoia. Life continued with minor adjustments to indulge the new CEO.

After one month, the CEO cancelled three large R&D projects, diverted that money to internet-based technology fields. Next, he identified eight veteran employees who had built the technology that had made them world leaders. These people were highly regarded in their industry. The CEO did not fire them, but moved them to roles where effectively they had no power or influence. Soon, they all resigned one after the other.

All the employees were shocked, but settled into the new way of working. Two years later, the success that followed made those former star employees admit grudgingly that those changes were required and that they had not foreseen the impact the internet could have on the world of telecom.

RAGHU: That is a brilliant example of a leader destroying that which created him for the greater good. He must have struggled with his own conviction on the one hand and the weight of the wisdom represented by the 'respected elders' on the other. What a deep *dharma sankata* he would have gone through before doing what he did! The fact that he let these Bhishmas decide the time of their own 'deaths' – the moment when their time at the company would come to an end – was a good example of treating old ideas with dignity but still moving on.

This is the context in which the Bhagavad Gita is narrated: Arjuna articulates his *dharma sankata*, where he has to come to terms with destroying the old that has nurtured him and given him many gifts in order to champion the emerging context. Krishna speaks about the beauty of discovering the space and energy beyond outward appearances and acting from a place of deep Intelligence.

Many Indian companies struggle with transitioning from being family businesses to professional organizations. I have worked with a few of these transition challenges, and I find that professionals often fail to appreciate the dignity of traditions. The idea of a conquering hero is valued over the idea of a nurturing and inclusive heroism, one that can be contextually sensitive and systemically appropriate, and can find a balance between the subtle heart of a tradition and the changes occasioned by emerging technology or markets.

RANDHIR: Isn't this because we treat management and business organizations as a very modern phenomenon?

RAGHU: True, there is a misconception that management is a very new innovation. China and India were commercial powerhouses for millennia, the Arabs were great traders, and Europe had its own commercial traditions. Now we have the idea of heroism projected in Hollywood, in which there is always a threat, and a hero must kill off the villain. There is also a clock ticking! People and property on both sides have to be sacrificed for the Rambo-hero to save the day, and all such losses are dismissed as 'collateral damage'.

It is important to build models of leadership around business continuity and not around short-term crises. We need to value Arjuna's approach to the decision-making dilemma in the context of larger human concerns. Indra tells Arjuna to not just learn 'new technology' but also how to use that technology responsibly. We must look at heroism in a holistic way rather than merely as conquest and destruction. Arjuna's ability to ponder over the profound meaning of life and human existence before seeking to define his own purpose becomes a very important parable.

SAMIR: What about Duryodhana? Did he follow *neeti* but not *nyaaya* and *dharma?*

RAGHU: There is a difference between *neeti* and *nyaaya. Neeti* is the letter of the law and *nyaaya* is fairness. Duryodhana simply used rules, without regard for the context and without compassion.

SHRUTI: Do you mean to say that the Pandavas did not follow the book?

RAGHU: No, I mean that both sides claimed to play by the book, but the interpretation of the book is where the difference lies. One interprets purely by the letter, and the other uses a *dharmic* approach, the concept of fairness. When Arjuna questions, 'Who am I?', there could be many answers: he is the grandnephew of Bhishma, a student of Drona, among many other such relationships. He then says that he will not kill because of these identities. Krishna helps him understand who he is at that point of time, in that context.

The identities that we hold on to are all about our idea of self, our ego. Identities based on personal relationships cannot help us follow *dharmic* action. Duryodhana builds his army by insisting on relationships and quid pro quos. Yudhishthira instead asks people to join him only if they are convinced about the *dharmic* nature of the war.

Arjuna works to leave behind these identities one by one and finally understand who he truly is in that context, and why he is there. He realizes that the vibrant and enlivening self is beyond all these identities and that one must act on the basis of *dharma.* For him, the battlefield becomes Dharmakshetra, where the fight is for *dharma* and not for the kingdom. For the Kauravas, the battlefield remains Kurukshetra, in which the battle is for the kingdom.

SHRUTI: So, *dharma* is very impersonal, right?

RAGHU: Yes, because it is beyond an individual and temporal identification.

SHRUTI: That is why the story of a Dharmakshetra and Kurukshetra is so fascinating even today. We go through struggles or fights of various kinds, which are stressful because we act on the basis of personal identities. However, if we anchor these struggles to a larger purpose of enlivening life itself, then the perspective changes. If our choices are based on whether our actions will enable the unfolding of good, they then become *dharmic* struggles.

RANDHIR: What does 'enlivening life' mean here? Is it happiness?

RAGHU: Enlivening life has a much deeper meaning than immediate happiness. If one engages with life mindfully, there will be a deep sense of satisfaction in having done the right thing for oneself and for others. For example, Duryodhana and Karna's course of actions are based on envy and victimhood, respectively. These actions are not enlivening for the person and the context, but they give these characters a sense of immediate happiness.

RANDHIR: Are we talking about right or wrong here?

RAGHU: Not really, as here is nothing right or wrong except as defined by us. But we can ask if something is *dharmic* or *adharmic*.

SAMIR: True power also lies in how one finds a space beyond fear without disowning the fear. When I try to shut out fear, I am in conflict with myself on the one hand and insensitive to the real dangers of the situation on the other. However, if I face up to it, it is very empowering and energizing because it will not allow me to do anything arrogant or take blind risks. Knowing the real possibilities of defeat and the true strengths of our position helps us to fight heroically.

Arjuna is able to go into *vishaadha* (depression) and ask fundamental questions such as 'Who am I? Where am I? And why am I here?' He tries to accept the grief and sadness he feels at the thought of killing and causing havoc. Arjuna can enter these depths without losing balance or acting unreasonably because he has faced his deepest feelings.

RAGHU: Powerful emotions like grief, guilt and sorrow can pull one down. Arjuna is able to listen to Krishna's voice even as he voices his deep depression because he is not overcome by this emotion. Rather, he faces up to it and becomes deeply aware of these feelings. This enables him to listen to the voice of Intelligence. This is an essential quality of a hero: to be fully cognizant of the reality confronted him, but facing it from a deep inner space of tranquillity.

SHRUTI: Facing our fears is a good thing as long as we are not overawed by them.

RAGHU: Arjuna did experience self-doubt, but another way of looking at it is that he is strongly anchored in his deeper self, which allows him to consider all sides.

The Pandavas were looking for a father figure and found it in both Drona and Bhishma. It is difficult to give up this connection that was so deeply yearned for. It starts to cloud one's judgement. That is why Arjuna asks Krishna to take him to the centre of the battlefield, so that he can choose the right thing to do only after evaluating both sides carefully from a neutral position.

This is the point where doubt exists. In Sanskrit, there are two words for doubt. One is *ubhayakotispraha* (literally touching the two ends of a line), which means running from one end of a dilemma to another in deep inner conflict without being able to come to a conclusion. The other is *aashrayabhuktha* (that which supports the fire is burnt away), which means suffering in one's effort to find a resolution for the dilemma. Thus, the neutral location is where we can step back and view the dilemma dispassionately, in spite of the immense difficulty we will experience between the two pulls. Only then can we question the assumptions we are making and the compulsions driving us.

Imagine Bhishma asking himself why he is so rigid about upholding his vow. Maybe the immense power needed to hold back his natural drives when he was in the prime of his youth became an obsession. We can only speculate on what it would have taken for him to allow doubt to enter his mind.

Arjuna's enquiry does not give space to something that burns him up nor does it tie up his energies in an inner conflict. He looks at each side of the *dharma sankata* completely and deeply before making a choice. He does this by going into *shaantham* to evaluate the context with a meditative mind.

SHRUTI: At the start of the war, Yudhishthira says, 'If anyone feels that they should join the side of *dharma,* they should join us.' One of Duryodhana's brothers by the name of Yuyutsu understood the context and chose to switch sides and join the Pandavas.

RAGHU: During the war, Yudhishthira asks people to act from their conscience, but Duryodhana asks people to act because it is what they owe him. Both Drona and Bhishma confess later that they felt blackmailed into obliging.

RAGHU: It is important to ask these questions and reflect on them. How do we make our life a Dharmakshetra rather than a Kurukshetra?

Dear Reader, let's pause and think about the 'Arjuna moments' in your life. How did you respond? What insights did they offer you about your ways of using power and your leadership style?

SECTION 6: Karna, the Victim

The story of Karna is, in essence, tragedy. From the time of his birth, Karna is wounded by circumstances beyond his control. He is the victim of his mother's decision to abandon him. As he grows up, the elders of the Kuru dynasty discriminate against him repeatedly. Even as he tries to heal his wounds of deprivation and denial through developing his extraordinary capabilities, he runs into the shadow sides of the system.

Karna's story is also one of sacrifice, of courage in the face of adversity, of magnanimity in the face of discrimination, of positivity in the face of negativity. It is a cautionary tale about what happens to the meritorious in a system that misuses power.

Karna is born to Kunti and Surya, the Sun God. Kunti receives a mantra as a boon from the rishi Durvasha. If she recites the mantra, whichever god she thinks of will appear before her and bless her with a son endowed with his own fine qualities. Out of curiosity, she tries this mantra while thinking of Surya, the Sun God. Indeed, Surya appears to bless her, and Kunti immediately gives birth to a son.

The child is wearing a *kavacha-kundala*, an armour filled with divine nectar. This armour will protect him and make him invincible. Kunti, still unmarried, is afraid of the social stigma that would accompany such a birth. She puts the baby in a basket and prays that the gods protect this child. Then she sets the basket afloat on the river.

The basket is discovered by Adhiratha Nandana and his wife Radha. They adopt him and name the child Radheya. Adhiratha is a charioteer and a poet serving Dhritarashtra. Because of his *kavacha-kundala*, the child comes to be known as Karna.

After being rejected as a student by Dronacharya for being a *sootaputra* (a low-born), Karna learns the art of warfare from Parasurama. Karna excels in the art of warfare. He appears in the royal court during a competition, to challenge Arjuna as the best warrior in Hastinapura. Karna is not allowed to compete and is humiliated for being a *sootaputra.*

However, Duryodhana recognizes Karna's immense talent and bestows legitimacy on him by anointing him as the king of Angada. Karna's gratitude creates a deep bond with Duryodhana. Karna is known as a good king, and his unbounded generosity wins him great renown. He becomes known as a *dhaanavaan* (a great giver).

The Pandavas fear Karna the most because of his great abilities with weapons of war and his mastery of archery. A strange animosity develops between Arjuna and Karna. It runs very deep.

During the twelfth year of exile, Yudhishthira spends every night worrying about Karna's might. Yudhishthira watches Karna closely and sees his *kavacha-kundala* protecting him. He feels that Karna is unbeatable and as a result the Kauravas will win the war.

Story 1: Karna's Benevolence

Indra is a well-wisher of the Pandavas, especially his son Arjuna. At the start of the Pandava's thirteenth year of the exile, Indra hatches a ploy to take away Karna's strength by asking for his divine gifts, his earrings and his armour. He knows that Karna will never refuse a gift asked of him. Surya, aware of Indra's intentions, decides to warn his son about the danger that awaits him.

As Karna lies asleep at night, Surya shows himself in his dream as a Brahmin. 'O son, my dear Karna, listen to the words I speak,' Surya says. 'Indra, ever desirous of the welfare of the Pandavas and knowing your quality of giving whatever is asked for by the Brahmans at noon, will come seeking the earrings and armour that you have worn ever since you were born. When he asks for them, please do not part with those.'

'Who are you, showering such great affection upon me?' asks Karna.

'I am Surya and I say this out of affection for you, for your benefit.'

'I am indeed fortunate to have you come to speak to me today,' says Karna. 'Please do hear me out. I am known the world over for my generosity. You are well aware that I will give my life for the best of the Brahmins. If Indra were to come in the guise of a Brahmin to beg for my earrings and the armour, I shall not refuse him. The world will honour me with fame. I will sacrifice my life for everlasting fame.'

'It is not the dead but the living who enjoy the fame,' said Surya. 'Since you have been a great devotee of mine, I am inclined to share this for your well-being. Speak to Indra with sweet and reasonable words and turn him away. If you are desirous of defeating Arjuna in the battle, do not give away your earrings and the armour.'

'O Lord, knowing me to be your devoted worshipper, you are advising me thus? Pardon me, sire. I am ready to sacrifice my life rather than break my vow. I shall definitely defeat Arjuna with the weapons that Parasurama has given me, even without my earrings and armour.'

'If you must part with them, you should tell him that you will do so under a condition: in return, you must receive a weapon that will destroy your enemies. There is an arrow of the Lord of the Gods that does not return to one's hand without killing thousands of enemies,' says the Sun God and vanishes.

The next day, Karna waits for Indra to appear. Soon, Indra shows up as a Brahmin and says, 'Give me alms.'

'What do you seek?' asked Karna. 'Gold, jewellery, land or cows?'

'I wish for none of those,' says Indra. 'If you truly wish to honour your vow, then cut off these earrings and armour that you were born with and give them to me. This is what I want.'

'What you ask for is what makes me invincible. I do not wish to part with them. Take half of my precious kingdom instead.'

The Brahmin dismisses all else that is offered and insists on receiving the earrings and the armour.

Finally, Karna smiles and says, 'I know who you are, O Lord of the Devas. I cannot bestow what I was born with without a boon in return.'

'What do you seek?' asks Indra. 'I shall grant you anything other than my thunderbolt.'

'In exchange for my earrings and armour, grant me that great weapon that you possess with which I may kill a great and powerful enemy.'

Indra thinks for some time. Then he says, 'In exchange for what I have asked for, I give you Shakti. When hurled by me, this great weapon kills thousands of enemies and returns to my hand. When hurled by you, it will kill one powerful enemy and will then return to me.'

'I do seek to kill one powerful enemy.'

'It will kill one powerful enemy. But the one you seek to kill is protected by the great being Krishna.'

'I understand, yet I seek that weapon.'

Karna then says that he will be scarred if he cuts away his armour and earrings.

'You will not bear the scars,' Indra reassures him. 'You will be splendorous like your father, as you keep the truth of your vow. Use my boon with care. If you were to hurtle it in anger, or when you have other weapons, it will come back and fall upon yourself.'

Karna proceeds to cut away his earrings and armour, and offers them to Indra. In return, he receives the great weapon Shakti. The celestials are pleased by this action and Indra, in deceiving Karna, makes Karna's fame last forever.

RANDHIR: Karna's whole life has been about giving whenever people have asked. It clearly defines who he is and has given meaning to his life. If this meaning goes away, then life becomes hollow.

SAMIR: I understood how Arjuna and Yudhishthira viewed Karna. Arjuna always viewed him as competition, and it was always about how to outdo him, whereas Yudhishthira was immensely fearful of Karna's power.

SHRUTI: Why is Karna considered the counterpoint to Arjuna? In this story, he is almost like Nakula, who is always so generous and yet remains unrecognized.

RAGHU: Karna is also versatile like Arjuna. He does show characteristics of others as well. Karna is a *daanaveer*, someone whose selfless giving was celebrated. In the war, Karna encounters all the brothers and defeats four of them, the same way Arjuna is able to fight all the warriors on the Kaurava side.

SHRUTI: Karna worked hard to master his capabilities. But it was soured by all the humiliation he received.

RANDHIR: Karna did not want to be judged by his birth, but by his virtues. He wanted to be known as a *daanaveer* and not as a *sootaputra.*

SHRUTI: When Karna says, 'I would rather die than not be known as the most generous person,' it seems as if he is living only for the fame he would like to have after he dies.

SAMIR: It's similar to how some people try their best to be included in certain elite circles. For example, certain companies have a culture of elitism. The managers who are members of the 'company elite' are treated differently from the others. The rest aspire to join that category, and until they do, they often feel small and ashamed of themselves.

RAGHU: This kind of behaviour in organizations is quite common wherein people keep on compromising to belong to the exclusive club. If a manager understands this behaviour, he or she can manipulate you to any extent in return for admittance to the elite.

SAMIR: Even if one does certain things to belong to the club, one may still feel uncomfortable and live in fear of being exposed as an impostor.

RAGHU: When only one's offerings and skills are valued, one's true self remains in the shadows. It causes a huge sense of hurt. Many Karna managers stress themselves out trying to prove themselves worthy of what they perceive as 'higher society'. Unfortunately, how they try to prove themselves is contrary to their authentic self.

They lose their source of inner power when they try to become what they are not. In the process, they do not nurture their real talents and lose out both ways. The individual often realizes this, but the fear of being shamed is very high. Unfortunately, Karnas get trapped into proving themselves in a system that does not appreciate their worth, and this only reinforces their sense of rejection.

SHRUTI: I also see this as a major difference between organizations that have a healthy work culture and those that don't. In the former, employees are valued not only for their skills but also for who they are as individuals. In the latter, employees are only valued if they fit into the management culture.

RAGHU: Even though organizations talk about diversity and inclusivity, many don't realize the extent to which certain employees must continuously disown who they are to fit in. The concept of 'inclusivity' is often taken to mean conformity to externally visible parameters, instead of respect for differences in propensities and backgrounds.

When one does not acknowledge one's own *svabhaava* and instead seeks approval or acceptance from others, one takes on the ways of a Karna. Despite being accepted a great warrior, Karna cannot get over the humiliation brought by the label of '*sootaputra*' that has been attached to him. Therefore, he tries to find further acknowledgement by being extra generous.

Whenever we yearn for external affirmations to compensate for deprivation and self-doubt, we leave ourselves open to manipulation by canny people. Many of us yearn for appreciation, and this allows organizations to manipulate us through their schemes of reward and punishment. We become trapped in looking for outer recognition over intrinsic rewards.

RANDHIR: During performance appraisals, I asked employees about their weaknesses. A regular answer was: 'I trust people too easily.' I used to ask people to turn it around and ask themselves if they are too naive. By feeling that they were too trusting, they were externalizing their own lack of judgement. It was due to their inability to value themselves.

SHRUTI: Does hurt and humiliation prevent Karna from acknowledging his strengths?

RAGHU: He had the choice to take pride in his unique armour and other gifts. But he gave too much importance to what others said about him. Karna never listened when Kunti told him the story of his birth because he had deeply internalized the humiliation that came from being abandoned. This humiliation is carried by him until his death. However, Steve Jobs was also an adopted child. The difference was that he could convert the angst into a positive force.

RANDHIR: I am reminded of a popular retelling of an encounter between Krishna and Karna. For every recounting of Karna of his unfortunate circumstances, Krishna shares one of his own. Karna says he is abandoned at birth. Krishna counters it by saying that he was born in a prison and abandoned by his parents. Karna then laments that he did not have teachers. Krishna responds by saying that he was living with cowherds and got formal schooling only when he was much older.

The difference between the two is that Krishna found in himself the intelligence and power not to convert any of these deprivations into deep wounds. I guess that is what we call a divine quality.

Story 2: The Unconvinced Karna

When Krishna is requested by Yudhishthira to stop the war, Krishna has a discussion with all the Pandavas. Though quite bitter, all brothers are willing to give peace a chance. After the discussions, Krishna goes to the Kaurava camp as an ambassador of the Pandavas. However, Duryodhana blocks all possibilities of peace.

Karna goes to see Krishna off on his way back to the Pandavas. Krishna asks Karna to join him on the chariot.

'A woman has two categories of children other than the ones she begets through marriage,' says Krishna to Karna. 'One category is of those who are begotten before marriage, and the other is of those who are begotten by a man other than her husband. You are born that way, and thus, you are morally the son of Pandu. Accompany me from here, dear friend, and let the sons of Pandu recognize you to be the first son of Kunti before Yudhishthira.

'The kings and princes assembled by the Pandavas will accept you as their lord, and so will the five Pandava brothers, the five sons of Draupadi as well as the son of Subhadra. Then, I will anoint you as the king and lord of the universe. Yudhishthira will be your heir-apparent, holding the chamara *(the royal umbrella) for you and driving in the chariot behind you. Bhima will hold the umbrella over you and Arjuna will drive the chariot, guiding the horses. Abhimanyu (Arjuna's son) will be by your side while Nakula and Sahadeva will follow you, and so will I. Rule and enjoy the kingdom with your brothers and delight the heart of Kunti. Let there be fraternal feelings with your brothers, the sons of Pandu, today.'*

'Krishna, I do know that you speak these words out of goodwill, friendship and warmth in your heart for me,' says Karna. 'I know myself to be the son of Pandu, born to Kunti before her marriage, begotten by my father Surya and then abandoned by her immediately upon being born, without a thought for my welfare. When Adhiratha found me, he took me home and my mother, Radha, found milk in her bosom for me, even though I was not of her womb.

'Adhiratha, the charioteer, looked upon me as his son and I loved him as my father. He performed all the ceremonies for me, and I married the wife he chose for me. My children play upon his lap, he is their grandfather. How can I neglect my offerings of pinda[6] *to their souls when my parents depart? Neither for the sake of this entire earth, nor for the sake of heaps of gold can I forsake those ties that are close to my heart.*

'Under Duryodhana, I have enjoyed sovereignty for thirteen years with all comforts. For the fear of being slain or captured, I cannot act treacherously towards my friend Duryodhana and embrace infamy forever. You speak for the benefit of the Pandavas and I. Please keep this conversation only

6 Pindas are balls of cooked rice mixed with ghee and black sesame seeds offered to ancestors as part of funerary rites.

between us. If Yudhishthira were to know that I was the eldest son of Kunti, he will never accept the kingdom. Even if I were to accept this large kingdom, I will in turn offer it to Duryodhana. Let Yudhishthira and Arjuna live forever. Let this earth and this great kingdom belong to the one who has Bhima, Nakula, Sahadeva and Draupadi by his side.'

'This world will truly come to an end, as my words are not acceptable to you,' says Krishna.

'If I am alive after this battle, O Krishna, I will meet you. Else I will surely meet you in heaven. I now see that I will only meet you there.'

Karna embraces Krishna and walks away with his heart filled with sorrow.

Krishna tells Kunti about the conversation. She makes up her mind to meet Karna and tell him all that had happened. She goes towards the banks of the Ganga, where Karna is offering his prayers to the sun. She stands behind him at a distance, waiting for him to finish his offerings.

Karna finishes and turns around to see Kunti waiting. Surprised, he says, 'I am Karna, son of Adhiratha and Radha. Why are you here? And what it is that I could do for you?'

'You, Karna, were born of my womb, fathered by Surya when I was unmarried,' says Kunti. 'Owing to your ignorance of the nature of your birth, you are serving the sons of Dhritarashtra. Let them bow down when they see you together with Arjuna. You are the eldest among my sons. Do not call yourself the son of a charioteer, you are indeed my son.'

Unmoved by the words of Kunti, Karna says, 'Royal lady, I do not respect your words nor your behaviour towards me, owing to which I sustained infamy for long. Born a Kshatriya, I received none of the great things accorded to me, because of your actions. Not having shown kindness when it ought to have been shown, you come to me now when it suits you, urging me for your own good. I was celebrated and worshipped by the sons of Dhritarashtra. Why would I turn my back upon them? How can I abandon them? The time has come for those who have been living off the earnings of Duryodhana to be there for him.

'I shall fight your sons with all my power and valour. Your efforts today will not go waste, lady. I shall not kill those sons whom I do not consider

my equal. Yudhishthira, Bhima, Nakula and Sahadeva are no match against me. Arjuna alone is one whom I consider my equal as a warrior, and thus I shall fight to kill him.

'At the end of the war, you will still have five sons. You will have either Arjuna or me. If I were to kill Arjuna, my reputation will grow further, and if he kills me, my fame will only increase.'

Kunti embraces him and says, 'May you be blessed, and may all be well with you.'

She leaves her first-born and returns to her palace.

SHRUTI: This is a story that embodies all the characteristics of Karna. There is clarity of thought in his dialogues, be it with Krishna or Kunti. Here is a man who is given a kingdom on a platter, but his motivations are different. He is not fighting for the kingdom like the rest.

SAMIR: Karna is fighting this war for himself, not to gain a mother, brother or a kingdom. His clarity of thought is tremendous, but it seems to be entrenched in feelings of hurt.

RANDHIR: It's as if he wants to redeem himself through self-destruction.

RAGHU: I am finding it a bit difficult to relate to this story, even though Karna demonstrates clarity of purpose. He seems to be unable to give up vengefulness. He knows what it means to be disowned and discriminated against. Thus, he would rather get what he really deserves on his own terms than live on other people's terms. The victim's voice is definitely there when he speaks about the years of humiliation he has endured.

RANDHIR: This would have been a great opportunity to emerge as a hero. He could have stopped the war and saved both sides.

SAMIR: If I were Karna, how could I think of abandoning Duryodhana? Kunti and the Pandavas were not there for him at his most difficult time.

RAGHU: But Karna is not protecting Duryodhana, if you think about the larger destruction the war would cause. It would lead to the loss of Duryodhana's life. Karna choosing to go to war and die fighting is completely self-destructive. This self-destructive tendency is very common among people who have a feeling of victimhood and they find it extremely hard to overcome it. They get into a spiral of negatives, despite knowing how destructive it is.

If he had transformed himself deeply, he would have made the choice to stop the war. In the Jungian theory, when the archetypal energies take over, one's consciousness gets overwhelmed. You can call it destiny or whatever you like. Essentially, your mind is clouded. Deep and strong compulsion takes over and leads you to a path of destruction.

SHRUTI: If Karna had listened to Krishna and stopped the war, what would have happened to the collective angst of the Kauravas?

RAGHU: When negative archetypal energies take over, they lead us to destruction. If we find a light below all these negative energies, there is a scope for real transformation. Karna showed extraordinary capabilities in trying to deal with the angst of the hurts he had been subjected to.

If Karna had decided to back off, would the poison in the system have ended once and for all? Duryodhana had a very high opinion of Karna. If anyone, it was Karna who could have influenced Duryodhana to stop the war. If Karna had found the strength to let go of the deep hurt to his identity and reclaim it on his own terms, maybe he could have changed his own narrative and stopped the war.

Every system is designed to have intended positives for its members. However, inevitably there are unintended negatives. There has to be a dialogue between the ones who represent the intended positives and the ones who experience the unintended negatives for a new system to emerge that is truly evolutionary and can include and embrace those affected by its present state.

In the Mahabharata, it means a dialogue between Bhishma, the icon of the system, and Karna. Bhishma has to listen to the hurt and pain of Karna, and acknowledge that they are the creators of the oppression. Karna has to speak, not from a need for retribution and vengeance, but from the depth of his feelings. Through a dialogue that is neither defensive nor offensive, a new and creative way of designing a system can emerge. From it, we can have a system that does not violate the vulnerable, nor discriminate against true merit.

RANDHIR: If Karna had decided to dissolve his hurts and sought Krishna's divine counsel for doing this, the Bhagavad Gita could have been about what it takes for a Karna to transform himself and the system rather than Arjuna's dilemmas around taking up the battle. Perhaps Bhishma was not ready to have a discussion, but Karna did have the opportunity to seek Krishna's advice.

SHRUTI: Yes, I can imagine a dialogue between Karna and Krishna where Karna asks: 'If I accept your offer, Krishna, then what about Duryodhana and my commitment to him? How do I embrace people I have hated for over so many years? How do I dissolve the hurts of discrimination and denial?' Karna will list a different set of *dharma sankata*s than the ones Arjuna articulated.

RAGHU: Absolutely. It was certainly a moment of *dharma sankata* for Karna, but he did not recognize it. He was so deeply entrenched in his hurt that he did not listen to his deepest Intelligence. In some sense, you can say that his clarity was his undoing. And that was a major difference between him and Arjuna.

RANDHIR: I think many managers with Karna propensities often become stuck in number two positions. They are often very capable, but unable to perform without a protective umbrella. They feel insecure when they have to let go of the dependency. It is like the symbiotic relationship between Duryodhana and Karna.

RAGHU: Yes, many struggle with the fear of how they would be received if they leave a situation in which they are protected and become more visible. On the one hand, they realize that their capabilities are not being fully valued, but on the other, they want to avoid the risk of losing their job. They end up making themselves indispensable to their senior partner. It takes a lot of self-reflection and inner healing for them to take a step out of this symbiotic relationship.

In the Yoga Sutras, this is the space of real *dhyaana* (profound attentiveness) from which one can see the deep hurt and stigma one is caught up in. One must see the *karma vaasana* (seeds of one's action patterns) and *samskaara* (behavioural habits). This *dhyaana* enables the person to see that he has the choice to act in ways that are not bound by his old patterns, which may be defined by hurt, craving or aversion.

SHRUTI: Unlike Karna, Krishna did not remain stuck in the same situation. Instead of being a cowherd all his life, Krishna found his way through many difficult situations without a benefactor.

RAGHU: True. Karna continued to hang on to the angst of being abandoned. If he understood his great heroic abilities and the gifts from Surya, the story would have been very different.

Maybe all of us have a Karna within, that part of us that feels unappreciated and discriminated against. We struggle to shut out the voice that cries for vengeance.

RANDHIR: Often in the corporate world, people get so indebted to the organizations for providing them with a career that they stop trusting their inner consciousness. They are scared of losing all the privileges that come with their jobs.

There was a listed company where the founder CEO took huge risks on his personal investments. The bets went wrong, and he landed up in a lot of debt. He then tried to take the money out from the company through spurious transactions. There were people who knew what he was doing, but only one of them mustered the courage to tell the board members while quitting the company.

However, the board comprised people friendly with the CEO, and they tried to bury the issue. They said, 'What has happened is wrong, but let's move on. We will put in stronger processes.' Unfortunately for them, the media got a whiff of it, and they had no choice but to ask the CEO to leave. The company never recovered from that loss of trust.

SAMIR: It is a difficult situation when you find the person who has done so much for you embark on the path of *adharma*.

RAGHU: As they say, 'the path to hell is paved with good intentions'. We need to have the ability to recognize and confront a *dharma sankata* honestly and seek a solution based on our values. This is where the contrast between Arjuna and Karna becomes stark. Arjuna found the courage within to acknowledge his dilemma and seek out his deepest intelligence in the form of Krishna. Karna instead allowed his shadow side to take over and became deaf to the voice of his own inner clarity.

Dear Reader, let's pause and think of the 'Karna moments' in your life. How did you respond, and what insights did you get about your leadership style?

SECTION 7: The Indomitable Will of Draupadi

Draupadi represents the immense power and resilience of Nature. She is the foundation on which the structure of *dharmic* action is built. The Pandavas are mortal heroes who are enlivened by the power of Nature and protected by divine intelligence, Krishna. When those who wield power through kingship violate the vulnerable through their acts, Nature loses patience and becomes enraged. Draupadi symbolizes this power of Nature.

It is Draupadi who constantly reminds the Pandavas of their *dharmic* responsibility. Some commentators on the Mahabharata see Draupadi as the central force behind the war. She relentlessly holds the Pandavas to their word and ensures that *dharma* is reinstated.

Story 1: *Vastra Apaharan*: The Disrobing of Draupadi

In the final rounds of the game of dice, Shakuni prods Yudhishthira to stake Draupadi, saying that it can help Yudhishthira win back his and his brother's freedom. Yudhishthira foolishly agrees.

As soon as the rolling dice proclaims that Yudhishthira has lost Draupadi, Duryodhana thunders, 'Go, Vidura, bring Draupadi, the beloved wife of the Pandavas. Let her sweep the chambers and live in the maids' quarters!'

'O wicked man, you are provoking a venomous snake that is upon your head. You will bring ruin upon the race of Kurus. Slavery does not attach to

Draupadi as Yudhishthira couldn't have staked her to the gamble, having lost himself first,' says Vidura.

Intoxicated with pride, Duryodhana ignores Vidura's warning and turns to a messenger, commanding him to bring Draupadi to the hall. The messenger enters Draupadi's chambers like a dog entering a lion's den.

'O Draupadi, intoxicated by gambling, Yudhishthira staked and lost you to Duryodhana,' says the messenger. 'He first staked his brothers and lost them too. He then staked himself and lost himself. With none left, he staked you and lost you as well. You have been commanded to come to the court.'

'Intoxicated!' cries Draupadi. 'Surely no man would stake his wife. Go back and ask him whom he had lost first – himself or me?'

The messenger returns to the hall and poses the question to Yudhishthira, who sits in silence, demented and deprived of reason.

'Let the Princess of Panchala come here and pose the question. Let the assembly hear what passes between them here. Go, bring her!' orders Duryodhana.

'The assembly wants you to come,' the disturbed messenger says in a low voice after returning to Draupadi's chambers.

'Go, ask the assembly if this is dharma, *' says the princess. 'Ask them if this is what the Kurus would like to be remembered for. I will listen to the words of the virtuous in the assembly.'*

The messenger stands in great discomfort as Duryodhana commands, 'Bring her to the hall; we will answer her directly here.'

'What should I tell her, sire?'

'Dushasana, my brother, this foolish one is afraid of what Bhima might do to him. Go and bring her by force here. They are our slaves,' cries Duryodhana.

Commanded by his brother, Dushasana walks into Draupadi's chambers.

'Panchali, you have been won by us legitimately,' he says. 'Cast aside your modesty, come to the hall and look upon Duryodhana, your master.'

Draupadi covers her face with her trembling hands and runs towards the quarters of the ladies of the Kurus. Dushasana runs after and catches her by her long wavy hair. He starts to drag her to the court.

Her body bent awkwardly, Draupadi says while sobbing, 'I am in my season and in a single piece of cloth. Do not take me to the hall!'

'You are our slave and it matters not if you are in season or not, nor whether you are in a single piece of cloth or without even that,' roars Dushasana as he throws her inside the court.

'You wicked wretch!' Draupadi says, simmering with anger. 'This court is filled with virtuous men and some here are my gurus. In bringing me like this, you have brought ruin upon yourselves. Yudhishthira is rule-bound and he may stay silent, but even if Indra were your ally, the other Pandavas will not pardon you. It is unworthy of you to bring me here in front of many virtuous Kurus. But I see that there is none here who rebukes. The morality of the land has been destroyed here and now. Else, why would the great Bhishma, Drona and Kripa remain quiet? They have lost their greatness and the dharma *lies wasted on the Kuru shores!'*

The enraged yet silent Pandavas cannot meet the distressed and tear-filled glances of Draupadi that fall upon them. They are pained more by her state of anguish than by the loss of all their wealth.

Seeing her look at her hapless husbands, Dushasana laughingly drags her around, calling out loudly: 'Slave, slave!' while Karna and Shakuni laugh. Everyone else in the hall is filled with great sorrow.

Draupadi finally confronts Bhishma, who speaks slowly, filled with shame. 'O blessed lady, a man cannot stake someone else's wealth, but a wife belongs to her husband,' he says. 'Yudhishthira himself proclaimed that he had been won. He does not state that Shakuni won him by deceit. I cannot decide what is right in this case.'

'The king, unskilled in dice, was called and asked to play a deceitful, wicked game like desperate gamblers and has been manipulated. How is that voluntary and right? Let the men in this hall with wives, daughters and daughters-in-law answer,' Draupadi says in anger as she weeps piteously, running her eyes over her husbands.

Bhima explodes, 'Gamblers do not stake even the loose women that roam their homes. Yet you did stake our dear Draupadi, Yudhishthira. It is for your sake the Kurus are treating this remarkable woman thus. It is you who is to blame! Sahadeva, bring me fire, let me burn his hands.'

Arjuna intervenes. 'Your anger has been stoked by the acts of these cruel foes,' he cries. 'Summoned by the Kurus, the unwilling king played the game by the Kshatriya dharma, *and lost.'*

At this point, Vikarna, Duryodhana's brother, suddenly stands up and says, 'I ask Bhishma and Dhritarashtra to speak amidst themselves and decide how to answer her question. Why do the great Drona, Kripa and other virtuous kings in the hall stay silent? O kings, O great men, answer,' he asks. He repeats himself loudly. But no one offers a response.

'Since no one is answering here, I say my bit,' continued Vikarna. 'Yudhishthira, maddened by the vice of gambling, staked Draupadi, who is married to all the Pandavas. He had lost himself before he staked her and was urged to do so by the avaricious Shakuni. Considering all these, I proclaim that Draupadi has not been won, and certainly not fairly.'

The hall roars and applauds Vikarna.

'Vikarna, brother of Duryodhana,' shouts Karna, waving his arms in anger, 'you are but a boy speaking like an old man. The great men present here have stayed silent. Why? She belongs to her husband and when he staked all his possessions and himself, she was won by us. Shakuni merely suggested it but Yudhishthira willingly accepted, staked her and lost. Why do you say she was not won? A woman should be married to one man, but she is married to many. Thus, she is unchaste. An unchaste woman may be taken anywhere in a single piece of cloth, or without even that!'

Turning to Dushasana, Karna thunders: 'Take off the robes of the Pandavas and that of Draupadi!'

The Pandavas, silent and sullen, take off their upper garments and throw them on the floor. Dushasana pulls at Draupadi's sari.

In her panic, Draupadi begins to pray to Krishna.

'Govinda, Keshava, Krishna, Srinatha, Janardhana,' she cries, 'save me from sinking in the ocean of Kurus.'

Moved by her tear-filled calls, the great Krishna saves Draupadi's honour by ensuring she is never unclad. As Dushasana continues to pull each piece of cloth off her and discards it on the floor of the hall, another one appears. The cloth in her saree will not end!

The astonished hall rises in a great uproar. Bhima, shaking in anger, shouts at Dushasana, 'I will tear open your chest, wretched beast, and drink the blood from your heart. This I vow!'

The stirring words stun the audience and the fatigued Dushasana falls down in the middle of the heap that has gathered from the boundless fabric.

Karna says, 'Drag this servant woman to the quarters where she belongs, Dushasana.'

Dushasana hauls the piteously weeping Draupadi away as she keeps looking at her husbands.

'Wait!' she shouts. 'I still have a duty to perform, which I had forgotten while being dragged by this strong man. I have not paid my respects to the superiors in the court. I was seen once by the assembled kings on the day of the swayamvara *(choosing one's husband from among eligible suitors), and until today, none has seen me. We have never heard a wedded wife being dragged to an assembly before. All that is virtuous has been destroyed in the land of the Kurus today.*

'I am high-born and chaste, yet have been treated like this. Where is the dharma, *O kings? The wife of Yudhishthira and born in a lineage of queens, tell me if I am a maid? Tell me if I have been won? And I shall do as you say.'*

Bhishma speaks. 'The complex and delicate nature of the situation makes me incapable of answering your question. The folly and greed of the Kurus show that their destruction is not far off. Though persecuted, you have still pointed to us the path of dharma, *O blessed lady. The family you have married into has not departed from the path of virtue. Men like Drona sit as though their life has left the body. In my opinion, only Yudhishthira is qualified to answer your question in the best way possible.'*

'Panchali, let me put your question to the Pandavas,' says Duryodhana. 'Let Bhima, Arjuna and the twins declare in this hall that Yudhishthira is not their master, and you will be freed of slavery.'

Bhima says with a heavy heart, 'If Yudhishthira were not our lord, we would not have been silent even if a hair of Panchali had been touched. He is the lord of our lives, and if he considers himself won, then we are won too. We are bound by virtue to our elder brother.'

Duryodhana exposes his right thigh and shows it to Panchali, gesturing her to sit on his lap, with an intention to spite Bhima.

Bhima roars, 'I shall not go the way of my ancestors before breaking that thigh in the battle!'

A jackal cries aloud, donkeys bray, and birds make fearful noises. All of them herald adharma.

The great men of the court are alarmed by the warnings. Vidura and Gandhari rush to Dhritarashtra and tells him what had happened. The king says, 'Duryodhana, you have been engulfed by your wickedness and you bring great destruction upon us for insulting this blessed wedded lady of a Kuru chief.'

He then calls Draupadi and consoles her. 'You are the foremost of my daughters-in-law. Ask me for a boon and I shall grant it.'

'If I were to ask for a boon, it is this,' replies Draupadi. 'Let the great Yudhishthira be set free. Let not the great prince, a superior man, be called a slave ever.'

'Yes, blessed lady, so be it,' declares the king. 'My heart desires that you seek another boon. Ask, my child.'

'O king, grant me that a Bhima, Arjuna, Nakula and Sahadeva be not slaves.'

'Let it be so, child. Ask for a third, as my heart is not satiated with what you have asked.'

'O king, it is said that a Kshatriya woman may ask for two boons and a Kshatriya man, three. I shall ask for no more. My husbands can find prosperity as free men.'

'This woman is a saviour!' Karna exclaims. 'When the sons of Pandu were sinking, she became their boat and brought them safely ashore. She is the refuge for the sons of Pandu.'

Yudhishthira approaches Dhritarashtra. 'O king, you are our lord,' he says. 'Command us. What should we do?'

'O child! Be blessed,' replies Dhritarashtra. 'Go in peace and rule your kingdom with dharma. *Do not remember the harsh words of Duryodhana. Remember only what is good in Gandhari and me. In you is virtue; in Arjuna, patience; in Bhima, prowess; and in the twins, pure reverence and service. Bear no ill will towards your cousins. Go forth and rule your kingdom in peace from Indraprastha.'*

SHRUTI: One has heard this story so many times, but every time I hear it, there is such a rush of blood. How can a society come to such a pass that they can let something as horrible happen? Except Draupadi, there is no real hero here.

SAMIR: This story affects me deeply. Many times I have felt ashamed and powerless when people who have been wronged stand up and question me if what is happening to them is right. Even if I was not the perpetrator of the wrongs, by my silence, I am complicit. All of us do this when we don't really speak up to address an injustice because we have something to lose by doing so.

SHRUTI: Drona, Kripa and others were silenced because they were beholden to the Kauravas. Often, one is ambivalent in such situations and hopes that the situation will pass. But when it doesn't, one is helpless. There is no shame on the part of the victim. The moment they speak up, it is the system that has to acknowledge their shameful actions and make changes.

However, the victim can easily be intimated and give in. They may think that finding ways to live within the limited space that the oppressor offers would be better than confronting them. This creates a mutually reinforcing cycle of victimhood and oppression, with the victim choosing submission over conflict and the oppressor stamping out the smallest sign of rebellion.

RANDHIR: The whole story is an extraordinary one! Draupadi's vulnerability did not prevent her from taking a stand in front of the court. By questioning what *dharma* is, she was taking the high road when everyone was going low.

SHRUTI: It is very difficult to understand human propensities in the face of such brutality and horror. It is a case of extreme courage and inspiration. However, other aspects of that incident can capture our attention, and we do not always do justice to Draupadi's bravery.

RANDHIR: Dushasana trying to disrobe Draupadi but failing tells me that however hard a person may try, they cannot strip you of your dignity if you don't give them that power. Despite being stripped, Draupadi was the only one standing with her head held high in that court. It is everyone else in the assembly, despite being dressed in regal splendour, who actually lost all their dignity. If Krishna represents our innermost Intelligence, what this tells us is that if you are in touch with your innermost Intelligence, no one can take your dignity away.

RAGHU: When such a confrontation happens, if you manage to keep your dignity, the other person simply gets angry, loses their reason and falls from grace. Yes, one can get overwhelmed. However, if we can ask ourselves the critical questions – 'Who am I, where am I, and why am I here?' – we will discover great power. This is true heroism.

RANDHIR: Draupadi knew, in doing what she was doing, what she was really doing. Knowing how rule-bound the assembly will be, she first confronted them about the rules and laws. Only when it was established that laws do not cover such a situation did she question them on the grounds of *dharma*.

SHRUTI: Draupadi was let down by the system, but she refused to be a victim.

SAMIR: Interestingly, Draupadi's fight was not about resisting or striking the enemy, but standing her ground with poise and speaking powerfully in a way that shames everyone around her. What is the meaning of strength here?

RAGHU: Strength here is being in touch with the fundamental questions and having awareness, calmness and balance in order to find a solution. This is remarkable strength and courage. It is exactly what leadership is all about.

No leader can hold power if he loses moral authority and the trust of the followers. Here the Kurus lose both. They display their greed and their inability to respect the boundaries of dignity.

SHRUTI: Can you give me an example of this kind of leadership?

RANDHIR: There is the case of Nadia Murad I read a little while back. She was a young Yazidi farmer who was kidnapped, enslaved, sold and repeatedly raped. She managed to escape after a few months. Instead of being filled with shame or hatred, she chose to spend her life highlighting how society over centuries has accepted sexual violence as a weapon of war. She was awarded the Nobel peace prize for her work.

RAGHU: She could have easily slipped into simply remaining a victim for the rest of her life. It happens all the time. The degree of provocation and fear we can handle without losing our inner anchorage is contingent on our integrity, inner strength and commitment to do the right thing.

This is where Krishna comes into the picture. It is not Draupadi, the visible persona that is staying poised, but a deeper and higher Intelligence at work. She is feeling the pain, angst and pressure of the situation but inside her is a higher energy that manifests because she remains anchored. We can access this energy too. It lies within all of us.

SAMIR: Sometimes, being outwardly aggressive may not be the best way to stop brutality. Rather, we can use internal power wisely.

RAGHU: The power of a Draupadi comes from a place of deep quietude, a space where one accepts one's vulnerabilities and limitations without any fear. Time slows down, a deep peace takes over and an intelligence much deeper than thought empowers one's actions.

When we are faced with daunting challenges, we first try very hard to fight it. It is only when we let go without feeling any sense of failure or dejection that we allow ourselves to get anchored. This escape from a desperate, repetitive and often inadequate place within opens up the possibility of discovering new unrealized potentials and allows new perspectives to emerge.

Great leaders often speak about humility and a power greater than themselves. They stay aware of the context and alive to the opportunities, threats and dilemmas. They accept their own feelings of inadequacy and helplessness. When they stop trying to force an answer, often described as giving up ego, they get insights. Their intuition becomes powerful. This knowing is not derived through thought and reasoning. They perhaps feel that some divine energy showed them the path.

SHRUTI: How can one bear all that turmoil?

RAGHU: You will feel the heat, the pressure and the fear. You must allow yourself to feel it all and yet not succumb to it. It is not easy. In my experience, no external help can come through because the situation creates fear in all the people around you. Rather, you may be abandoned by people who just cannot comprehend the reality, or feel overwhelmed by it. At this point of time, it is something within that helps you say, 'I am alone in this, and I will take full responsibility for myself. I will accept reality. I will neither defy it nor deny it.'

This immediately frees the mind from thinking like a victim, getting reactive, or judging others. Whether one's actions were correct or not cannot be determined at that point of time. We just have to ask ourselves if we really tried the best we could at that time.

SAMIR: It is critical that people discover this space within themselves. It is not obvious, but it is there all the time. Draupadi discovered the depths and intensity of her heroism alone. Once she acts from that space, no one can do anything to her.

RAGHU: The heroic possibility is presented to everyone around in that context. In the court, the intensity of the brutality was felt by every person, but they are unable to bring out their heroism and confront the system that is *adharmic*. They unwittingly collude with the brutality by staying silent.

Bhishma, in particular, was in a position to change the situation if he chose to, since he was the one upholding the legitimacy of the court. Instead, he rigidly held on to the old meanings of the system and made everyone captive to it.

RANDHIR: True, the best and worst of any person comes out in such difficult situations. It brought the best out of Draupadi, and the worst out of all the Kurus, especially Bhishma.

RAGHU: One of the mistakes I see organizations make is that they do not know how to redefine heroism when the context has changed. For example, Bhishma holds on to an idea of justice that could be seen as heroic from a dogmatic point of view, but it became a perpetrator of *adharma* in Draupadi's case. Seeing the dysfunctional aspects of a system is difficult as only its victims understand it, and they are often voiceless.

The ability to see the context afresh is the first step. The second step is to be able to redefine current systems so that it becomes *dharmic* and healthy again. A good leader is someone who senses these shadow sides of the system, can understand the current negatives and propose a better system.

Redefining the idea of heroism is very important. It is for the system to realize how power is being used and review it. The question of heroism comes in only when we understand the deeper nuances of the situation and then take action that not only arrests the rot but also enables a shift to a higher level of functionality.

RANDHIR: Is this what is referred to as Arjuna's propensity?

RAGHU: Yes. In the Mahabharata, there are three people who are in constant touch with a deeper Intelligence called Krishna: Karna, Arjuna and Draupadi. All of them articulate the negatives of the system clearly at different points in the story. But the one who goes through the process of having the conversation with Shri Krishna and awakening to the divine Intelligence within is Arjuna. To radically redefine a system, one needs to first dissolve one's own shadow sides so that one can judge things clearly. Second, one needs to see profoundly both the visible reality and the invisible dynamics of a system. This then enables one to envisage a more *dharmic* system.

Karna does not make any changes to the system; nor does he stop the system from breaking down. He is entrenched in his victimhood. He has great heroic potential, but his actions do not reinstate *dharma*. He is in touch with his innermost intelligence, but he does not act from it.

Draupadi confronts the *adharma* and calls it out. Her stand ultimately leads to war, in which the dysfunctional people and their ways have to be destroyed. There are various points of time when the Kauravas could have listened to reason and given up their envy and greed. Things need not have come to the stage when a destructive war was needed. Each of these moments calls out for heroic action, but instead of acting for *dharmic* reasons, the powerful men act out of self-interest and self-preservation.

SAMIR: A couple of decades ago when my start-up failed, I was staring at the possibility of going bankrupt. But the moment I gave up fear, possibilities opened up. I made a few difficult decisions but survived, confronting the worst-case scenario without fear and letting myself stay anchored in *shaantham* and it worked.

RAGHU: These are the moments when we stop fighting a situation and allow our minds to calm down, so that a higher Intelligence takes over and we can see newer possibilities.

SAMIR: Being able to accept our helplessness without sinking into the victim mode is probably the critical ability.

SHRUTI: But how does one explain this whole thing about Draupadi having five husbands? Even Karna commented on it.

RAGHU: Draupadi is the manifestation of *prakrti*, the primal mother energy. We must go past today's moral framework and try to understand the symbolic meanings. Each Pandava represents an element: Yudhishthira is earth; Bhima is fire; Nakula is water; Sahadeva is air; and Arjuna is a fifth element, space. Draupadi represents the *prakrti* by integrating all these elements. She was the binding force for all the brothers.

Dear Reader, were there any 'Draupadi moments' in your life? How did you respond and what did it tell you about your leadership style?

PART 2

The Five Seats of Power in their Contemporary Avatars

Having understood the five Pandavas, we now look at their behavioural manifestations in an organizational context. With the story of the Mahabharata as the backdrop, we will explore each of the Pandavas in their heroic potential.

Before we move further, let us quickly recap what we have learnt so far.

- Each Pandava has a dominant propensity that personifies a role archetype.
- Each archetype manifests a form of power intrinsic and unique to that archetype.
- Each archetype has a particular relationship to the overall system and manifests the relationship through behaviours that can be heroic, functional or dysfunctional.
- In the process of manifesting these powers, there are aspects of oneself that are repressed and suppressed, and one is not conscious of these disowned parts of oneself.

- The most compulsive and strongly disowned parts of oneself are referred to as the shadow.

There are three critical aspects to every role archetype:

1. The part that is acknowledged: It reflects the positive and the constructive behavioural manifestations of the energy.
2. The part that is disowned, or unacknowledged: The shadow represents the deeply repressed and suppressed parts of the archetypal energy that have a destructive potential.
3. Replenishment: This must be mastered for the archetypal energy to manifest itself in its full glory. Often, in the demand for action, we deploy the 'doing' aspects of the archetype and lose touch with the 'being'. Unless the being part is also embraced and owned up, replenishment and regeneration become impossible.

The visible, action-driven 'doing' has to be complemented with inner, meditation-driven 'being'. 'Doing' refers to an expending of energy in order to accomplish tangible goals. 'Being' refers to regenerative energy, a healing and nurturing process, in which one experiences renewal from within.

This inward movement involves resting the mind in *shaantham* and allowing the meditative mind and self-healing processes to generate power. If we take for granted the source of our energy, we risk losing our innate ability to replenish ourselves by accessing our intuition and wisdom.

The 'doing' energies are action-focused. In this expending of energy towards outcomes, we experience the depletion of energy over time. We have to acknowledge the need for replenishment with humility, healing of wounds and easing of pain. When we need healing, we have to turn to our 'being'. This part of us helps us to deal with shame, hurt and fear, and opens the path to being the best we can be.

Only by embracing the disowned aspects of 'being' can heroic behaviour emerge. When we fail to understand and integrate these aspects into ourselves, we are unable to reach our highest potential. These disowned parts block the flow of energies and create inner conflicts that one is not conscious of. When they are triggered, the negativity is projected on to others. This leads to dysfunctional behaviour. It severely impacts teamwork as the parts disowned in ourselves are held in shame, guilt or fear.

In times of stress, these shadow energies can overtake one's consciousness and one can behave totally out of character. In order to reach our heroic potential, it is crucial to reclaim those parts of ourselves that have been disowned. Our full heroic potential energies are available only when we embrace our shadow with compassion.

The case studies that I will share with you are drawn from real experiences but presented in a narrative form with names changed. These are people whom I have known intimately through long-term consulting and coaching relationships. I have, therefore, been able to influence and witness the transformations in them.

You might have different ways of understanding the case studies and propensities than how they are shown in the book. The aim is to not simply accept the given conclusions but instead understand yourself better through the conversation.

A reminder of how we will use the following terms to refer to different aspects of the archetypal hero:

- Archetypal energy covers all the possible behaviours that can be exhibited by an archetype.
- Propensity refers to the more tangible and cognizable actions that emerge when the archetypal energy manifests in a given context.
- We will use phrases such as 'Yudhishthira will act/think/feel' as a shorthand for 'The Yudhishthira archetypal energy will manifest through action/thought/feeling in the following ways'.

The Power of Order and Stability: Yudhishthira

The name 'Yudhishthira' means 'one who is unshakeable even in the time of war'. A Yudhishthira leader provides stability to the organization and ensures that the team members are clear about what is expected of them. He understands how to use structural power appropriately, and therefore knows how to derive power from the position he holds.

An Overview

A Yudhishthira is bound by the system in which he operates. However wise he may be, in his action he exercises discipline and holds back his subjectivity and feelings. He may, therefore, come across as rigid and operating only within the boundaries of his role. The archetypal energies of the 'King' and the 'Judge' manifest as a Yudhishthira. He has an awakening of forethought and an ability to plan for the future.

Systems that nurture this energy of engagement function like clockwork. Yudhishthira anchors the rules and procedures of the organization and ensures predictability, stability and safety. He is idealistic and capable of sacrificing much in order to create a stable future. He is, therefore, a great steward of the system.

The Heroic Yudhishthira

The heroic Yudhishthira has a great ability to go into chaotic environments and bring in predictability and stability. He handles the anxiety of the chaos without getting swayed by its intensity, and thus becomes a pillar of strength. He can identify systematic deviations and bring in the relentlessness needed to ensure conformity to rules and procedures.

Though a heroic Yudhishthira values control and compliance, he handles the tension between the reality that is unfolding and the need for ensuring ongoing structural anchorage and operational clarity. He keeps himself aware of the emerging context and makes appropriate changes to structure, roles and procedures to address this context. He reviews continuously and takes feedback on the objectives of current roles, structures and processes, and will fine-tune if the objectives are not achieved. He enforces the rules and sees to it that they are followed.

However, a heroic Yudhishthira does not become a slave of the existing way of doing things. Though he may be willing to change the structure and rules, he will not accept any deviations until they are changed. Even the changes have to be brought about in a structured manner through a reliable process. Leaders with the Yudhishthira propensity are great consolidators. Their role becomes absolutely necessary when change for its own sake is undesirable, and creating a strong foundation is called for. The energy of Yudhishthira also makes a person accept authority and hierarchy as part of the organization.

A heroic Yudhishthira understands structural processes and defines policies that are fair and create a sense of stability. He has a very good understanding of the role-appropriate action. He will not act beyond the defined role and will expect others to respect role boundaries. He is a very good enforcer of systemic discipline. A heroic Yudhishthira has great control over his behaviour and tends to stay within tradition and norms. It is difficult for others to know his real self. Self-control becomes a prized practice.

The Functional Yudhishthira

The Yudhishthira propensity could be played out by a person who does not deploy its full potential. When the archetypal energy becomes an unconscious framework within which the person is acting, a Yudhishthira is not in touch with his heroic potential. He becomes a dependable applier of rules, procedures and practices as they are handed down to him, but without understanding their relevance to the context.

A functional Yudhishthira's life entails strict discipline. He follows the personal regimen he defines for himself with rigour. He tends to go by the letter of the law, committed to upholding the rules and accepted practices and traditions of the system. He does not judge the writers of the law but enforces what is written. He follows the procedures as best as he can and is loath to be seen as unfair or manipulative for selfish reasons.

The functional Yudhishthira grows in ways that the system defines. He views the system primarily through the lens of order and disorder. He is very sensitive to aspects of the system that do not uphold the rules and norms of the system and have the potential to disrupt stability. A functional Yudhishthira may get righteously offended if he sees people overstepping boundaries or not adhering to set procedures. The primacy of control becomes the overriding theme of a Yudhishthira manager who does not invest in the heroic potential of this archetype. Such a Yudhishthira will represent the mindset of a standard operating procedure in the organization. The structure, processes and role boundaries become not just the means but an end.

As organizations grow older, stakeholders start to value stability and continuity over excessive dynamism. Organizational design is based on the classical theories of management enunciated by thought leaders such as Henri Fayol, Fredrick Taylor, Max Weber and Adam Smith; their theories have defined modern management practices. The principles they set forth largely attempt to capture the Yudhishthira energy that is essential for task completion and predictability. Efficiency is valued over efficacy and inspiration.

The Shadow Side of the Yudhisthira Power

A Yudhishthira constantly engages with the non-conforming and deviant aspects of the system. This constant engagement with the undesirable, unwelcome and ugly elements and processes in the system makes Yudhishthira feel as if he is scavenging. He wonders why he has to do the dirty work of making everyone follow rules and punishing those who don't.

However, scavenging is an integral part of his role. If a Yudhishthira does not acknowledge his unique ability to audit the system, he fails to find ways of dignifying the role. He then experiences a dissonance within and becomes a mechanical and clinical enforcer of conformity.

When Yudhishthiras take up leadership positions without having come to terms with the overactive judge within them, they will supervise their subordinates excessively. They are also likely to judge others and reject and condemn anything that does not fit their framework and conclusions about reality. They stay imprisoned within the norms and traditions and feel guilty if they question or act contrary to these norms.

A Yudhishthira's commitment to the codes of the system often makes him disown his own originality. Ultimately, he gets separated and distanced from his intuition and emotions. When Yudhishthira acts in a cold and controlled manner, lacking compassion for himself and for others, he fails to see the multiplicity and dynamism of life and will continue to experience it within a narrow and restricted range. He then falls back on his position and status in the system to give himself legitimacy.

The Dysfunctional Yudhishthira

In most situations, a Yudhishthira tends to get drawn to the tension between external situations and the expectations of his role. A Yudhishthira who is not in touch with his inner self will not contribute his own knowledge and will only act within the boundaries prescribed by the current system. This might sometimes have disastrous consequences for both him personally and the system that is dependent on him for leadership.

In his focus on precedence and procedure, he stops being concerned about individual well-being and becomes insensitive to human emotions. His actions become restricted to those that are required by the role and he absolves himself from the responsibility of the consequences of these actions. The outcome of the lack of coherence within is dysfunctional and compulsive behaviour. The suppressed and repressed parts get triggered, and it becomes very difficult to control their expression.

When a Yudhishthira loses the flow of energy between his inner processes and the situational demands, he can become very rigid, turn a blind eye to the contextual needs and mindlessly enforce conformity. He then treats himself as the proxy of the system and acts like the prisoner of his position in the hierarchy. Even when his intuition tells him to do something else, he tends to ignore it and keeps to his custom-bound behaviour. This behaviour could be seen as cold, unfeeling and passive-aggressive. A Yudhishthira can be manipulated by people around him by doing things that are in accordance with the rules but go completely against the spirit of fairness.

When a Yudhishthira becomes very rigid and normative, he represses and suppresses his own drives, needs and impulses. Because he does not acknowledge them, these impulses can burst forth in times of crisis and when he is challenged. He loses all control and is incapable of listening to anyone. At these times a Yudhishthira is a man possessed. When his shadow side takes over, he can create havoc in a moment of madness.

Insufficient Identification with the Yudhishthira Propensity

People with low Yudhishthira propensity will be devoid of intrinsic discipline and will be resentful of authority. Their need for freedom of expression could result in erratic and impulsive behaviour. This may predispose the person to deploy themselves in socially inappropriate ways.

They will tend to be blind to the implicit social conventions that are important to a community, and when they are aware, they may tend to disregard them. Making fun of traditions and being irreverent are ways in which these people will violate the tradition. Respect for authority could be absent. Such people are disrespectful to structures and systems in irresponsible ways.

Integration and Replenishment

Yudhishthira's deepest pathos is having to make judgements of right and wrong in a world full of dilemmas, paradoxes and irreconcilable polarities. When Yudhishthiras sit on their chairs, sombre and thoughtful, searching for the right decision and the right judgement, what lies invisible to the common eye is their inner anguish.

A Yudhishthira would have to seek replenishment, regeneration and the wisdom of his being when he is torn between the two opposing sides of an argument. The ability to value the disturbance that inevitably accompanies a questioning of one's assumptions will enable a Yudhishthira to act from wisdom while managing his fears.

Case Study: Yeshwanth

Yeshwanth was a respected and seasoned finance professional who had grown to head the finance operations of a firm. He was known to be meticulous and methodical. He interacted with his teams and inspected their work daily. His daily rounds were feared by the rest of the organization. They would often wonder how his gaze came to fall on exactly those areas that were non-compliant.

Yeshwanth had set up very clear processes. He would have meetings every morning of the week, one day for each of his direct reports along with their teams. The teams had to prepare presentations based on templates that Yeshwanth had defined. His managers found this very useful, but also quite restrictive. When the operations went according to expectations, they found the templates very easy to work with, but when they did not, they did not know how to report the issues.

Yeshwanth was fond of protocol. He expected his team to be as disciplined as him in the way they worked. In his managerial style, hierarchy was respected. Managers at lower levels waited for the instructions from their bosses.

Yeshwanth was fascinated by Japanese methods of managing operations such as Total Productive Maintenance (a method of physical asset management focused on maintaining and improving manufacturing machinery, in order to minimize the operating cost to an organization while maximizing up-time) and Zero Defects (a way of thinking and doing that emphasizes the notion that everyone should do things right the first time).

He went to Japan to study their methods and came back thoroughly impressed. He started implementing some of these methods.

Matters took a turn for the worse. There was a palpable dissatisfaction in his team, but Yeshwanth responded to this by relating stories about what he had learnt in Japan. Yeshwanth soon found his growth in the organization stalled. He also started losing respect among his juniors. Yeshwanth's boss told him that he was not performing up to expectations, and his team management skills had to improve.

Yeshwanth became more disciplined in his approach but results were elusive. He felt stuck, and his enthusiasm for maintaining discipline began to wane.

How did Yeshwanth discover the best he could be?

The Transformation

When Yeshwanth realized that he had hit a wall, he decided to seek help. He signed up for a leadership coaching course. 'The world is not what it was any more,' he declared during his first conversation with his coach. 'People don't respect the wisdom of experience. They come up with new-fangled ideas and act on them without sufficient testing. They don't understand how it disturbs the operations.' Yeshwanth appeared most disturbed by what he called the uncooperative attitude of his peers.

It was not easy for Yeshwanth to see that the changes proposed by sales were in response to the demands of the customers. The customers were facing an uncertain context and were not able to make clear commitments. Yeshwanth could not see that the ability of the operations team to anticipate latent needs and create flexible solutions was the most important differentiator in the market. Predicting markets, and therefore enabling a steady process, was becoming almost impossible.

Yeshwanth found himself getting very angry and this upset him even more. He saw his anger as righteous and being triggered by the capriciousness of others. When Yeshwanth was introduced to self-reflective thinking, it took him time to see that the judge in him was very dominant. It enabled him to be rigorous and be very good at planning on the one hand, but on the other, it also made him contemptuous of what he saw as a lack of discipline in his team and his peers. It made him very closed off to different ideas and ways of thinking.

Yeshwanth realized that he was holding on to the idea of a manager that he had internalized early in his career from a senior he respected. Yeshwanth was deploying a service-oriented part of himself to solve problems and issues, but ended up implementing processes that further rigidified the operations thinking.

It was Yeshwanth's time to see that his efforts to help were making his team dependent on him instead of empowering them. He eventually understood that his own fear of making mistakes and his overzealous sense of accountability of not being held responsible were making him anxious to not give up control.

He took time out to start early morning mindfulness and breathing practices. That got him into a space of quiet where he could spend some time on self-reflection. He had set aside his interest in music and theatre when he started working.

Yeshwanth decided to get back in touch with his hobbies. He finally took a couple of weeks off from work and spent more time with his wife and on his hobbies. It helped him feel rejuvenated. 'I became tense when I gave up my love for the arts, but hardly noticed it. I realize now how important self-replenishment is. I saw it as a waste of time!' he commented.

With help from his family and coach, Yeshwanth navigated this inner shift very well. He became more tolerant at work, relaxed his strict regimen, and started enjoying the challenge of creating a flexible and responsive workplace. He came to realize how he had become a captive of the injunctions and rules that he lived by and how change and uncertainty made him anxious. Doing something wrong had been a constant source of worry. By awakening his intuitive and artistic side and discovering how it could harmonize with the disciplined side, Yeshwanth developed a very engaging and demanding style of leadership that his team loved.

Coming to terms with the shadow side of the Yudhishthira archetype and acknowledging his inner feelings allowed Yeshwanth to value what he brought into the context without being defensive or protective. He was able to be more open to the demands of his workplace, less judgemental and far more approachable. Yeshwanth's career moved back on track.

Summary

When Yudhishthira leaders internalize the heroic potential of this archetype, they become capable of bringing order, predictability and efficiency. This capability is extremely important in organizations that need consistency of performance. Innovation and experimentation must be harmonized by the Yudhishthira capability of creating certainty and repeatability.

Conversely, leaders who reflect the shadow side of this archetype are continuously insecure and anxious when they are not in a stable and secure environment. They have perspective and can anticipate the future, and are also able to plan and execute their agendas, but are tripped up by their judgemental and righteous nature.

This dysfunctional focus on rules and structure causes them to create procedural barriers when none exist. This could make others in the system feel oppressed. However, these Yudhishthiras will tend to entrench themselves in righteousness and defend themselves by deploying role-sanctioned power and quoting rules.

I, Yudhishthira, the King: Power of Order and Stability
I listen to the call for stability and balance from a sense of duty and commitment to the system. I give and receive gifts of responsibility that enhance the effectiveness of my role. My core values are built around fairness, justice and role-discipline. My questions focus on deviation, a quest for new roles and appropriate stances, and how one creates predictability and certainty. My purpose is to protect myself and the system from uncertainty and chaos.

Enablers	Derailers
I value structure and stability. I value the framework of roles. I stay within the legitimate boundaries of the system while making demands on the system.	Without structure, I feel lost and confused, so I compulsively demand and impose structural boundaries irrespective of context. I dislike the uncertainty and messiness of unstructured situations.
I value the standards set for role behaviour and expect everyone to play by these standards. I define standard operating procedures to ensure predictability.	I find myself imposing standards in punitive ways. I dislike deviations and resist changes. I wish to eliminate all strange, surprising and unpredictable occurrences in the system.
I believe that power and authority are given by the system, and they must be respected and exercised in a responsible, dignified and dispassionate manner. I am impersonal and correct. I am a good administrator.	I resent power and authority that are not formal, and become entrenched in finding rules and procedure to stymie these. People must remain in their role-defined boundaries.
I respect the status that one acquires by virtue of one's position in the structure. I consolidate my position and build my career through carefully planned and incremental steps.	If my entitlement is not honoured, then I become resentful and reactive. I make my power felt by withholding the performance of my roles and responsibilities or dragging my feet over them.
Emotions and intuitions have no place in my performance of the roles. My actions are within the frameworks provided by the system. I seek the advice of wise people when in doubt.	I freeze when my emotions are triggered. I blindly follow precedence and become a mere proxy of the person in authority.

The Power of Passion and Action: Bhima

'Bhima' means 'one with formidable might'. A Bhima brings passion and action into the system. His power enables him to be vigilant and to respond quickly to danger. He has emotional intensity and courage and infuses life into the system. Bhima thrives on romantic inspiration. Entrepreneurs such as Steve Jobs come to mind when one thinks of people who exemplify this power.

An Overview

The archetypal energies of the Warrior and the Adventurer manifest as a Bhima. The warrior energy is vital, primal and emotional, but at the same time, such emotions could blind a person. When this energy is directed properly, it makes for agility and responsiveness to challenge. Bhimas celebrate strength and invest a lot of energy in honing their skills and building capabilities in order to stay ahead of the competition. They thrive on competition and challenges.

Bhimas love life and express themselves with a lot of energy, drive and assertion. The Bhima propensity does not place importance on the method used, but merely on the outcome. Differences are not tolerated, and the discomfort of others remain unimportant as long as their goals are met.

A Bhima can, therefore, be highly integrated, sophisticated and self-directed when he is helped to anchor himself in the right role; or he can go on a rampage and become disruptive and destructive.

The Heroic Bhima

Bhima is a person of great vitality and courage. He is a great friend, very loving and full of emotional intensity. Exploration and adventure bring Bhima to life and routine depresses him. Once a Bhima has been aroused and sets a goal to achieve, he plunges into action. He prefers to figure things out as he engages with action and gets impatient with rules and processes that come in the way of quick results.

Bhimas are the quintessential self-starters who love to challenge themselves and their followers to go into uncharted territory. They have a high appetite for risk and drive organizations to accomplish great and inspiring goals. People operating under this archetype sometimes tend to be lone heroes. They are self-reliant but crave recognition, appreciation and affection.

The heroism of the Bhima is inspirational and makes people aspire for greatness. The heroic Bhima is the proverbial romantic who will move mountains for the love of his life. Once they offer their love and respect to someone they consider worthy, the Bhima will be steadfast and committed.

A Bhima explores new worlds and can, therefore, expand the boundaries of the system. At the same time, he is vigilant and protects the system from enemies. A Bhima with heroic potential accepts systemic discipline and invests his energies to respond better to external threats and challenges.

The Functional Bhima

People with the Bhima propensity who have not explored its full potential often seek independence from the system in a reactive manner. However, a functional Bhima is aware of his own impulsivity and the fact that he is prone to being aroused emotionally. He, therefore, recognizes the value of respecting boundaries. Accepting systemic boundaries enables him to grow in a disciplined way, accept role definitions and channel his energy in constructive ways.

Bhimas view the system primarily through the lens of opportunities and threats. In organizations, these are individuals who play the role of trouble-shooters, hunters and explorers. They can also be defenders and protectors. A Bhima values action and derives energy and meaning from confronting challenges to the system. Hence, he is capable of responding well in crisis situations, where immediate action is required.

Bhimas are willing to fight the odds to get a desired outcome. He is capable of acting alone, and often prefers not to be encumbered by the responsibilities of building and maintaining teams.

The Shadow Side of the Bhima Power

Since those functioning under a Bhima archetype are ruled by powerful impulses and emotions, they lose touch with their rational sides. Forethought is abandoned or even held in disdain, and a lack of courage is seen as a sign of weakness. Bhimas can be rebellious and not show respect for systemic rules and traditions. This then makes the Bhima unpredictable or even uncontrollable.

Bhimas wear rebellion as a badge. In a system where he is valued for his courage, a Bhima is placed in a position where he has to be constantly alert for any signs of danger. This constant vigilance causes burnout. Since Bhimas are valued for their ability to fight, they are often put forward in situations that call for brutal action. Bhimas have to find the balance between blood lust and fear to gain mastery over this archetypal energy.

Bhimas can also get trapped in fierce competitiveness and feel a need to win at all costs. Every engagement becomes a test of strength, and the joy of play and discovery that could make exploration enjoyable is lost in the process. Their propensity for aggressive action can make Bhimas oppressive and create fear in others.

Arrogance can make them self-destructive. Such Bhimas are often more feared than loved.

The Dysfunctional Bhima

Because of his passion for action, Bhima avoids forethought and strategy. He rarely thinks things through before acting and thereby shows little regard for processes and procedures. Since he is usually successful in his actions, this is often overlooked.

Bhima's tendency to act first and think afterwards often makes him do things that he may regret later. This leaves him open to being emotionally blackmailed and manipulated into fighting for causes he has not thought through. His need to accomplish heroic actions often makes him ignore his anxieties and fears and just act from bravado.

Bhima tends to magnify his own strengths and capabilities whenever there is a challenge and ignore or even hide his own fears and anxieties. Even if he has apprehensions about the enemy, he covers up his fears, which he sees as cowardliness, and presents a false front of bravery. He tends to be overconfident, and this makes him boastful.

Insufficient Identification with the Bhima Propensity

An excessive detachment from the Bhima propensity leaves people anxious in the face of confrontation. They avoid shaping themselves through the rough and tumble of engagement with harsh reality.

These people end up feeling fragile and tentative. Any use of power and authority becomes problematic. They lack the conviction and courage it takes to confront a chaotic reality.

Integration and Replenishment

A warrior he may be, but Bhima has his fears too. He has to acknowledge his feelings of inadequacy and his fear of failure. Bhima can become possessive. When he enters the arena looking supremely confident, what the eye cannot see is the love and compassion of his being that fills his heart.

Without his emotional self, Bhima would feel empty. But, in discovering his own freedom and love of the world, Bhima will release himself from narcissistic self-absorption and find the joy of exploring the world around, entering the new and unexplored with childlike enthusiasm.

Case Study: Bhaskar

Bhaskar was a young and very successful human resources and industrial relations manager who was drawn to the challenge of turning around an ailing organization in the agriculture industry. The company had a long history and was very well-known in its field. However, it had been stagnating for a while. Recently, the company had been taken over in an attempt to revive it through financial and sales discipline.

While these measures stabilized the situation, it soon became apparent that the organization needed a drastic improvement in its work culture. The new owners decided to put a Bhima on the job. Bhaskar was offered this very difficult task and he took it up as a challenge.

The initial processes were difficult. Bhaskar put together a team of people with a can-do attitude to help him with his work, and then began a close study of the employees' past performances, attitudes and potential to identify who the real contributors to the organization were. But instead of relying on the copious reports his team put together, he went directly to the shop floor to identify the problem areas and involve himself in solving the problem.

Bhaskar was able to douse many fires and move the operations ahead through his acumen for tactical responsiveness. His style was directly in contrast with the earlier culture of the organization. The protocols of status, hierarchy and privilege were done away with. The older managers, who prided themselves on upholding the legacy of a glorious past, were disconcerted. Their approach was getting exposed by Bhaskar's energetic and hands-on style of leadership, and they could not protect themselves behind the facades of positional power.

While he lacked the patience to read through long reports or learn from academic studies, Bhaskar was very quick to grasp things. He loved to involve himself in debates, and this was his learning style. Every Saturday afternoon, he would call in managers from across departments and levels and put forward a provocative proposition. He would then lead a process of cross-questioning them, pushing for evidence and challenging the outcomes of these debates by setting out practical projects for the managers to engage with.

The managers initially felt intimidated but soon understood Bhaskar's deep passion. The place was buzzing with competitive energy and employees were taking up challenges to prove themselves. Bhaskar established a strong personal connection with the employees. He was not averse to accompanying the sales managers or their juniors on sales calls. This move enabled him to elicit a willing response from them when he asked them to be more dynamic.

Then came the painful part: asking people to leave. Through his direct involvement in every aspect of the organization, Bhaskar had assessed the capabilities of his managers. Many of the ones who found themselves redundant had stagnated for years and were probably unemployable. They were middle-aged and had families to support.

But Bhaskar steeled himself for the ordeal and started wielding the sword on behalf of the organization. The other managers held him in awe and fear. Soon, Bhaskar was being secretly referred to as the 'butcher'. Towards the end of this terrible chapter of the turnaround story, Bhaskar came to know about this nickname. He was deeply hurt, but he hid his pain and carried on with the task.

However, within about a year of this event, Bhaskar's performance started deteriorating. He became moody and irritable. As the system started to stabilize, Bhaskar's style of direct involvement and quick tactical decision-making began to prove counterproductive. His tendency to make quick decisions meant that he often gave solutions that worked in one area and contradicted the needs of other areas.

Soon, standardization of shop-floor operations became problematic. Bhaskar realized this and tried to introduce TQM practices. However, he found it increasingly difficult to be patient and let the organization find new stable ground. He was unsettling processes that needed time to settle before improvements could be brought in. His style of engaging directly with people from across the organization was disturbing a more predictable and orderly way of managing.

While he had cleared all the crisis areas, Bhaskar had not created a scalable working culture. The organization was starting to depend on the ability of a few smart and highly energetic managers who thrived in the new dispensation. The owners realized this and were concerned. They advised Bhaskar to take a break.

How could Bhaskar discover the best he could be?

The Transformation

As he enjoyed active learning, Bhaskar decided to attend a few 'learning laboratory' groups. Learning laboratories are spaces for group dialogue where one learns about and practises how to develop shared understanding, collaborative problem solving, team building and empathy.

He liked the highly interactive nature of these learning processes and engaged himself intensely in the labs. The learning was not easy, as Bhaskar had to listen to the feedback others gave to him about his aggressive nature, his self-absorption and his domineering ways. He learnt how his enthusiastic way of engaging with life could actually be bothering people who preferred other approaches.

As he slowed down and started listening to others, Bhaskar started appreciating the stability of a Yudhishthira, the inclusivity and selflessness of a Nakula and the thoughtfulness of a Sahadeva. It took a while for Bhaskar to comprehend the world of an Arjuna and to appreciate the nuances of deeply interconnected systems.

As he started uncovering his feelings, Bhaskar started practising the art of looking at reality from various lenses. He realized that the core issue draining him emotionally was a feeling of betrayal by his teammates. He had done what needed to be done, and yet those people had not understood and had been calling him a 'butcher'.

When Bhaskar let go of his strong warrior stance, he had a cathartic moment. He got in touch with the deep sense of anger and loneliness that he felt when he was intensely engaging with the difficult and urgent task of the turnaround. Whilst examining this feeling further, it became clear that behind this anger was pain and guilt that stemmed from having to leave men without a way to provide for their families.

Bhaskar could then understand that the treatment meted out to him by his erstwhile colleagues was a reflection of their own fear and envy of his strength. They had taken protection under him and played the roles of good implementers. However, they were not willing to stand by him in his most difficult hour. Like a great Bhima, he had to fight the bloodiest battles alone.

By understanding the archetype of the Warrior, Bhaskar came to realize that the Oppressor/Executioner was the inevitable other side of the coin. Once he realized this, he could release himself from the guilt he felt for having ended the careers of the employees he had to fire and the resentment he had towards the people by whom he felt betrayed.

With these negative feelings gone, Bhaskar was able to see what his strengths were. He reclaimed his conviction to action and recovered his zest for life. He decided to surround himself with young and bright people, and hired accordingly. By allowing this team to become his sounding board, Bhaskar was able to shape a new style of working and be more measured and strategic in his responses.

Bhaskar then hired an operations manager who was a solid Yudhishthira and gave him a lot of freedom. This ensured that his own disruptive style was held in check. Eventually, Bhaskar was appointed as president of the company.

Summary

Bhima leaders are courageous and engage energetically with challenges. They are expressive and affectionate and build loyal followers who are inspired to greatness by these Bhima leaders.

However, a Bhima leader who has not dealt with his shadow side becomes a restless and impulsive seeker of action. This can lead to confrontational and aggressive stances. Because he is restless when there is no challenge, such a Bhima can create a crisis out of nothing by being too trigger-happy.

I, Bhima, the Warrior: Power of Passion and Action
I listen to the call of adventure from a core of vigilance. I listen for opportunities and threats. I give and receive gifts based on my desires and fears. My motivation is competition and challenge, and taking up heroic causes for the system. My questions focus on impact, strength, weakness and raw power. My primary concern is establishing territory and expanding it. I need to protect my vulnerability by engaging with my fears and paranoia. My purpose is to establish territory and expand it.

Enablers	Derailers
I am adventurous, decisive and action-oriented. I don't like wasting time on analysis; I see it as a lack of courage to act.	I hide my cowardice. I expect my subordinates to play along with the facade I show. I could become ruthless and create fear in others.
I am hardworking and loyal to my superiors. I act as a trusted agent. I am resourceful, and I get things done. I am also protective of my subordinates, and I expect them to be loyal to me.	I become an unquestioning fan of my heroes and can easily become an instrument in their hands.
I am alive to power and influence in the organization. Politics is a reality of organizations, and I know how to play the game.	I get entrenched in the 'what's in it for me' question. I can become greedy for power.
I am sensitive, emotional and alive. I like vibrancy in my team. I like to celebrate success. I hate failure.	I like to hype up situations and enthusiasm even when it rings hollow. I lose myself in impulsivity and reactivity.
I value competitiveness and come alive when challenged. I believe that real talent and capability must be rewarded.	I am bored when there are no challenges. I am contemptuous of voices that call for caution and rush into situations without any strategy. I sometimes cheat so that I don't lose.

The Power of Compassion and Service: Nakula

Nakula is the quintessential healer. His source of power comes from the ease with which he can empathize with others. Nakulas ensure that the infrastructure is maintained for the Arjunas, Bhimas, Yudhishthiras and Sahadevas. A Nakula is moved by a genuine desire to help others. He strives to keep harm away from himself and those he loves.

Nakula acts from the premise that the organization is more important than the self. He does what is required in a necessary situation, without being invited to do so, because of an inner commitment to uphold the system.

An Overview

The archetypal energy of the Healer manifests as a Nakula. A Nakula genuinely cares for others and takes care to ensure that no suffering comes to them. A sense of compassion makes him very sensitive to the needs of others and ensures that these needs are always fulfilled in unobtrusive ways.

The great Nakulas convert toxic tensions between people into meaningful bonds by evoking in them the ability to be inclusive. They ensure that the hurts and wounds that are inevitable when people are engaged in intense action are healed so that they do not lose sight of the bigger picture.

The Heroic Nakula

A heroic Nakula heals the system through facilitation and resolution. He permits disagreements to surface and enables resolution through consensus-building. The toxicity and tensions that confrontation often generates is absorbed by a heroic Nakula and converted into the energy needed for new agreements and creative dialogue. However, disagreements are kept within limits, so as to maintain the dignity of the system.

Nakula leaders are great institution builders. They plant the trees for future generations to enjoy the fruits. The ability to be sensitive to the feelings of others makes Nakula leaders inclusive, and creates a strong sense of belonging in the members of the system. However, their efforts in ensuring that the system is free of tension leads them to absorb a lot of toxicity silently.

A Nakula's ability to bring compassion and empathy into the team allows each of the team members to appreciate not only the strengths and capabilities of others but also their limitations and vulnerabilities. This creates a very powerful emotional infrastructure for the team, and leads to mutually supportive behaviours.

Nakulas are great enablers, as they make it possible for each person in the team to excel and the team as a whole to rise to great heights. People in systems that are efficient and smooth tend to take this efficiency for granted, and the Nakulas who are constantly enabling it remain invisible. A heroic Nakula accepts this and rarely lets it come in the way of his commitment to the system's needs.

The Functional Nakula

A Nakula who has not explored his heroic potential acts as a functional and important member of his team. He naturally senses the kind of supportive behaviour that would facilitate efficient, harmonious action. This enhances inclusiveness and cohesion in the team.

Nakulas are great team builders. They can enable others to perform and succeed while keeping themselves in the background. They are valued for the proactive emotional support they readily provide to their team members. A Nakula views the system through the lens of inclusivity and harmony. A manager who falls under this archetype is a silent, tireless and committed worker.

Nakula's commitment to the system could make him sacrifice his own aspirations and needs. He rarely makes demands on the system. A Nakula who is appreciated for his readiness to be helpful will tend to be self-effacing and will readily share the appreciation with others.

Team members who act for themselves or without regard for the common good disturb Nakula, but he cannot confront people easily. Thus, he tends to take on himself the negative fallouts of any lack of cohesion, thereby feeling overburdened and unrecognized.

The Nakula archetype grows through service. Therefore, when a Nakula's own aspirations, which are never apparent, converge with the goals of the system, he thrives.

The Shadow Side of the Nakula Power

Since a Nakula puts the system before himself, he ends up disowning his own aspirations. He even feels selfish in acknowledging them. Thus, while tending to and healing others' pain, he may be prone to downplay his own pain. However, his yearning to be seen and appreciated does not go away. It remains suppressed.

Nakulas are unable to seek help, even when they are feeling overburdened. This leads to exhaustion. They often feel a deep loneliness and a sense of sacrifice that is not recognized and honoured. A person deeply identifying with the Nakula archetype will evoke the martyr self. It leads to a feeling of being used. He may withdraw from all conflict and retreat further into the background of the system.

A Nakula often ends up relating to the system only through his usefulness. He ends up looking for those tasks and activities that are not prominent but are vital for the organization's success. He tries to makes himself indispensable. As Nakulas are remembered only during crises, they may at times withhold resources to force the organization to recognize them.

Nakulas who bury themselves in the task of healing could wallow in the pain and suffering of others and lose touch with their own being. In the compulsion to serve others, they forget to be compassionate to themselves. These Nakulas lose their graciousness and tenderness.

The Dysfunctional Nakula

Nakulas unquestioningly make the system's goal their own. This often makes them blind to the consequences of their choices. Their world is circumscribed by this one purpose of serving the members of the system. They silently seek the love and recognition of their community but do not ask anything for themselves. They have a penchant for avoiding pain and conflict. However, if their help is taken for granted, Nakulas feel resentful.

Unless they acknowledge their own aspirations, managers who show Nakula characteristics rarely succeed in the number one position. They end up as the helpers of the leader they dedicate themselves to. This way, the Nakula's functional efficiency becomes eroded. Their silent inner yearning for appreciation blocks their natural propensity to be helpful.

Coming to terms with his own aspirations enables the Nakula to find a balance between nurturing the system and nurturing himself.

Insufficient Identification with the Nakula Propensity

An excessive detachment from this archetypal energy makes the person self-centred. They always look for what is in it for them. They often feel they don't have accountability for the rest of their teams.

Integration and Replenishment

The 'being' aspect of Nakula is his ability to grieve for the sorrow he feels for himself and to let it go. This enables him to value the joys of life as well. Nakula's emotions have to not only absorb the pain of others, but also challenge and awaken him when he becomes dependent and self-pitying. This could be a difficult process to negotiate and call for a lot of wisdom and patience.

Awakening the ability in himself to use anger appropriately and proactively will be Nakula's greatest challenge. When is pride essential for empowering a person, and when does it become a dysfunctional vanity? How much compassion is too much? These are the kind of questions a Nakula needs to ponder over when he sits in communion with his being.

Case Study: Neil

Akash had taken a boutique consulting company and made it into a powerhouse in its field. However, he had a tendency to show his preferences and prejudices. He either loved people or disliked them, and these feelings were reciprocated by the recipients of his attitude.

Neil was his second in command. He was able to understand Akash and become the bridge between him and the organization. Neil absorbed the tensions and the toxicity, converted potential arguments into creative dialogues and built the platform for growth. He showed the typical Nakula behaviour of keeping the needs of the organization paramount. He did not make a big show of it and remained invisible.

Soon, Neil was appointed CEO, replacing Akash. In comparison with his predecessor, he appeared very down to earth and pragmatic. But soon, he was facing the issues faced by many who take over from charismatic founders. Many of the accomplishments that were actually achieved by Neil behind the scenes, such as building of teams and diffusion of conflict, were attributed to the brilliance of Akash.

Because of this, Neil had a difficult time as the new CEO. He felt unappreciated and did not have the control and respect that he needed to fulfil the duties of the position.

How did Neil discover the best he could be?

The Transformation

Neil took part in a workshop, which helped him recognize his Nakula leadership style. The coaching enabled him to understand his dilemma, which stemmed from the tendency of managers to see leadership as an assertive and demanding position. He realized that his self-effacing service to the organization had made his contributions invisible, and that his style of functioning had predisposed him to remaining in the background. He had ignored his own aspirations and needs for recognition.

Neil's martyr self was seeking recognition for all the pain he had endured and the toxicity he had absorbed and transformed. Instead of being drawn into this shadow self, he explored the other side of his propensity. This released Neil from his secret need for others to tell him how good and important he was.

Neil made up his mind to view the CEO role as an opportunity to improve the infrastructure that had been neglected so far. Once Neil realized that this was his way of making a difference, he was able to truly appreciate the immense gift he had for creating stable teams and practising situational leadership.

After a period of introspection, Neil also came to realize that in order to build a stronger organization, he needed to supplement his skills with the skills of other propensities and powers. Neil appreciated the Sahadeva and Yudhishthira propensities, but his preference to be understated made him distrust the Bhima tendency to be aggressive and expressive. When he understood that within this dislike there was also an envy of the Bhima archetype, Neil was able to gain a deeper appreciation of that power.

Neil realized that by creating a space where these propensities could express themselves freely, he could put together a very powerful team. The operations became very efficient, and his own Nakula style was very evocative. The employees felt valued and soon the company was flourishing.

This came about only after Neil, a Nakula leader, confronted his shadow side and drew on his strengths to be a heroic leader.

Summary

The heroic Nakula is capable of absorbing the toxicity of the system and converting the energy into a positive force. Nakulas genuinely seek to serve the interest of others and enable others and the system to be the best it can be. The operations become smooth and teamwork is more efficient since Nakula, at his heroic best, ensures that conflicts are minimized and the tensions that come in the way of collaboration are absorbed and nullified. Nakulas are great institution-builders who invoke a great sense of belonging in the members of the organization and create a strong and committed community.

When a Nakula wakes up to the heroic healing power of this archetype and confronts the compulsive energy of his shadow side, he becomes a great servant-leader. Once he acknowledges his own aspirations, Nakula also learns how to negotiate for himself and does not feel guilty about asking for his due.

<table>
<tr><th colspan="2">I, Nakula, the Healer: Power of Compassion and Service</th></tr>
<tr><td colspan="2">I listen to the call for healing and understand the difficulties of the people in the system. I give and receive gifts of understanding, compassion and inclusiveness. I am an invisible hero who lives for others and those around him. My questions examine the human context, the world of suffering and possible ways in which one can be of service. My purpose is to ensure the wellness and safety of the people in the system.</td></tr>
<tr><th>Enablers</th><th>Derailers</th></tr>
<tr><td>I value equity and teamwork.
I am proficient at developing teams and creating a shared group purpose.</td><td>I devalue myself and allow myself to be taken for granted.</td></tr>
<tr><td>I value the attitude of service.
I serve others even if it means making my own needs secondary.</td><td>I am very uncomfortable with centrality, and I sacrifice what is rightfully mine in the guise of being humble.</td></tr>
<tr><td>I am alive to the prerequisites and preparation essential for tasks to be effective and efficient. I am willing to give the lead to others when they show greater expertise for the tasks at hand. I invest time and resources to create robust infrastructure that enables task efficiency.</td><td>I tend to become a compulsive provider in order to derive self-worth. I crib in private for not being recognized for my efforts. Sometimes I silently withhold essential services to let the system know my importance.</td></tr>
<tr><td>I am sensitive to the pain that people experience because of systemic issues. I sympathize with them and nurse them.</td><td>In constantly wanting to address others' pain, I find it difficult to acknowledge my own hurts and pains. I find it very difficult to seek help and nourishment for myself, and I get burnt out.</td></tr>
</table>

Enablers	Derailers
I value harmony and inclusivity. I invest in creating a sense of safety and belonging.	I avoid all confrontation even when I know that confrontation is important. But when I do express my disappointments, I become reactive and start accusing others.

The Power of Curiosity and Knowledge: Sahadeva

A Sahadeva has curiosity and a passion for learning. He is a thinker, a seeker and an innovator. He loves a challenge that requires him to look for creative solutions. However, while he does all the intellectual work, he doesn't initiate action or make decisions. He likes to remain in the background, and hence he is often invisible.

Many times, a Sahadeva's contribution is not seen or acknowledged, yet many modern organizations are built upon their innovations. A great example of the struggles that Sahadevas go through can be understood by reading the book *The Social Life of Information* by John Seely Brown and Paul Duguid (Harvard Business School Press, 2000). In this book, the great work done in the Palo Alto Research Centre of Xerox is described in detail. The reason why much of this research was not used by Xerox but went on to power the whole computer ecosystem reads like the pathos of the Sahadeva who is not understood and respected by the rest of the organization.

An Overview

The archetypal energy of the Seeker and the Hermit manifests as Sahadeva. For a Sahadeva, the world is full of objects to enquire into with childlike curiosity and excitement. A Sahadeva is not satisfied with accepting the boundaries of current knowledge, and will always be questioning and innovating. He values intellectual freedom.

While Sahadevas are adept at connecting with others, these relationships depend on a mutual love of enquiry and curiosity. His relationship to the system is dispassionate – he functions as an observer. A Sahadeva manager is committed to knowledge-building and continuous innovation. He functions as a knowledge centre for the organization.

The Heroic Sahadeva

A Sahadeva has many qualities that make him a valuable member of any organization. In times of crisis, he can provide major contributions to finding solutions through creative problem-solving and deep study and analysis. However, the real contributions of the great Sahadeva come in wherever research and innovation are important for the organization. His curiosity and urge to study a phenomenon, to understand it deeply, make him restless and prone to looking for intellectual excitement often without going into the depth of an enquiry.

A heroic Sahadeva is capable of a relentless search for new and reliable knowledge. He is extremely meticulous in his work, and tests and confirms the validity of the knowledge before he offers his inputs to others. He can provide an objective viewpoint in any situation. Sahadeva's love for experimentation leads him to create innovative solutions. As a dispassionate observer, he offers creative insights in many situations.

The Functional Sahadeva

By sharing knowledge, a Sahadeva has the ability to increase the capabilities of his team members so that they can take on bigger challenges. He explores various ways of looking at situations and studies different methods to face a challenge. He does not rest till a solution is found to the problem at hand.

However, a Sahadeva does not contribute his perspectives until he is invited to share his ideas and insights. This makes him come across as reserved and dispassionate. Sahadeva instead focuses on proving the validity of his knowledge, viewing the system in terms of skills, technology and data. He is sensitive to lacunae in technical expertise and learning.

The functional Sahadeva manager is seen as a good performer, but he requires supervision as his tendency to become self-reflective leaves him tentative in action. Once in a while, he surprises his superiors with his astute and erudite perspective and appropriate choice of action. While these observations and actions might be noticed, as an individual, Sahadeva does not always get much recognition.

Among peers, Sahadeva acts as a silent supporter. He does not create tensions, conflicts or threats. In fact, he remains invisible unless he is asked for. Leaders with the Sahadeva propensity rarely create large organizations, except when their technological insights become the starting point of new organizations. Even here, the Sahadeva managers tend to stay with their research and not get pulled into the rough and tumble arena of action.

The Shadow Side of the Sahadeva Power

The shadow side of the Sahadeva archetype manifests in an extreme worry that his knowledge is incomplete or flawed. This makes the Sahadeva hoard the intellectual treasures that he possesses rather than run the risk of being proven wrong. Sahadeva prefers to stay within elite intellectual groups. He may not attempt to communicate his understanding, insights and knowledge in ways that an average person can understand; his language is intelligible only to a small community of experts. The absentminded professor is a cliched portrayal of the Sahadeva lost in his own inner world of abstractions and theories.

If a Sahadeva withdraws from emotional engagement, he comes across as dry, distant and lacking in warmth. In extreme cases, he gives up all action and cannot apply his deep insights to the organization, nor is he interested in doing so. Researching and gathering knowledge becomes an end in itself. This tendency to get self-absorbed makes a Sahadeva incapable of using his ability to make an impact within the organization.

Though knowledge is power, Sahadeva tends to disown his need for power. He can, therefore, become the one who stays behind the scenes and be the most important advisor to the one in power. A Sahadeva not rooted in *dharma* can use the power of his knowledge and intelligence to fool others, sometimes just to get the pleasure of seeing the discomfort of others. He could become cunning and scheming.

The Dysfunctional Sahadeva

Sahadevas sometimes manage their fear of offering incorrect knowledge by shutting themselves in and indulging in the joy of intellectual challenge without taking any responsibility for the system. That can lead to a cynical outlook on life, as despite having a good intellect, they do not find motivation to act and make a difference.

A Sahadeva's need for knowing before acting can lead to 'analysis-paralysis'. This could result in a deep unexpressed anxiety. He manages this anxiety by shrugging off all responsibility. Sahadeva's pursuit of knowledge and objectivity leads to poor people skills. He can come across as being antisocial, elitist and arrogant. This lowers his ability to lead others into action.

A dysfunctional Sahadeva flits from one area that excites his interest to the next without delving deeply into any one enquiry. This inevitably leads to the feeling that he has wasted his talents.

Insufficient Identification with the Sahadeva Propensity

Individuals who undervalue the Sahadeva propensity display disdain for abstraction and theorizing, thereby losing the ability to gain knowledge and skill for themselves and for the system.

These individuals do not discriminate between untested assumptions and reliable knowledge. They lack forethought and end up with a strategy that is not backed up by thorough study and testing.

Integration and Replenishment

The curiosity and insatiable appetite for learning and knowledge that a Sahadeva has can reach its full potential if he anchors himself in self-belief. This comes from his 'being'. Sahadeva's being has to help him take his own thought processes seriously and bring his innovative ideas to fruition.

A Sahadeva's ability to enquire deeply also leads him to question his own identity. Often, a Sahadeva will withdraw deep within himself. This is when he needs to appreciate his ability to be alone and still remain anchored as he lingers deep within his inner spaces. It is this inner anchor that will bring Sahadeva back to reality and enable him to give concrete shapes to his thoughts.

Case Study: Shanti

Shanti was a very talented filmmaker. She started her career making insightful documentaries on very controversial subjects. Shanti was particularly good at researching a subject in depth before setting out to do her filming. She planned her work meticulously and her shooting was focused. However, Shanti took a long time to complete her films because she liked to work on her edits in great detail until she was fully satisfied.

Her talents and abilities resulted in a scholarship to study and work with some of the very best filmmakers and film teachers in the US. On her return to India, she was surprised and thrilled to be offered a leadership role in setting up a television production house by a prominent film producer. It was the opportunity of a lifetime. She accepted and began work, selecting independent professionals like herself to create scripts and pilots. Before long, two of her ideas were accepted and the shows were aired.

Shanti's work soon gained a lot of respect. The production house decided to build a team around her. However, all kinds of small irritants soon started to surface. Shanti found that the production value of the work turned out by others was not to her expectations. She started to supervise the work turned in by others more directly, and this led to budgets being overshot.

Shanti tried to work out ways of increasing the efficiency of the shoots and editing. At first, her financiers were willing to play along, but it soon became evident that their investments could not provide the infrastructure that Shanti was looking for.

When they pointed out that she was way over budget, she would get impatient and insist that it was a temporary problem and that soon viewers would agree to pay premiums for quality. It is true that Shanti produced some of the best work in Indian television, but the paths of artistic self-expression and business pragmatics did not converge.

Eventually, Shanti began to feel that she did not understand the television business well enough, and her conviction deserted her. Finally, she took a sabbatical to introspect.

How did Shanti discover the best that she could be?

The Transformation

With the help of a business coach, Shanti realized that when she had to work within the constraints of time and fixed budgets, she became anxious. She had fixed ideas on what was acceptable, and she was imposing that in every situation, even where it was clearly not required. Others used to find it hard to work with her as she never liked what they did.

It dawned on her that she was constantly looking for adulation and recognition by her peer group of filmmakers and was ignoring what customers wanted. This desire for peer recognition made her put significant effort into production quality and authenticity. The more she perfected the final product the more it won critical acclaim, but the less accessible it became to the general public. She wanted to be commercially successful too, and this dilemma was tying her into knots.

Shanti had to ask herself many searching questions. Firstly, what did success mean to her? Who was she making her films for? What is the purpose of being in business? After a lot of contemplation, Shanti decided that what gave her joy was working on themes closer to cultural reality. She left TV to start a small boutique consultancy and began to make sensitive documentaries portraying the Indian reality.

Summary

The heroic potential in the Sahadeva propensity is the ability to convert knowledge into innovative and insightful application. In an organizational context, these individuals shine in areas that primarily require research and reflection.

The Sahadeva is a constant learner and a great innovator. However, they could have a fear of emotional engagement and become reluctant to convert ideas into concrete outcomes. Sahadevas often prefer to watch from a distance and avoid the rough and tumble of engagement with the world.

<table>
<tr><th colspan="2">I, Sahadeva, the Seeker: Power of Curiosity and Knowledge</th></tr>
<tr><td colspan="2">I listen to problems that need to be solved. I give and receive gifts that are focused on knowledge acquisition, enquiry and theories. I am passionate about learning and experimentation. My purpose is to advance my own understanding and share knowledge.</td></tr>
<tr><th>Enablers</th><th>Derailers</th></tr>
<tr><td>I value learning and knowledge and am driven by a sense of curiosity. I believe that the pursuit of knowledge for its own sake is important.</td><td>I can get fascinated with intellectual challenge and the intricacies of abstraction and, in the process, lose touch with reality.</td></tr>
<tr><td>I value rigorous analysis and like to create conceptual frameworks of reality. I respect people who value enquiry and am willing to contribute to their learning.</td><td>I get caught in analysis-paralysis. I procrastinate and withdraw from action.</td></tr>
</table>

Enablers	Derailers
I am excited by the challenge of experimentation, discovery and problem-solving. I value quality work done with care that goes into creating products and services of intrinsic worth. I dislike acting in a hasty and haphazard manner.	I am never sure when experimentation is enough. I tend to wait until I am fully sure that what I offer will be accepted. I am afraid of being accused of deficiencies and inaccuracies in my solutions.
I tend to be an observer in most situations. I give a lot of space to others and do not interfere unless invited to join in.	I tend to become a spectator, get lost in my own world and refrain from taking action, even when the situation demands it.
I tend to be a loner, and enjoy deep conversations with people who show a genuine interest in things I am interested in.	I am sensitive about how I am received by others. I love my loneliness and use it as a cloak to avoid the rough and tumble of life.

The Power of *Dharma Sankata* and Integration: Arjuna

'Arjuna' means 'light' or 'clarity'. Arjuna seeks to integrate and balance all opposites. He has a great deal of potential and resources but must choose between self-oriented action and system-oriented action. His choices and actions are backed by great conviction.

The four powers discussed so far represent the four pillars on which an organization resides in the present. While they are essential for daily functioning, those four powers largely uphold the present. The job of balancing these four essential roles and anticipating the future is done by Arjuna.

An Overview

The Meditator and Visionary archetypal energies manifest as an Arjuna. Arjuna's source of power is conviction, generated from within.

An Arjuna anchors deep introspection and self-expression from this conviction. He starts from the position of not knowing, and enquires deeply. Since he is aware of the subtle aspects of reality, Arjuna is able to grasp things that are not easily visible to others. He listens from a space that is open and unbiased, and can understand and embrace paradoxes and polarities.

An Arjuna is capable of dissolving ego boundaries. He can be joyously spontaneous or full of doubt and uncertainty. Systems that reflect the Arjuna propensity of holding multiple realities in balance resemble ecologies where many diverse but mutually supportive elements collaborate to create a vibrant space. There is proliferation of life and the growth of varied forms of self-expression. A sense of harmony, mutual appreciation and spontaneous organization emerges.

The Heroic Arjuna

People who act from heroic possibilities of the Arjuna archetype are not only inspired by great vision, but also instil in others the drive to excel and exceed themselves. In the context of the organization, they are referred to as leaders who create and nurture other leaders. These leaders discover the path that the system must take to evolve and transform to the next level. The vision that Arjuna articulates has to constantly bridge seemingly opposing polarities, such as short-term effectiveness versus long-term viability, and people-independent system versus people-oriented culture. This is the power that the heroic Arjuna wields with poise.

The heroic Arjuna will ask fundamental questions about the nature of the system and turn his gaze towards the intended and unintended consequences of its functioning. He is sensitive to the often invisible and unarticulated dysfunctionalities of the system. This is the place from which Arjuna experiences the *dharma sankata* that confronts the system: its paradoxes, competing priorities and conflicting goals pursued by different subsystems. Every new possibility has to be weighed against other equally compelling possibilities, as well as its consequences on both the individual members and the whole system.

Arjuna is the quintessential hero of the Mahabharata. He faces the ambivalence of the contrary pulls of the different voices in every context, while continuously looking at what is emerging. He does not shy away from asking the fundamental question. What is the way forward? Is the present paradigm sufficient? He is willing to explore the unknown, and moves the organization forward through dialogue and negotiation. This is more difficult than the choices that Yudhishthira makes between what is clearly right and wrong, Bhima's responses to challenges, Nakula's focus on service, and Sahadeva's observations and studies.

The Arjuna inside oneself grows out of the search for balance, and the conviction that the self and the system must find mutually beneficial growth. He may, therefore, not draw clear lines between self and the system until he finds an inner resolution. Because he is always looking at the growth of the system, by finding a resolution between the various voices that represent different aspects of the system, he enables systemic integration.

Arjuna agonizes over the limitations of the current system and constantly looks for change. This is the power of the process of acknowledging a *dharma sankata* and the intense pulls and pushes it creates in order for a new resolution to emerge.

The Functional Arjuna

An Arjuna can bring in great energy and conviction when he is able to comprehend polarities and dilemmas. The functional Arjuna relies on the advice of people he trusts. He performs best in fulfilling tasks of integration, orchestration and change.

Functional Arjunas are capable of taking up very difficult organization transformation roles if their conviction is clear and they experience the trust of the stakeholders. They are committed to their organizations and derive their satisfaction from this commitment. Given their ability to hold divergent viewpoints, they have to work very hard to find the right balance.

Unlike others, a functional Arjuna questions systems and traditions. He is capable of articulating the need for changes in organizations.

To do this, an Arjuna envisages many alternative scenarios. His ability to remain open-minded while examining a situation allows him to view the system and the context from different perspectives. However, unless the Arjuna awakens his heroic potential and listens to his deeper intelligence, he comes across as articulating the ambivalences of the system but not really providing the answers.

The functional Arjuna displays great versatility. However, he needs to commit himself to gaining mastery over one specific skill and bring an internal convergence so that his many talents create a focused power. This gap between the potential he holds and the hesitation he displays before he acts often bewilders others who are looking at immediate action.

The Shadow Side of the Arjuna Power

The Arjuna archetype is able to see realities that are often invisible to others. When such people lose their inner balance, they can become overwhelmed by this capability. The burden of managing their insightful understanding of the invisible and unintended impacts of the way the system works combined with the responsibility they feel for systems at a holistic level makes them internalize the negatives of the system. They then articulate the negatives of policy and practices in ways that are sharp and bitter. As a result, they get associated with these negatives.

An Arjuna's versatility can become consumed in inner indecision and make it very difficult for him to act. An Arjuna beset with self-doubt could become a pawn in the hands of the system, or a slave to those affirming him. He is torn between how he thinks others see him and how he experiences himself. Arjunas can then become depressed by their sense of inadequacy and try very hard to make amends for the systemic ills through personal acts of largesse and protection. These acts of generosity come from a compulsion but never fills the inner void. These Arjunas live tragic lives full of angst, suffering for the systemic ills and hoping to find a way to create a better future for themselves and the system.

The Dysfunctional Arjuna

An Arjuna can become enmeshed in doubt, leading to hesitation or procrastination. He anchors the processes of questioning without a push for resolution. The need for deep enquiry and making a balanced choice sometimes leads him into a state of 'analysis paralysis'. When he gets caught in his shadow side, Arjuna undermines his ability to change the system.

The force of his inspirational vision could blind an Arjuna from other key factors that are important for the system. Entrepreneurial organizations led by such Arjunas could overextend themselves by taking on goals and strategies that may seem heroic but are, in fact, flighty and not grounded. Given their ability to hold divergent viewpoints, Arjunas have to work very hard to find the right balance. Arjunas who are not able to find a balance within seldom convert their immense potential into anything substantive either for themselves or others.

Insufficient Identification with the Arjuna Propensity

An insufficient identification with the Arjuna propensity can lead one to see no value in scepticism and doubt and, therefore, to become dogmatic. Such individuals end up debating with others who differ from them and remain closed to new possibilities. The fact that reality has many faces and all of them have equal potency and meaning becomes very difficult for them to understand. A weak identification with this propensity also makes a person judge others on the basis of their own perspectives and expect others to be like them.

Integration and Replenishment

Arjuna's ability to listen deeply and with empathy awakens his vulnerability, and he seeks an inner space where this vulnerability is held in grace. In order to make sense of the many voices, Arjuna seeks an inner quietness. As he discovers a way forward that is wise and *dharmic*, Arjuna also needs to discover his conviction to act. These are intense engagements with his insightful 'being'.

The being is then called upon to experience the hidden and shadow sides of the archetype. The self-reflection enables the discovery of wisdom and forbearance by transforming the angst into nourishing energies. It is from this inner ground that an Arjuna finds the flexibility and firmness needed to enable the propensities of his brothers to converge. In this feeling of being grounded, he can acknowledge his doubts and can ask the difficult questions. In embracing the 'being' – the meditative stillness – Arjuna awakens his inner Krishna, his divine intelligence.

Case Study 1: One Such Organization 1 (OSO1)

This is a midsized Software Services company with an excellent record of producing high-quality IT services in the manufacturing domain. It has been in business for more than two decades. The Managing Director started his discussion with what he called the 'statement of the problem'. 'We are at an inflexion point. We have successfully negotiated similar crises earlier, but this one requires greater attention. We have to redesign the organization so that it can become capable of being a global player and be seen as a "co-maker" by large manufacturing corporations. I think our strategy is clear, but we have a mindset issue. We have to think and act very differently across the organization.'

As the story unfolded, the 'problem' became clear: the organization had invested heavily in becoming a 'level 5 CMM' certified organization, created a set of semi-independent delivery systems and become a preferred vendor to some of the large players in India and abroad. Further growth required a much deeper connect with the customers at the level of the 'New Product Development' processes of the customers. Their service-oriented business model needed to change to a shared development model. Only this would ensure a continuity of business. Many of the senior managers who had grown with the business may not be able to make the necessary shifts. A new CEO had been hired but failed to integrate.

What are the issues of OSO1?

The MD, by anticipating the challenges that lie ahead, shows great foresight. He sees an 'inflexion point', i.e., he sees a number of dilemmas that confront him. The Mahabharata tells us that the mark of a leader is not one who is great at solving problems like a Hercules, but one who can understand a *dharma sankata*. Inflexion points call for wisdom and re-anchoring of one's values, finding new inner resources to make the right choices, and investing one's full conviction and energy in that choice.

OSO1 has grown by investing in creating structures and Standard Operating Procedures (SOPs); clear policies and well-defined role boundaries. It values certainty and predictability. The modal role that has been nurtured is that of a 'good soldier'. Dependability and reliability are its calling cards. Now the MD sees that this way of working and presentation to the world fostered over the years will not take them too far. It may well become a liability. The future lies in the organization being innovative and responsive, an organization whose modal role is that of a 'customer delighter' backed up by 'experimenters' and 'innovators'.

But in the shadow of the 'good soldier' lurks the person who is comfortable in a box and who creates a degree of indispensability around their roles. Knowledge is a security deposit to be held on to; sharing it is dangerous. The discourse in the organization has a tacit set of rules: 'do not rock the boat', 'status is to be respected', 'be deserving and wait', 'adjust and accommodate', and so on.

The MD has modelled many of these behaviours and shown great discipline. However, the future organization has to have these features: it has to be a 'value chain' and not a hierarchy; it has to be able to anticipate and even trigger changes in the customer space. Moving from a 'good soldier' to a 'customer delighter' shifts the view of the person from the supervisor to 'the customer' in the value chain; it requires the person to not just follow an SOP, but to constantly look for ways to improve and innovate. Status consciousness and hoarding knowledge will become toxic; challenging and sharing have to characterize the new discourse.

The design brief articulated by the MD was: 'Move the organization from being a set of well-oiled structures to an aligned customer-centric system.' When viewed as a problem, the required shift will create an unhealthy tension between the two orientations.

The challenge the CEO placed before his team was how the new could evolve from the old, without large-scale negation of the old (which could destroy the organization). The *dharmic* way would mean an understanding of the functional aspects of both orientations and presenting opportunities for a creative dialogue that leads to the discovery of an 'and'. The unstated change that is required in the ways of thinking, feeling and acting is significant. The shift from structure-centric silos to customer-centric value chains through changing the visible and tangible aspects of the organization, is comparatively easy. What is hard is reorienting the way people think and behave.

Case Study 2: One Such Organization 2 (OSO2)

The second company we look at is again midsized, and it is in the life sciences sector. The MD is a second-generation entrepreneur. Her father leads a mature organization that is an established player in the 'injectables' domain. She has entered a new area of operation that relies on DNA mapping. It is time for her to step out of the penumbra of the parent and the parent organization.

A new company is set up to take advantage of the new domain. As the young woman starts to take the next steps, she becomes aware of many 'organization design' issues: she has imitated the structures and processes of the larger organization; in fact, some of the more experienced and high-potential younger managers nurtured in the parent organization form the core of her team. They have imbibed the ways of the older organization and recreated many of the practices. She realizes that she has been filling in the gaps between the new ways and the old in many areas, especially in building the research orientation and nurturing people. Growing means unpacking these roles and finding incumbents who will play them; it also means charting a clearly independent course and leaving the safe harbour.

What are the issues of OSO2?

The MD of OSO2 has proved a concept. She has taken an intellectual route in choosing a fairly sophisticated technology, created a very competent research team and, with the help of some from the old guard, established a sizeable company. Her first step has been very successful, but the next step is daunting. She now finds herself at a threshold. She has to stand on her own feet, go out into the battlefield as it were without the security of a fallback. She has to seek investments for the expansion, expand the market and create a brand. While all these are the measurable and tangible changes on the cards, she is discovering that her credibility as a leader needs to be established. 'I have been accepted as a leader in technology; it is only now that I am realizing what business leadership means. I must dig deep within me to develop these capacities.'

Her direct reports were a mixed lot. Some of them had some idea of what the next steps would involve and were excited by the prospect of taking up leadership positions. Others were satisfied to leave it to the 'senior management', little realizing they were soon going to be the 'senior management'. A few were sceptical of the MD making the transition. 'She is not like her father,' was their assessment. Perhaps they were not conscious of their own biases, but were right to the extent that the MD had not been tested in difficult times!

OSO2 did not require too much redesign; a few positions had to be filled. Since these were senior positions, this would be a difficult but not a great challenge. The real transformation was in developing the leadership qualities of the MD and then helping her grow her team.

OSO1 Revisited: Nurturing the Arjuna Within

The MD of OSO1 has a high Yudhishthira orientation. He is comfortable with being a Nakula. We can safely say that his success so far has been due to a very functional anchorage in a leadership style based on these two propensities. The alignment between the propensities of the MD, the organization culture and the environment has been deep. The clients of OSO1 also encouraged and rewarded this behaviour so far. The Yudhishthira-Nakula leadership style is 'benevolent patriarchal'. Role discipline is the credo of the followership. The dynamics of the Clan and the Clockwork systems energize the culture of the organization.

The environment is now going through a great deal of uncertainty. Software services in their domain are not the future; digital apps, products and specialized capabilities are in demand. The context is unpredictable and unforgiving of lacunae in an organization's ability to be innovative and proactive. A leadership style that emphasizes Bhima and Sahadeva in an appropriate mix is what is demanded. Can OSO1 and its MD make the shift?

The ability of the MD to clearly define his challenge and state it in terms of an inflexion point shows the latent Arjuna waiting to be nurtured. One aspect of Arjuna is being disruptive of the present ground while the new paradigm that he has envisioned gets established. The other capability is to orchestrate the deployment of the right kind of leadership at the right time, by understanding the relationship between the organization and its environment. Is the MD OSO1 capable of evoking these capacities from within himself? To address some of these issues and to create scaffolding within which the new ways can emerge, we designed a series of forums based on the concept of a *Koodam*. The *Koodam* is an old Indian institutional practice, similar in many ways to the Ringi System of Japan. A *Koodam* brings alive an 'ecological' space, where dialogue and exploration become possible. The Arjuna behaviours of questioning and expressing self-doubt are encouraged.

Mutliple workshops were held, games organized across levels and functions to help overcome internal organizational boundaries.

A context of safety was created where empathy was encouraged. People were, therefore, able to express their fears openly. Dialogues and discussion around critical issues became possible.

This process culminated in a formal and facilitated visioning process. Groups were encouraged to write scenarios that included specifics on the new knowledge, the new growth process, the new people interface, the new governance and the wealth interface, i.e., the essential questions of the five archetypes. Through these workshops and dialogues, the people with a natural flair for leading the future emerged. The different types of leadership required for the future was subtly imbibed. The functionality of the different propensities was recognized.

Several shifts in the thinking, feeling and action modes took place through this initiative: the security and safety experienced in the 'patriarch leader' was subtly replaced by the safety of a discussion/dialogue process, and old habits of retreating behind role boundaries was replaced by contact, and central authority by peer discussion. The MD endorsed and legitimized the emerging ways of managing the boundaries of an engagement, and role boundedness had to be cast aside in order to engage in the discussions. The MD not only joined in as a member of a few groups, but also visibly gave up much of his decision-making power as the process evolved. Not only was the vision a collective endeavour, but also the strategy had clear contributions from many of the senior members of the team.

By engaging in workshops and dialogues from time to time, the MD modelled the behaviours that were critical for the new culture. The MD himself went through a coaching process concurrently where he confronted his own fears of letting go, his need for centrality, and his limitations. The MD loved music but, in the process of becoming the kind of leader he chose to become, he had repressed his own emotionality and love of aesthetics. In rediscovering this, he also rediscovered his innate ability to read patterns and make subtle connections like an artist. This became a key capability when he had to understand trends and shape the emerging scenarios. The MD's potential to open up his Arjuna propensities was awakened. An unintended benefit of this opening up was the ease with which he started mixing with people from his own organization and with existing and potential clients. What he gave up of his Yudhishthira-Nakula ways was filled in by an emerging Arjuna.

The design process that the organization went through had three features. First, the central pillar was anchoring the process: the 'benevolent patriarch' who was slowly morphing into an 'orchestrator' and was visibly participating and making significant efforts to change. Second was the safe practice space of the workshops, and third, the self-introspection in the coaching sessions. The whole team needed to internalize new skills, of course, but the skills without the change in the culture, i.e., ways of thinking, feeling and action, would be water on a duck's back, not providing the necessary nutrients for the new seeds. The shift in culture was thus a critical element of the organization's journey.

What of OSO2?

OSO2 had to cross a different threshold, both as individuals and as an organization, since they had invested in being Sahadevas with more than a sprinkling of Yudhishthira discipline. Comfortable with hi-tech instruments and analysing data, they made a name for themselves in a comparatively rarefied field. The MD had obtained her PhD in genomics and was a good researcher. There was very little competition in the field, but that only meant that growth would depend upon the ability to define and nurture a market. It required a combination of Bhima and Nakula capabilities. Did the MD have this? Her father had overseen much of the business end of deal-making and facing the banks and shareholders. MD, OSO2 had to move her *energy* centre from a natural facility with the research, experimentation, dialogue and networking with technologists to the rough and tumble of the arena-fighting for market share and engaging with competitors! And in that process win the admiration and loyalty of a set of older heads of the support functions like finance, business development and HR, who saw themselves as the proxies of her father.

Though MD of OSO2 loved dancing, she was encouraged to learn martial arts. One of the lacunae of people drawn to the Sahadeva-Arjuna propensities is their aversion to power, the very stuff that a Bhima loves. She had to develop a love for the heroic and, therefore, inspire her team to follow her. This could not be done by risking the present operations that she had successfully nurtured. Her father saw the wisdom in creating a space for this to happen. She was asked to head the turnaround of a small but potentially profitable tablet-making unit. This meant that she had to pass on some of her present responsibilities and grow her team to replace some of her roles; it meant working on strategy and business planning while transfering the anchorage of technical excellence.

Learning to be a strategist in a turnaround situation meant learning to fight battles on the ground as well as understanding the narrative of the war. A turnaround requires the leader to absorb the feelings of anxiety and inadequacy of the top management team and convert it into a will to fight. It requires one to calmly study a situation and understand it, but also to stay action oriented and not wait for the perfect solution – a Bhima trait.

The turnaround of the MD and the tablet business took two years, but at the end of it, a hero emerged. The combination of Sahadeva and Bhima made her a formidable strategist. The experience made her overcome her aversion to confrontation. That, coupled with her innate feminine leaning towards inclusivity made her Nakula capabilities a natural part of her repertoire. Her father continued to stay on the board as the chairman of the organization, and some of the members of OSO2 Top Management who had seen themselves as the 'proxies' of the father were reabsorbed into the parent organization.

How Does One Work with This Lens?

The Mahabharata is a 'myth to live by' (borrowing Joseph Campbell's terms). It is called a *puraana,* which is literally 'ancient yet nascent', and the word mythology, with its associations of a dead story, does not capture the power of a *puraana*. The heroes are archetypes, and these archetypes lie dormant in each of us. Situations that carry emotional intensity and are potentially life changing bring them alive in us and become the driving algorithm of our perception, meaning-making and choice-making. Using a metaphor like 'Arjuna', for example, awakens a whole host of inner and outer prototypes of 'being' and 'action'. Thus, when one sits with the MD OSO2 and asks, 'Can you awaken your Arjuna?', it allows one to allude to the intense penance that Arjuna undertook before he stepped into the battlefield. It allows one to ask: 'What are the dilemmas that you see in your context? How have your ways of being that were appropriate for that context created the ground on which these dilemmas stand? Can you consult your inner Krishna, the wise person within to ask fundamental questions regarding your ideas of self, others and the world before you formulate solutions? Will your solutions resolve the *dharma sankata*, or will they be a problem-solving exercise that converts a dilemma into a polarity, or worse, into a stand-alone issue?' One can ask how the feminine and the masculine are being held within, because Arjuna had the courage to deeply encounter the feminine within before he could emerge from his introspection. It allows 'soft options' such as exploring the arts as a way of discovering one's subtle resources, and awakening compassion. Arjuna was a great dancer, not just a warrior. Through this process, the dynamics of the subtle energies are awakened. Through the practice of *aasana, praanaayaama, dhyaana* and artistic expression (if the person is so inclined), these subtle energies can become embodied. The inner algorithms are subtly altered.

The coaching process, as well as the dialogue, becomes less threatening, since the reflections and the symbolic similarities are explored through the Mahabharata or any other shared narrative (discussions of popular films often came up in the collage sessions) before looking at one's own narrative. Scenario writing is a process of initiating one's own saga, and evoking one's own heroic potentials. This is an iterative process. It takes time and persistence.

The broad steps in the process are:

- The initiative starts with a meaningful assessment of the situation and the propensities of the key players in the ongoing drama of the organization.
- Depending upon the assessment, one starts with the leader as the starting point of the transformation (OSO2) or the organization culture (OSO1) as the context for the initiative, with the leadership team as central players.
- The coach uses narrative and storytelling as the facilitating mediums.
- The individual coaching gives space to the individual to choose his level of comfort; however, the bias towards uncovering identity processes is stated up front. This allows the coach-client conversations to include the entire life-space of the client.
- Identifying one's identity processes through looking at similarities and differences between one's role models and heroes, and the five archetypes is an important part of the conversations.
- The importance of an 'embodied learning' and the need to embrace a mindful practice/*saadhana* is emphasized. Encouraging the person to awaken artistic interests, hobbies such as sports, yoga, adventure tourism, gardening, is at the heart of the mindful practice. But this has to be through active engagement, not as a passive recipient. For example, the MD of OSO1 was an ardent music lover, who loved to attend concerts 'as a way of relaxing'. He was encouraged to resume his singing lessons, something he had enjoyed doing as a youth. The MD of OSO2 cannot just be aware that she needs to be more like Bhima; she has to learn martial arts, and maybe she will go on to read Sun Tzu's *Art of War*.
- Mindful practice is not just a 'personal practice': mindful listening, for example, is applicable equally to one's own inner dialogue, the conversations with friends and family as well as roleplaying in the organization.

- The coach/consultant only acts as a '*sutradhaar*' – the person who has the liberty to be without a specific role, takes up any role temporarily, be a mirror to the process, articulate the meta-narrative and be the 'sacred clown' in the emerging drama.

Summary

When these two internal blocks – hesitation to act and self-doubt – are resolved, Arjuna's heroic qualities start to grow. He can absorb the intense pressures of the *dharma sankata* and look beyond the current methods to study the system and the environment carefully. He can then identify the dysfunctionalities of the system and offer new paradigms of thought and action.

An Arjuna seeks new ways of interpreting reality and challenges himself to find new responses. He is able to refashion his identity and role appropriately, and set out on new paths.

<table>
<tr><th colspan="2">I, Arjuna, the Hero: Power of Dharma Sankata</th></tr>
<tr><td colspan="2">I listen to the call for systemic change and to the many voices and conflicting perspectives that reveal the unfolding pattern. I give and receive gifts that enliven myself and others simultaneously. I engage in deep enquiry to understand the whole system and its relationship with the evolving context. My purpose is to ensure that the system and I evolve as we grow.</td></tr>
<tr><th>Enablers</th><th>Derailers</th></tr>
<tr><td>I listen without judgement , and with an intent to understand deeply.</td><td>I get caught up in the negatives of what I see.</td></tr>
<tr><td>I act from a deep sense of commitment to the whole system.</td><td>I end up questioning my own legitimacy.</td></tr>
</table>

I ask questions and explore deeply to find answers; I engage in an intense questioning of the invisible practices and processes of the organization.	The loneliness of the process leaves me burdened and blocked.
I enter the unfamiliar without seeking guarantees; I am willing to be alone in the search for the new.	I end up seeking advice and affirmations from others.
I engage in a dialogue with the system to initiate change; I am a proficient orchestrator and an agent of change.	I find myself constantly having to prove my credentials.

PART 3

Discovering the Best That You Can Be

Draupadi, Arjuna and Karna, the Centre of the Vortex

Before we examine the idea of the process of inner transformation, we need to revisit the meaning of the three heroes in the Mahabharata who have deep encounters with Krishna, the Divine Intelligence. They are Draupadi, Arjuna and Karna. While Draupadi and Arjuna integrate the Divine Intelligence into themselves through their friendship with Krishna, Karna confesses his inability to embrace the wisdom of Krishna. The hurts he has received from society are too deep for him to find the ability to heal inside and forgive the perpetrators of the grave violations.

Draupadi, Karna and Arjuna represent three aspects of the heroic possibilities of the Arjuna archetype. Draupadi is the feminine aspect and Karna is the counterpoint.

The Mahabharata refers to Arjuna as *vibhooti purusha* – a titan who is half-divine. His brothers are great, but are mere men. Draupadi is referred to as the inner Krishna, and during the Mahabharata war, the confrontation between Karna and Arjuna symbolizes the many ways in which they are counterpoints. Unfortunately, Karna gets trapped in his victimhood and stays with the Kaurava and their *adharmic* stance.

Let us now examine the Draupadi-Arjuna-Karna triad and its relevance to leadership.

Denial, discrimination and deprivation are Karna's constant companions. He discovers and expresses his greatness in spite of this constant torment. When he prepares to enter the battle on the seventeenth day of the war as the head of the Kaurava army, his mother, Kunti, finally acknowledges him. However, she does so only to extract a promise to not kill his brothers. Karna promises that he will spare all except Arjuna.

Shalya is a great charioteer and is chosen to drive Karna's chariot. However, Shalya does not like this job and says so in no uncertain terms to Karna, even as he walks up to the chariot on the morning of the battle. He discourages Karna before each of his encounters with the Pandava princes.

This is in direct contrast to Arjuna, who is not only the favourite of his elders and teachers, but is also showered with all kinds of advantages from society because of his noble birth. And if that weren't enough, he is empowered by Krishna throughout the battle. Krishna encourages him and his doubts are answered.

If we observe these two heroes from a larger perspective, it is evident that if Karna, who was Arjuna's equal in every way, had been appreciated for his heroic capabilities and not humiliated for his birth, maybe there would have been no war. But for that, Karna would have had to transform his deep hurt and stop looking for legitimacy and external validation.

The Two Great Failures

The Mahabharata highlights two great failures of society that lead to violence and war. One is not judging people on their abilities and deeds, and instead humiliating and undermining them because of their birth. In the epic, there are no changes made to the laws and norms that allow such discrimination. We see this in the life of Karna. The other failure is not protecting the most vulnerable. This is illustrated in Draupadi's humiliation after Yudhishtira's misadventure with gambling. This decline in governance and societal norms is referred to as a change in *yuga dharma,* the *dharmic* ways that were relevant to a bygone age.

Any society, civilization or system that allows these failures has reached its nadir. If the people holding positions of authority in this system can recognize these failures for what they are and find ways of changing for the better, the system can evolve. However, if they continue to stick to what worked in the past, the system has to be destroyed for a new one to emerge. It is better if this destruction is done by someone from within the system than by an outsider.

Organizational Evolution

Placing this in a contemporary context, organizations need to recognize when they are failing to recognize or protect their employees and other stakeholders. A wise leader can understand these failures. He treats the system as a work in progress and listens carefully to the various voices that may be hidden in the system. This makes him aware of the unintended shadow aspects.

He then pulls himself away from the pressures of the present and reflects deeply on the current paradigm through a process of *tapas* (intense introspection), where he examines his own assumptions, conclusions, biases and motivations. If this deep self-reflection does not happen, he will only make some superficial changes to the system without developing a transformative paradigm.

The wise leader then has extensive discussions with knowledgeable and intelligent people who understand the emerging reality and, most importantly, remain above all personal motivations. Through this process, he evolves a thorough understanding of the system as well as the context that the system has to thrive in. This enables him to develop a new and more inclusive and powerful paradigm, as well as the conviction needed to put his insights into action to deal with the emerging context.

If the unintended negatives in the governance of an organization are not acknowledged and are allowed to accumulate and fester, they cause the organization to suffer. Organizations that have been successful over long periods of time have found ways of engaging in this agonizing re-evaluation of their foundations and regenerating themselves.

Exile: The Space to Own the Disowned

The *tapas* that the Pandavas undertook during their exile (*vanavaasa* – retreating to the forest for contemplation) allowed them to discover new potentials within. They had deep discussions with sages and went into periods of intense self-reflection. The process ends with a period of discovering their shadow sides, acknowledging them and dissolving them.

A very important meaning of the word '*tapas*' is 'using the heat of the psyche to ripen'. When a fruit ripens, it naturally falls off. If the fruit is broken off the branch before it is ripe, it leaves a wound in the tree. In the Yoga Sutras, this ripening refers to our psyche and body. Yoga does not recommend harsh austerities that weaken the body and mind. Self-development is not about pushing oneself to become something that one is not.

In Yoga Sutras, there are three types of heat, or fire, that have to be protected and tended so that they burn in a healthy manner. They are

1. Heat of existence: *deha-agni*
2. Heat of digestion: *jaatara-agni*
3. Heat of deep contemplation: *dhyaana-agni*

Yoga defines the middle path of tending the three fires to bring the mind and body into a state of maturity. Then the mind becomes capable of subtle insight and the body does not retain toxins that trigger compulsions. This is very different from rigorous self-condemnation and self-correction.

In the Mahabharata, everyone, including the Kauravas, has heroic potential. The difference between the Kauravas and the Pandavas is that the former remain deeply engaged with their personal agendas and vendettas, which colour the lens through which they make choices and give meaning to their world. All their actions, and their relationships with others, are exploitative. They do not undergo *tapas*, and thus their fires are untended and burn too bright. These fires ultimately consume the Kauravas and destroy them.

The Pandavas do get pulled towards their shadow sides too. However, they recognize it when it happens, and they introspect and work to transform these energies. Their exile symbolizes tending of their existential fires in a place far away from the disturbing influences of society.

Once the three inner fires are tended to properly, the Pandavas discover their real potential, gain wisdom and master their talents. However, they have not really confronted their deeper shadow side yet.

How do we know this?

The Shadow Overwhelms the Psyche

In the great game of dice, Yudhishthira gives in to his shadow energy. In Draupadi's humiliation, many shadow sides are exposed, most noticeably that of Bhishma but also of each of the Pandavas. At the end of this terrible travesty of *dharma*, the Pandavas embark on another exile to confront their inadequacies and shadow sides. However, the Kauravas, whose indulgence in their shadow energies is the cause of the *adharma*, stay put in their palace. They do not move out of their habits and remain entrenched in their self-centred ways.

During exile, the Pandavas acknowledge their unresolved compulsions and shadow energies and try to transform themselves. It is an intense process of self-discovery. When Arjuna undertakes a very difficult *tapas* to acquire special weapons, it symbolizes his shadow energies being transformed into positive forms of power.

In the final year of exile, they have to live incognito. This is a period in which the Pandavas discard all signs of their high birth and live as servants. They do not carry their weapons and cannot be in communication with each other, nor with Draupadi. In a sense, the Pandavas are left with nothing except their own selves, devoid of all external pretence. In exile they gave up their power; but it was this one year of living incognito, where they had to give up their identity as well, that helped them to truly discover who they are.

Yudhishthira becomes an advisor to King Virata. He becomes a gambling companion who has to play dice with the king. Through this, Yudhishthira has to confront his shadow side and transform it.

Bhima becomes a cook to confront his lust and greed; at the end of the year, he has to confront Keechaka, the lustful brother-in-law of King Virata, in a battle unto death. Keechaka intends to violate Draupadi, but unlike in the court after Draupadi's humiliation, this time, Bhima takes action and defends her.

Nakula tends to the horses and lives in the stables, and through this work, he confronts his shadow propensity to ignore his own needs when absorbed in the service of others. Sahadeva becomes a cowherd and goes away into the forests to confront his shadow propensity of withdrawing and becoming invisible.

Arjuna, the greatest warrior of his times, disguises himself as a woman called Brihannala and works as a dance teacher to discover his femininity. This allows Arjuna to become a complete person.

Every great leader must experience and deeply understand servanthood, to be in touch with how the use of their power affects those who are dependent on them. It is only by confronting and transforming one's shadows that one can wield power with grace and dignity. This is a critical step in unleashing one's heroic potential to fight a *dharmic* war.

If one does not do this, one will constantly be pulled into personal agendas and find ways to collude with the current paradigm and let things continue as they are. Inner compulsions and appetites will take over. To fight a *dharmic* war, we need to be anchored in *shaantham.* As we have learnt, this is the deep meditative core of our being from where divine intelligence can be accessed. To be anchored in *shaantham,* you need to transform the *asuric* forces into *daivic* ones.

Anchoring oneself in *shaantham* nourishes the process of discovering one's inner *sakhi* (friend) and *saakshi* (meditator). This process is called *saadhana* – a lifelong journey to seek the true, the good and the beautiful.

Let's look at this through the life of Bhishma, who is the real power behind the throne. As Devavrata (his birth name), he promises away his right to the throne and his virility because his father was blinded by his desire for Satyavati. He is hailed as Bhishma, the one who has made a terrible vow. The rest of Bhishma's life is lived carrying out this promise, living that entrenched identity.

Bhishma nurtures a very rigid and righteous judgemental persona. He is a mighty warrior, but all his wars are fought as a proxy for the one occupying the throne. Slowly the beautiful and powerful energies of Bhishma become congealed and inert; he does not look at the context, nor does he introspect and question himself. Instead, he continues to hang on to his past promises in a frozen form even when the context has changed.

We all do this to ourselves at times, when we make promises to ourselves and to others. We build and cultivate an image around it, and keep on sticking to that image despite the changing context. We pat ourselves on the back for remaining strong and not getting tempted. We get stuck in old promises and images we have created for ourselves. It gives us a powerful sense of being.

Bhishma thinks he is great because he did not break his vow even under the greatest provocations and seductions. The world also applauds him for this and reinforces this identity. Even today, we often see high praise offered to Bhishma Pitaamah: the greatest upholder of *dharma.*

He is, though, just representing the power of dogma. He holds on to an idea that, over time, has lost its relevance. He refuses to intervene when Satyavati, because of whom he made the promise, wants his help to continue the Kuru dynasty. He sticks to his vow and what the rule book says when a grave injustice is done to Amba. He dilly-dallies and fails to protect Draupadi despite the forces of *adharma* playing out so shamelessly in front of his eyes. And finally, driven by his sense of loyalty, he knowingly ends up fighting on the side of *adharma*. He had the power vested in him by the system, and his own personal power, to stop the Kauravas from sliding into the world of *adharma* – but he didn't use it.

We tend to build our identities in the same way. We get affirmed, rewarded and celebrated for our abilities that are meaningful in the eyes of significant people in our lives and extremely relevant for a given context. Circumstances challenge these deeply held codes, but we fight to protect these ideas all the time. In doing this, we are merely reinforcing methods that have become dysfunctional and keep our potentials locked in to serving a self-centred purpose. The world also continues to applaud us for being an upholder of the identity that makes us a willing instrument of its purpose.

When one is blinded by one's own compulsions or dogma – like the Kauravas – one's choices are bound to be detrimental to the context and the people who are dependent on one. However, if one is capable of accepting failures and limitations as the starting point for self-reflection – like the Pandavas – one can walk on the path of self-mastery. The Pandavas go on exile every time their actions reflect immaturity.

What are the key accomplishments of the Pandavas during exile?

1. **Purification and clarification of intent:** The Pandavas and Draupadi have several intense discussions about why they should fight a war. Each of them goes through periods of doubt, restlessness and guilt. Yudhishthira bears the brunt of these intense highs and lows. But in the end, they emerge with great clarity about their *dharmic* intent.
2. **Discovering their true self:** Many sages visited the Pandavas during their exile and taught them yogic practices. They provided profound discourses on matters of *dharma*. The one year spent incognito is when each of them has to finally confront and understand their true selves.

3. **Discovering true power**: Each of the Pandavas go through *saadhana*. The stories about the mastery of many weapons are symbolic of the inner transformation of energies that are locked up.
4. **Becoming aware of the context**: The Pandavas used the twelve years of *vanavaasa* to speak with wise sages and send emissaries to different kings, and deployed their own spies to study the context, assess their strengths and strategize. They understood the importance of timing, of alliances with reliable friends. The brothers went on many expeditions to friendly lands to make alliances. This helped them understand the contextual relevance of their stance.
5. **Creating a community**: The alliances they made during their travels were based on a shared understanding of *dharma* and the conviction that *dharma* must be upheld, and not on convenience and compulsion as with the Kauravas.

Any strategic action must have the following factors – ABCD – for anyone to become the best they can be:

- **Awareness** of self that enables an unhindered flow of one's energies.
- **Balance**, an inner calmness that enables accurate perception.
- **Contextual Intelligence** so that one's actions are in harmony with the emerging reality.
- **Direction** to be anchored in one's inner self and deal with decision-making dilemmas.

What Does Exile Mean for Leaders in Today's Context?

Each one of us has an ongoing internal dialogue. The higher the stakes, the more intense and confusing this dialogue becomes. What voices do we hear in this cacophony?

- The voice that reflects old hurts and fears, that entreats us to not venture into anything, lest we get hurt

- The voice that reflects anger, that is vigilant and ready to fight and protect us from real or perceived danger
- The voice that is full of judgement, that can invoke guilt and shame
- The voice of the escapist that throws up fantasies and distractions
- The voice that speaks through dreams and visions
- The voice of the compassionate and honest inner friend who will give wise counsel – the voice of *sakhibhaava,* as it is called in Indic literature
- The voice of our deep inner intelligence that can only be accessed through meditative silence, which is called the voice of *saakshibhaava*

The first four voices are disempowering derailers. The inner dialogue that takes place between the first four voices – the voice of the victim, the fighter, the judge and the escapist – traps our psyche and its energies into dysfunctional and self-defeating ways of being.

If they are not dissolved through retreat and contemplation, they get embedded deeply and slowly become powerful unconscious compulsions. Unless we discover the silence of the meditative observer within, i.e., the space of *shaantham* and *saakshibhaava*, the inner dialogue does not get resolved. Doubts and anxieties persist, and any actions taken will not be authentic and powerful.

The last three voices are empowering enablers. Transforming these frozen and congealed inner energies is the essence of the *tapa*s we must engage in. Every opportunity for inner reflection that is lost reinforces entrenched identity patterns. Leadership ought to be a lifelong journey towards being the best we can be. We have to deploy the heroic potential in us in a *dharmic* way.

The Five Questions

Authentic behavioural change or an unleashing of your greatest potential cannot happen without the *tapa*s you do in a period of exile. Obviously, it does not mean going away to a forest for years! A few minutes every day, a few hours every week, and a couple of weeks every year are all that it takes. I have found that for most brilliant leaders, this self-reflection becomes an unconscious habit.

The practice of *tapas* comprises creating a space of *shaantham* to awaken the *sakhibhaava* and *saakshibhaava* and asking yourself these five questions:

- Who am I?
- Where am I?
- Why am I here?
- In doing what I am doing, what am I really doing?
- How am I part of the problem, and how can I be part of the solution?

Who am I? The answer to this question is the foundation of life. Without a sense of self that is meaningful, that is built on a wholesome narrative of our own lives, there is no foundation for making meaning of the world and making choices. While an overly frozen construct of self makes for rigidity and self-righteousness, an unformed construct has no power.

Where am I? This is the enquiry into our context. Being sensitive to the visible and invisible dynamics of the situation we are entering is vital for formulating the right strategy and preparing ourselves.

Why am I here? This question has to be answered keeping in mind the short-term and immediate purpose for which one is engaging with the world as well as the long-term perspective of one's life journey.

When you answer these first three questions with clarity, you gain better conviction and your action becomes more strategic and focused. It is the inability to answer these three questions that lie at the heart of Arjuna's despondency. His dialogue with Krishna enables him to gain confidence and enter the battlefield without doubt or inner conflicts.

Before you enter any high-stakes situation, you must ask the first three questions for that context. A false, mistaken or old idea of who you are clouds the way you approach others. Being authentic starts with understanding and being anchored in yourself. This is where a good understanding of your propensities, limitations, enablers, derailers and shadow tendencies becomes crucial. You cannot understand others without understanding yourself.

Assessing your context and the terrain of an upcoming battle is critical to the formulation of your strategy. In today's context, answering 'Where am I?' could come from being aware of the expectations of the various stakeholders who impact one's role. Based on the answers to the first two questions, one can begin to formulate possible scenarios for the engagement. Out of this understanding, we can develop a preferred strategy and backup plans.

Being self-aware and truth-seeking while engaging intensely in a situation enables one to ask, even while engaging in action: 'In doing what I am doing, what am I really doing?' This is not a natural ability and has to be developed.

Asking this question after an engagement is very important. We can dive into our deeper motivations and inner compulsions, setting aside superficial reasoning. This will enable us to not only become aware of what is usually referred to as subconscious processes, but also become more authentic.

As this self-reflective process becomes second nature, you come to be in harmony with your emotional core. True personal power is the flow of emotional energy that is spontaneously aligned with one's intentions and action.

The last question: 'How am I part of the problem, and how can I be part of the solution?' is that part of the self-reflective process that enables us to discover our unique style. Introspecting on the question 'In doing what I am doing, what am I really doing?', enables one to go beyond superficial analysis and delve deeply into one's inner processes. This allows one to discover how one can be a part of the solution with a greater perspective.

Subtle exchanges that happen at subconscious levels influence us in powerful ways. Developing the ability for mindful contemplation is important to catch these invisible exchanges, which take place all the time. They may even be in the compulsive and disowned sides of ourselves.

As we become adept at listening to ourselves and being self-reflective even as we express ourselves, we will be able to sense and understand the unconscious undercurrents that characterize all human interactions. Without this ability, we are prone to be judgemental and not insightful. These introspective processes enable us to discover our unique style and make it an authentic and powerful way to become the best we can be. Asking these questions triggers an inner process.

Let us try this out?

Take up a critical issue you are facing.

Create a space for reflection and set aside a chunk of time. Prepare yourself by having writing materials handy.

Awaken your contextual intelligence. Ask yourself: 'Where am I?' map this out as fully as you can. What is the context? Who are the key players? What do you know about them?

Get in touch with your intent. Ask yourself: 'Why am I here?'

Based on your understanding of yourself and your power propensities, answer this question: 'Who am I?'

Use your imagination, go to the centre of the map you have drawn, examine different scenarios in a playful manner and envision different possible ways in which they might unfold.

Assess the different possible prognoses of the situation before committing to a plan of action.

As you engage with the issue at hand, keep a diary in which you write your actions through the process and then note down the lessons. Take a pause every few days/weeks and ask: 'In doing what I am doing, what am I really doing? Am I listening intently? Am I evoking the most heroic of my propensities? Am I getting derailed?'

Over time, the more powerful ways of feeling, thinking and acting will become spontaneous. It is essential to let the meditative mind dominate the process of self-reflection.

Move from self-condemnation and self-criticism to self-discovery, using methods such as slow breathing to become more tranquil. This has to be done as an honest witness of yourself.

However, trying to imitate or compare yourself with others, consciously or subconsciously, doesn't help. You have to be the best *you* can be, and you cannot do it by trying to be someone else. The Yoga Sutras reflect this idea by comparing inner transformation with the flow of water. There is a reservoir of talents that each of us is gifted with. We are all born with natural propensities that define who we are. The flow of propensities is blocked by the cacophony of the inner and external drama. When we practise the meditative way of observing our mind, we dissolve the barriers to the flow of our unique way of being. The voices of the meditator within and the friend, the *saakshi* and *sakhi,* dominate the inner dialogue. The cacophony of the victim, the fighter, the judge and the escapist dies down.

The Yoga Sutras

The Mahabharata is one of the earliest texts that explains the Yoga Sutras. It is a set of principles that are woven into the stories and the dialogues between the Pandavas and the sages they meet. The Yoga Sutras are the earliest texts on psychology and are concerned with the processes of transformation of one's self.

The philosophy of Yoga stands on two pillars: *satvaada and parinaamavaada*. While *satvaada* says that what we experience is real, *parinaamavaada* says that this reality is changing all the time. It, therefore, offers a way to live in a world that is unpredictable, a way to live without clinging to the past and the known. Arjuna is often called the foremost Yogi because of his ability to embrace these two aspects of life.

Yoga is nowadays confused with *aasana* practice. Sometimes *praanaayaama* is included in the word 'yoga'. However, the Yoga Sutras have less than ten aphorisms on these practices. Of the 195 sutras, more than 150 speak about topics such as the mind, how we perceive reality, how we distort it, how we suffer due to the inaccurate perception of reality, how we develop a mind capable of contemplation and meditation, and how we relate to our world and to other people.

It then offers many paths that take us from the current troubled ways of making meaning and choosing action – a state of *duhhkha* – to a more lucid and accurate way – a state of *viveka*. This lucidity and inner equanimity give us the intelligence to survive a world that is transitory and unpredictable. All *duhhkha* is caused by clinging to the idea of permanence and imagining that repeating what we did in the past will ensure happiness in the future.

Causes of Inaccurate Perception

The Yoga Sutras offer the idea that perception is critical to our existence. When perception is inaccurate, it leads to inaccurate assumptions and conclusions, which in turn impact all subsequent processes. This is referred to as *avidyaa*. It means a mistaken perception of:

- time (permanence and impermanence)
- quality (wholesome and unwholesome)
- experience (healthy and unhealthy)
- identity (real and constructed)

When Arjuna talks to Krishna on the battlefield, he is in *avidyaa*. All his questions at that point in time reflect confusion about what will create true and lasting happiness. In response, Krishna first tries to dispel the wrong notions Arjuna carries about the nature of the self.

There are seeds that take root in one's psyche. These seeds are called *vaasana*, but not all *vaasana* are dysfunctional. These seeds can be seen as the receptacles of our psychological patterns. When we initiate a process of engagement with the world, these seeds unfold and empower our psyche. It is as though our senses get covered by a coloured lens. The colouring is from our old habitual ways of feeling, thinking and acting. They drive the psyche into autopilot, choosing a preconditioned way of sensing, perceiving, and making meaning of the world. Different seeds get activated based on the context. There are both functional and dysfunctional seeds. Some of our habits are healthy, and we do internalize those too.

We can see the impact of negative *vaasana* when we look at the life of Karna. The idea of self that he constructs based on his feelings of deprivation and discrimination overwhelm his decision-making at critical times. He refuses to see the *adharma* in the one who provides him refuge and, in doing so, offers his considerable capabilities to the Kaurava side.

The functional seeds have the potential to enable self-reflection and introspection. When we strengthen these tendencies, we start questioning our own assumptions and conclusions about ourselves and our world. Insights that are founded on our own contemplation start to develop. This marks the very important step in which we cast away all external authority and take full responsibility for our ways of interpreting life and the choices we make.

It is important to analyse whether the feelings, thoughts and actions triggered by the conditioned seeds are functional or not. This is because they are created by habit and, therefore, lack freshness and power. If they are dysfunctional, these seeds could colour the entire process of perception and, in turn, can create more dysfunctional seeds. Our decisions could end up being enveloped by a conditioned set of reflexive processes. The understanding of ourselves and our world that comes out of our own introspection is the source of our authentic power.

What is commonly referred to as identity is the expression of the *vaasana* complex. It is important to recognize this and develop our own autonomous ways of being. When we are unmindful of this, we can unintentionally fall into the trap of selfish thought and action. One is driven by a focus on consequences by one's unexamined desires and aversions. This is referred to as attachment to the fruits of one's actions. Actions done without this attachment can create the inner context for insight called *viveka*. This is the central teaching of the Bhagavad Gita.

When the Pandavas are confronted with challenges, they respond with courage and conviction, but they also face the limitations of their understanding and capability. At these times, they retreat to re-examine themselves. This process of acting with our current capabilities while remaining open to learning is the essence of Yogic practice.

However, confronted with a similar possibility, Karna is unable to give up his conditioned self. He confesses this inability to change his mind when he talks to Krishna.

Understanding the Inner Game of Introspection

To have a more experiential understanding of the process of *saadhana*, let us do a thought experiment. Please do this as you read ahead.

Imagine that you are playing a game that you are very interested in. You would naturally play it with passion; you would study your opponents and plan your moves. You play to win. But, if you lose, it does not become an ego issue. You probably laugh, enjoy the challenge, and convert it into a learning opportunity.

However, imagine you play only to win, forgetting that it is a game. The game will become a source of stress. Whether you win or lose, there is no fun. There is only one of two feelings: a satisfaction of your ego or a feeling of hurt.

The approach of engaging with the game playfully and having a learning attitude is called *apavargam* (detachment) in Yogic terminology. The egoistic way of engagement is called *bhogam* (consuming). *Apavargam* is an essential component of the sustained and intense process of self-discovery needed for *saadhana. Bhogam* instead continuously reinforces the *avidyaa–vaasana* cycle.

Now imagine that the game you must play is a difficult conversation. The moment you are reminded of a difficult conversation, it is likely that your stress levels go up because there are real consequences if you make mistakes. High stress is not bad as it makes one more attentive. This is the level at which we play a game intensely and enjoy the challenge posed by the opponent.

However, stress that is not managed well invites our four internal voices to start their cacophony. The victim voice starts cautioning against any risk-taking, the fighter voice awakens defence mechanisms, the judge voice rationalizes, and the escapist voice looks for an easy way out. If this happens, you cannot listen to what is being offered in the here and now. The ability to build a narrative of the current encounter in the larger context of your life is compromised.

If you are sensitive to stress, you can feel your body tightening and your breath becoming uncontrolled. These are the same psychosomatic symptoms that Arjuna said he was feeling on the battlefield. If you can sense this stress building up, it gives you an opportunity to apply some quick relaxation techniques. But if you can't sense it, your compulsive fears will take over.

Many sportspeople speak about 'the zone' – the space where meditative attentiveness takes over. In his book *The Inner Game of Tennis*, Timothy Gallwey examines the application of Zen meditative principles and practices to playing tennis. This book transformed coaching methods in the sport. Temperament differentiates a player who can stay at the optimal level of stress from one who sinks into a dysfunctional level. *Apavargam* is that optimal attentiveness, a state that helps us to observe carefully, respond fully and learn as we engage. *Bhogam* is the compulsive engagement with all the attendant unconscious drives that distort our perceptions and actions.

Our conscious knowledge of the self is often just our conditioned being, the habitual patterns of engagement with the world. They are the tip of the proverbial iceberg. The hidden part of the iceberg is the *bhogam* cycle. This is what we refer to as unconscious drivers, or the shadow side. These can manifest as derailing behaviours that overwhelm a person. If we remain unconscious of our true drives, we remain unaware of our highest potential.

Becoming the Best One Can Be

If someone is gifted with the abilities of a Sahadeva but is unaware of it, they may wonder why others don't ask him for solutions, without realizing that he is not offering one either. Then they may start analysing the situation to allocate blame on other things, such as the stupidity of colleagues who do not think through. This pushes Sahadeva into the *bhogam* cycle.

A Yudhishthira propensity may make a person stand apart from others, judging them on the appropriateness of behaviour based on their social standing. They may wonder why the world is not behaving the way it ought to behave and feel quite disgusted seeing only the negatives of the world. Unaware of their shadow, they may try to push themselves to be perfect, starting the negative cycle of judgement, self-condemnation and futile attempts to become what they are not.

An individual with a Bhima propensity may often see systems and processes as unnecessary hurdles. They may wonder why the world is not supporting him in this fight and instead creating hurdles, especially when he is fighting for the larger cause and not his own. The more they fight, the more they encounter resistance. They may see threats where none exist. Unless the Bhima sits back and reflects, he will get stuck in a counter-dependent cycle.

A Nakula *bhogam* propensity will make one wonder why everyone can't live in harmony. Nakulas will rush to help someone in distress, but will also yearn for recognition for what they see as self-sacrificing service. They may feel internally torn between the feeling of being used and their natural propensity to help others.

An Arjuna propensity will make a person continuously debate the pros and cons of every situation. When they are not happy with the place they are in, but don't see any merit in being in another place, they would find themselves in no-man's land.

None of these ways is right or wrong; they are just a reflection of our propensities, who we are. Understanding our own ways of being and remaining authentic to them is the most powerful way to be. The context may trigger or support some behaviours. It does not *cause* behaviours. A particular context may not appreciate you, while another might celebrate you. You cannot manipulate yourself based on the context. However, you must be sensitive to the context.

It is our responsibility to discover our deepest potential and our unique talents, to master them, to embody them and deploy them in ways that are enlivening. This is a *dharmic* responsibility. Anything less is self-defeating. It is a disservice to your context and your community.

This doesn't apply only to those in positions of power and responsibility. When you commit to this inner unfolding, you will demonstrate leadership behaviours. You will not be satisfied with anything but the best from yourself and your context.

As you start to learn with an attitude of serious self-enquiry, you discover your innate patterns – both light and shadow – and your true gifts. You become adept at navigating the context: you act appropriately, seek help when needed and complement others when the team requires your innovative insights.

Let's get back to the example of Sahadava and his shadow side. What can Sahadeva do when he is caught up in a negative cycle? To start with, he should look at himself as a work in progress. He starts observing himself with care and curiosity. He watches the way he engages with his world and starts to enquire: Who am I? From where do my motivations arise? How have I arrived at the conclusions I hold about myself and my world? What untested assumptions am I hanging on to? Is my thinking really autonomous, or have I unquestioningly followed the ways of significant people in my life?

Since this is an ongoing enquiry, there is no hurry to conclude it. Our Sahadeva might discover that he has more than one propensity. He starts gaining a more rounded idea of himself and his world. He gains a larger perspective and develops a meaning for his life. He then starts the process of reflecting after every critical engagement. He asks: 'In doing what I was doing, what was I really doing?' and furthers his process of discovery.

Committing to this process of self-observation creates a space within and encourages self-reflectiveness, even as you are engaging with your world. Self-discovery is a lifelong process. Living life with a sense of *leela* – play – enables you to take the vicissitudes of life with equanimity.

Unfortunately, most of the advice we receive pushes us into the *bhogam* cycle. We want certain consequences and often strive to modify our behaviour by imitating others. When we try to modify our behaviour based on consequences, we remain unconscious of the compulsions and motivations that drive us. We act from the *avidyaa*. This way of attempting behavioural modification is not transformative; it is at best an accommodation, a coping mechanism. Modifying your behaviour based on a desired result is, at best, temporary.

We try to modify our behaviour based on either our experiences of pain and suffering or our desire for success, power and wealth. The urgency for results goes against the organic growth of your talents and deep potential. To grow a tree, you must know how a tree grows, the nature of the seed and the nature of the soil it is embedded in. Give the seed the right conditions, and it will grow into a magnificent tree!

Transformation should happen through self-reflection and a dispassionate search for 'the true, the good and the beautiful': *satyam, shivam* and *sundaram*. Once we start listening to ourselves from the meditative mind, the voice that reflects hurt and fear transforms into a voice of a healer, the vigilant voice becomes a warrior, the voice of judgement becomes wise, and the voice of distraction becomes a seeker. These are the uniquely heroic and powerful ways that we can manifest in.

Inherent in the voice that comes out of our memories of hurt and pain is our ability to feel hurt and pain. We need to acknowledge the hurt and not try to disown it. Once we develop the capacity to meditate upon the inner processes that compel us to hold on to the hurt, we also get a deep insight into the nature of the mind that gets us into a victim position. The insight releases us from being stuck in old patterns. Our ability to resonate with compassion to the pain and hurt of others remains, and this is the key to being a Healer.

Inherent in the voice of vigilance is a keen observation of our surroundings. Being aware of danger and having a readiness to respond to those dangers is key to survival. However, when this becomes a compulsive, reactive and overly defensive pattern, it becomes a liability. We see dangers everywhere. We see ourselves under attack all the time. We view the world as antagonistic and dangerous. Once we become aware of this compulsive behaviour, we can work on being released from these patterns. The same energy can make us observant, aware of the context, and relaxed. We can choose the right fight with wisdom and fight with intensity, like a true Warrior.

The voice of judgement gives us the ability to be rational, weigh pros and cons, and make meaningful choices. However, when this ability is submerged by a compulsive need to be right according to a set of rules and norms that we have accepted without discrimination, it becomes a judgemental voice. Everything becomes black and white; people are categorized as either 'good' or 'bad'. An opinion once formed of a person becomes difficult to change. People are expected to blindly adhere to set norms and processes, even when these norms and processes have become outdated. Wisdom lies in developing our own frameworks drawn from compassion, constant enquiry, context awareness and inner intelligence.

Inherent in the distractive voice is curiosity in disguise. Children have an insatiable need to find out new things; they love to be surprised and love the feeling of wonder when they encounter the unexpected. When this energy is not understood and invested in, it turns into a superficial seeking for novelty, impulsive daydreaming and indulging in fantasy. But if understood, the voice coming from our innermost intelligence becomes the voice of true and sustained enquiry.

By discovering the heroic potential with which we are gifted, by giving space to the dialogue between the friend and the meditator within, we develop mastery over ourselves. The inner space of *shaantham* from which the *sakhibhaava* and *saakshibhaava* arise is our permanent companion. Our own Krishna resides here, a friend who will sing to us our own Bhagavad Gita. As we go through the *tapas* of Arjuna, the gods of the four directions will bless us!

Turning the Dharma Wheel

All great Indian philosophers have called the path of transformation 'the warrior's way'. Those who conquer themselves are called the Mahaveera or Dheera. The Yoga Sutras say that conviction, courage, rational enquiry and contemplation are the essential prerequisites for walking the path. The Mahabharata teaches us how important it is to go into exile. When the Pandavas give themselves a little space, when they pause to ponder over the key questions, they have the opportunity to contemplate. Then they can get back into action with intensity and deep conviction.

You may have seen people in Buddhist temples turning colourful copper wheels. This action is called 'turning the Dharma Wheel'. It is a ritualistic action that reminds the person to go inward, into a contemplative space and have a conversation with one's Krishna. What is its relevance in the modern context?

We are moving into a world where several technologies are growing in an exponential manner. The early indicators of the emerging world are already here. What will be the form of the new organization, and therefore of the new leader? These are the questions that will confront us:

- Are we ready for a radically different world?
- Are we ready to engage with others in new patterns of collaboration very different from the current steep hierarchies?
- Will we respond from a fight-flight-freeze mode as the changes shake up our comfort zones? Or will we be able to go with the flow?

The Mahabharata is set at the cusp of momentous change, when the world moves from the Tretayuga to the Kaliyuga. While the Pandavas found a *dharmic* way to embrace the change, the Kauravas did not. They tried to defend the status quo. Arjuna studies both the old and the new from the centre of the battlefield and has a conversation with his deepest intelligence. From a place of *shaantham*, he reviews his assumptions about the world, himself and his life purpose. He then anchors himself in his convictions and acts in a way that is in total harmony with the emerging reality. He turns his Dharma Wheel!

When we face a disruptive world, we cannot predict what will emerge. For example, IBM notoriously underestimated the number of computers that would be needed, and those in the CD and music business didn't see the iPod coming. The idea is not to gaze into the crystal ball and say what the future will be. Instead, it is to create inner mastery that will allow us to respond to change with awareness, balance and contextual intelligence.

In life, when we find ourselves in the middle of critical events, we should go into a mini-exile: retreat into ourselves, shut out external and internal noises, and move into a space of *shaantham*. From there, we have to ask our innermost intelligence five key questions:

- Who am I in the context I am in? *The role I am playing.*
- Where am I today in this context? *The space I am occupying.*
- Why am I in this space? *The reasons for the context to exist, and for me to be here at this point.*
- In doing what I am doing, what am I really doing? *The inner processes driving me.*
- Am I being part of the solution by being the best I can be? *Awakening my heroic potential.*

You can go into such a mini-exile at any time of the day.

We can learn to play the game of life with passion and to treat every encounter as an opportunity to learn. I will take you through a few games and ways of turning the Dharma Wheel to learn about yourself. The games can become a mirror to consult every now and again when you want to look at yourself dispassionately.

On Becoming Powerful

We touched upon the framework of power in Part 2. Power comprises two components that have to work in harmony. The first is called *shakti* (inner force) and the second is called *balam* (outer strength). *Shakti* is intangible – it comes from deep inside us; *balam* is tangible and can even be measured.

There are three forms of *shakti: ichcha shakti* – the force of emotions; *jnaana shakti* – the force of intellect; and *kriyaa shakti* – the force of action. When we feel deeply moved by a cause, we are moved by our *ichcha shakti.* When we are drawn by curiosity to enquire deeply or when we enjoy the process of discovery, we are moved by *jnaana shakti.* When we feel the rush of adrenaline, we are responding to the awakening of *kriyaa shakti.* During their exile, the Pandavas undergo various forms of *tapas*, through which they nurture and enhance their *shakti.*

There are three forms of *balam: yoga balam* – the strength of alliances with powerful friends; *kaala balam* – the strength of good timing; and *aasana balam* – the strength of position and rank. The Pandavas plan out how they will create powerful alliances. Arjuna goes to the four corners of Bharat to cement these alliances. Numerous times during the exile, Bhima urges action, and Yudhishthira speaks about timing and readiness. Time used for preparation and learning is like storing potential energy. Yudhishthira also speaks about the need for the Pandavas to evoke the inner conviction of the people with whom they seek alliances, because, being deposed kings, the brothers do not have the power that comes from position and rank.

When we look at Duryodhana's behaviour before the war, it is clear that he relies on *balam* and does not comprehend *shakti.* During a meeting between Krishna, Duryodhana and Arjuna, Krishna promises to help them both. He asks them to meet him at the crack of dawn and says he will let the one he sees first have the first pick of the help he can give. Arjuna and Duryodhana come to Krishna's bedside at dawn the next day. Duryodhana seats himself beside Krishna's head and Arjuna at his feet. As soon as he wakes up, Krishna sees Arjuna because of his position by his feet. 'You can have either me or my entire army,' says Krishna to Arjuna. 'I will not carry arms.' Arjuna says he wants only Krishna and requests Krishna to be his charioteer. Krishna then offers his army to Duryodhana, who is overjoyed and gladly accepts this gift.

Every alliance Duryodhana forges is negotiated on the basis of quid pro quo. He uses his position as the ruler of Hastinapura to coerce kings to take his side in the war. In the process, he amasses a very large army, but this army has not prepared well and has a lot of internal friction. The inner force of *shakti* is missing. There is no conviction or a sense of a larger purpose. Bhishma and Karna are not able to set aside their animosity. The smaller Pandava army is anchored in conviction and has Krishna as a source of energy, power, and strength on its side.

Shakti and *balam* are not binary, but essential together. A leader with inner conviction needs to forge good alliances and understand timing. He has to learn to use social status and position. When *balam* is not energized by *shakti*, it becomes brittle. The use of *balam* without *shakti* will move the world towards greed, acquisition and divisiveness. Together, they will move the world towards the true, the good and the beautiful.

Dear Reader, if you would like to internalize the methods suggested so far, please refer to 'The Toy Story' in the appendix at the end of the book. We take you through the journey of Ranjan as he lives out his entrepreneurial dream. It has been my experience that anyone who has done the exercise with sincerity has seen lasting change.

Learning from the Masters

The interviews appearing in the following part of the book are open-ended. We did not ask the leaders to comment on the Mahabharata but only shared the context and overview of the book. As you read the interviews in the next chapter, you will see how the five questions that we have highlighted keep recurring in their life choices, and that they have converted seemingly simple business decisions into defining moments in the growth and evolution of their organizations because they asked themselves these questions at every fork in the road.

Life becomes enjoyable when every failure and success improves our capabilities. We become the best we can be when this self-reflection becomes a regular practice. When learning becomes more mature, we go beyond the tensions of light and shadow and discover a deeper integration, our gifts emerge spontaneously, and we become capable of heroic action.

PART 4
Inspiring Leadership Journeys

MS ANU AGA

I was born in Mumbai and have two older brothers. When my mother was expecting her first child, my father wanted a son. Fortunately for him, his first child was a boy, and the second one was a boy too. The third one was me. So, in a way, I was conditionally accepted because of my rank. If I had been the first-born, I doubt if he would have doted on me the way he did. He was strict with his sons but very nurturing with me.

Though I was good at studies, I was continuously told in subtle ways that one day I would have to get married and have kids. We had a family business, and my brothers were told that they would have to join it. Not once was I told that it was for me as well. In fact, not seeing any women in business, I thought that it was a profession only for men. I saw women doctors, lawyers, teachers and nurses, but there were not many women entrepreneurs in those days.

I got married to a wonderful man called Rohinton. He attempted to treat everyone equally and would always encourage me to express my own views. So, my growth as a person started only after marriage. Until then, I had been moulded into a compliant person, and I had readily accepted it. I was not raised to state my own opinion.

Once we were at a public meeting, and I openly differed with my husband. My father was upset with me and later said that I insulted my husband publicly. My husband responded, 'Why do you say that? I have not married a rubber stamp. I have married a girl who can and should speak her mind.'

My husband encouraged me to get a job. I did a course on social work and was at the top of my class. And I started working. But I did not have any belief that as a woman I should be working and have a professional career. I did it because I enjoyed it. I was even awarded a Fulbright scholarship to study abroad, but since I already had a child, I decided to go only for four months instead of a full year.

Meanwhile, my husband's business grew and we moved to Pune. I readily gave up my job and began playing Mah-jong and cards with affluent friends, thoroughly enjoying myself.

I lost my second child in between at five months. And then we had a son.

My husband was a workaholic. He smoked and drank alcohol every day. One day he came home and said he wasn't feeling well and wanted to go to the hospital. We had a very dear friend who was a doctor. At the hospital, our doctor friend predicted my husband would have a massive heart attack. I begged him to do something. He said he could not do a thing here as he did not have the equipment to do a bypass surgery before the attack. We felt a sense of helplessness as we knew something bad was going to happen, but we could not prevent it.

The doctor stayed the night with us. That night, Rohinton had a massive heart attack that badly damaged his heart. Since we could afford to, we were advised to go to England for the surgery. On our second day there, he had a stroke. He was on a ventilator for ten days. He was in hospital for three weeks instead of the one week we had expected.

My husband was a brilliant man, but when he came out of the hospital, he did not recognize me and did not remember basic letters and numbers. All his knowledge and memories were wiped out. In a situation like this, one could be sad or angry. My husband got angry, but that anger mobilized him. It made him determined to get well. The flipside was that my daughter and I had to bear the worst of his anger. That man who would never speak harshly began to yell at us. It was not easy for us.

Rohinton had lost about fifteen kilograms, and his eyes had sunk into his skull. He looked horrible. I felt sorry for him. One of his hands was still quite weak. He told the physiotherapist that he wanted to tie his shoelaces himself. She said it would take a month. She suggested that he starts by practising to tie a big bow on his thigh. However, Rohinton worked on it the whole night, and the next day, he could tie his shoelaces! The physiotherapist was amazed. The doctors had said that large parts of his brain and heart were damaged and that he would never be normal again. He proved everyone wrong. So, a very important lesson for us was to not take the experts' opinion as final! Have faith in yourself. This was a wonderful example of anger giving him energy to do things.

Though he improved over time, because of the scar on his brain, he had four major epileptic fits. Every time he had a fit, his self-confidence was a little shaken. He had to take so many medicines – for his heart, his brain, his epilepsy – that he always felt drowsy.

It took about two years for him to fully recover. In the meantime, people suggested that I take an interest in the company because my kids were young and we as a family were vulnerable. However, I did not want to replace my husband. Prasad Kumar, who was head of HR, encouraged me to join HR part-time and see how it works. Within a week, I decided I liked the job and also realized that if I wanted to be taken seriously, I needed to work full-time. That was how I became a full-time Thermax employee.

I was very happy with the job. Our company won many awards in HR and were said to have one of the best HR departments. We had very innovative training and team-building programmes. Those were fascinating days and I really enjoyed them. Five years passed, and Prasad decided to start his own consultancy. He told me that I was ready to take over as head of HR.

By then, my daughter, Meher, had married Pheroz, a nice boy from Pune. My husband and I thought the best training they could get was to go to England and manage a small business unit of ours that was not doing well. We requested Dr Joshi, our head of R&D, if he would go with them to help out. He readily agreed and moved to England for a year along with a very senior engineer, leaving their families behind. In fact, he even agreed to reduce his salary by half because the company was not doing well. They helped turn around the UK operations. The two senior executives came back after a year, leaving Meher and Pheroz to stay on and run the UK operations.

I had promised my daughter that when she had her first child, I would be with her for six months. Four years later when a boy was born to Meher and Pheroz, I went and stayed with them for six months. When it was time for me to return to India, Rohinton was so thrilled to have me back that he drove from Pune to receive me at Bombay.

But as destiny would have it, at the Bombay guest house, he had a massive heart attack and died before my plane landed. One of the company executives came to the airport instead and tried to soften the blow by saying Rohinton had had a heart attack. But my brother immediately told me that Rohinton was no more.

My son, Kurush, had returned to India from Venezuela just a week before his father died. Both my husband and I had told him that there was no pressure on him to join the company. If he wanted to, he could work with the company for a while and then decide. I think the main reason he returned to India was that he wanted to get close to his father. He was very close to me, but not so much with his father, despite looking up to him. He was quite bitter about not being able to get to know his dad very well.

Three days after my Rohinton died, I was nominated as the executive chairperson to replace him. I just did not want the role. It was an engineering company, and I was not an engineer. Unlike my husband, I hated numbers. I really felt that they were doing this because I now had the majority shares. I cried and cried and begged them to not give me this responsibility.

I had heard of Vipassana, but it was something I did not think I could do, to stay quiet for so long. But I felt that I was now ready for Vipassana. So, I went to the vipassana meditation centre at Igatpuri. I must say that being quiet was not at all difficult. In fact, on the eleventh day, it was speaking that was difficult!

But I was missing my husband. There are teachers at the ashram with whom you can talk if you have a problem or if you have not understood the technique. I cried and cried on one such teacher's lap. My mind was rebelling after meditating for eleven hours a day. I found that once I settled down, I got in touch with my inner strength. I felt I was constantly comparing myself with my husband, and it was not helping me. I had my own strengths so I decided to focus on them.

I used to be scared of death and used to touch wood if anything about death was spoken. Even on the highway, I would insist on my superstitions, and my husband would indulge me and stop the car so that I could find a tree and touch it. But now I realized that even if I carried the entire jungle with me, I couldn't change my destiny. I also came to accept that we make up so many rules about death that are not correct and only serve to make ourselves miserable.

I also realized what is meant by 'Pain is inevitable, but suffering is optional'. You suffer when you ask 'why'.

And 'why' has no answer.

You have to accept it. And whether you are Princess Diana or Anu Aga, death will come to everyone. It does not look at your power or your glamour, your wealth, your position. Nothing. So, God was not partial to anyone. Another thing I understood was that an apple tree cannot bear oranges. So, if I keep wanting to be like Rohinton, not only would I never succeed in doing that but also I would not be able to give the best that is in me.

I came back from the ashram very charged up. It was really a very important experience that helped me to get in touch with my internal power. We all have answers within, but we keep looking for answers from outside. Now I meditate for an hour every day. It is very important for me.

We had gone public a year before my husband died, but the company was not doing well. We had diversified into many businesses, which added to our top-line and growth, but eroded our bottom-line. One day, I got an anonymous letter from a shareholder. Normally I do not give anonymous letters importance, but this one bothered me for days. The letter read: 'Mrs Aga, I do not know your financial condition, but I am a small shareholder in your company and you have let me down.' For us, 'let me down' is a terrible phrase. I did not know what to do, but I knew something had to be done.

As luck would have it, a friend of mine, Arun Maira, the head of BCG (Boston Consulting Group) at that time, was coming home for dinner. He immediately offered his services. Their fees were exorbitant for us. When I told my executives, they declined and said it's just a temporary phase of poor performance. Ups and downs happen, and we will get over them. I insisted that since we had become a public company, we should consider the interest of all stakeholders.

I went to the board of directors, which in those days comprised nine company executives and four independent directors. Because of the majority of our own executives on the board, it was difficult for them to be objective. They kept coming up with various excuses for the non-performance. I could finally convince the independent directors, and we hired BCG.

The first thing they did was an audit with the senior executives. We had to take very tough decisions. We had to make big changes at the senior level. My husband could not be tough on people. He looked upon business as generating employment while I believed in investing in people and nurturing them. But if after a few years they do not perform, then they have to leave. I am very particular about this.

We also divested out of many businesses. We were in the software business before Infosys or Wipro, but we did not know how to run that side of the business. My husband also had the vision to move into wind energy way before there were any tax benefits for doing so. He was always full of ideas. I am not a visionary, but I can manage people and bring the best out of them. To understand technical and financial issues,

I will openly admit I know nothing about them and will ask people to explain them to me.

We reconstituted the entire board, which involved going to each board member and requesting them to step down. Luckily, not one of the executive board members left the company even after being removed from the board. In this way, we turned the company around. We made many mistakes, but I do not think that we knowingly cheated anyone. That is why we have tremendous goodwill among our stakeholders.

I decided that I did not want to be the executive chairperson, because, in a way, I was pretending to run the company. It really did not feel right and I decided to take on a non-executive role.

I also set a rule, that you either run businesses or you are on the board, and that applies to family as well. My daughter and son-in-law were wearing both hats, so they were very angry with me. They said, 'All these years we were running the business and were on the board too, so why this change now?' I explained that I was convinced that it was not a good combination. In the end, they decided to be on the board and step down as executives. Today, they think that is the wisest decision we made.

In between, for fourteen months my son Kurush joined the company. He was really immersed in it. Once, there was a client in Bangalore that we were about to lose, as they were having issues with the quality of our product. Kurush immediately drove to Bangalore with a service engineer. His sister and I asked him to take a flight. However, business was not doing well and also the service engineer's rank was not entitled to fly. So, he drove instead, fixed the issue and saved the order that we had almost lost. But on the way back, they met with an accident, and he died in that accident.

I was able to take the terrible shock because of Vipassana. I had accepted that death is inevitable for everyone. And then something beautiful happened. My son's friend from college in Bristol, whom I knew a little, called and said he had come all the way to Pune to be with me. He spent three weeks with me and I took that time off, unlike the time my husband died when I had to get back to work three days later. I could talk about my Kurush and had time to grieve, which was very helpful.

When I was sixty-one, there was a press conference, and I announced that I was retiring. My daughter was quite upset that I didn't tell her first! I explained that I did it that way because once a public announcement is made, there is no going back. If I had told her earlier, she and others would have persuaded me to change my mind.

The board wanted Meher to take over, but she said she wasn't ready as her children were still very young. I called her and said, 'Meher, if you are not keen to be the chairperson, I will find someone else. But I am retiring.' She asked if I meant that I would find someone outside the family, and I said I would. I can be very tough when I want to be.

Now Meher went for Vipassana! She found Vipassana much easier. She came back and took the role of the chairperson. I retired, but remained on the board. We have a rule that independent directors have to step down at the age of seventy-five. I said the same should apply to the family and wanted to step down from the board when I turned seventy-five. Some wanted me to become a 'chairperson emeritus'. I cannot stand all that, so I said, 'No, I am retiring.' Now I am retired and very happy with my life. Of course, I have my ups and downs, but with daily meditation, I am able to face life with equanimity.

My son used to be very keen that most of our earnings should go to social causes. He once said that we should give away most of what we have because we do not have an ostentatious way of living. This was not long before he died, so it played on my mind. I went to Bombay and met a lady called Shaheen Mistri, who had started a charity called Akanksha. Both of us took to each other. I was invited to join the board of directors at Akanksha.

Shaheen then started another charity called Teach for India (TFI) and asked me to partner with her. I readily agreed. I served as the chairperson of TFI for ten years. As a family, we give 30 per cent of what we earn from our Thermax shares to philanthropy. We are hoping to increase it to 50 per cent in a couple of years.

I think job titles and positions are what the world gives you, so if you overvalue that, you could become miserable after retirement. A leader has to offer wisdom, and all other skills can be hired. Wisdom comes from reflecting and learning from your personal experiences. One thing I do believe in is not interfering after giving up a position. Even if the new executive makes a big mistake, it is his or her prerogative. Unless they ask me, I will not step in.

Many wonder how I ran an engineering company without being an engineer. I managed because I am not afraid to admit it when I do not know something. Why should it make me feel small? I am not pretending. For everything you know, there will be ten thousand things you do not know.

It's not that I have resolved all my issues and I am perfect; not at all. I am not spiritual, none of it. I hate anyone saying I am spiritual. This is a journey. Nobody has reached there. If you have, you would be dead and gone and be part of God, you know. Going to temples or reading Gita does not make one spiritual.

I always say I am full of shortcomings, but my shortcomings do not bother me. I can live with them. So, I am reactive, judgemental, maybe a little less than before, but still. I am really human, full of mistakes. I fall very often and become judgemental, then I recover. Life is far more than the mistakes one makes. I think it's about seeing your life as an actor, as if you are outside. I can, I really can laugh at how stupid I have been.

Even after twenty-three years of meditation, I don't think there have been any dramatic changes in me. What has changed is that I accept my frailties. And because I accept mine, I can accept other people's too.

I used to think that I would never be able to live without my husband. One year after my husband died, my mother-in-law died. And a few years later, my son. After my son died, I did not want to live alone in that house. But Kurush's friend asked me to wait for a year. After a year, if I still wanted to move, he promised to help me move. I am glad I did not move. I lived there for twenty-three years. I am moving now because of logistical reasons, but not because of memories. I came to realize that it was not the house that was bothering me, it was the memories. But I will carry those with me wherever I go.

Now I love my solitude, which I had dreaded earlier.

Ms Anu Aga was chairperson of Thermax Limited, one of India's most respected engineering companies. She has also served a Member of Parliament (Rajya Sabha) and was awarded a Padma Shri in 2010 for her social work.

MR NARAYANA MURTHY

I believe that one's style of leadership emanates from one's culture. My leadership style has been to get inputs from the experts in the field and from people who are affected by that decision. I feel that everybody must have a say in their own future. Except in some confidential matters such as promotion and salary, I feel that any decision that impacts a class of professionals will have to be taken after discussing with those who will be impacted by these decisions. There should be a sense of fairness in whatever decision a leader takes.

I agree that many people do not get the opportunity to participate in decisions that make the context better. Very few people who get the opportunity of participating in such decisions open their mind, think deeply about issues, and speak out openly and honestly. But many who get such an opportunity are not able to open their mind. Most Indians who are intelligent and have been given the opportunity to speak out honestly still do not do so. There are many reasons. First of all, they may be worried that expressing one's honest opinions may hurt those impacted by the views expressed and thus incur the displeasure of these people. Some people do not express their honest opinion because they are afraid it may not be liked by their bosses and that they may become unpopular. Their view is to keep their bosses happy as that's what will bring benefits to them from their bosses. The second set of people are status-quo people and may not be afraid of their bosses. They do not want to stir the pot because they believe that any change would create extra work for them. They want to lead a simple and uncomplicated life and don't want any uncertainty.

But there is a third small set of people who will say, 'This is what I have been taught all my life. This is what my teachers have taught me. This is what my parents have taught me. I do not mind incurring whatever it costs me to exercise my beliefs.' These people are more concerned about the organization and not self-betterment. Such people are plenty in developed societies where institutions are strong and not in countries like India, where many times we barter the institutional betterment for individual betterment. These people operate as checks and balances when the leaders of an institution are involved in wrong, unjust and unconscionable activities. Unfortunately, we tend to blame this set of people who operate as checks and balances, and not the leaders who commit wilful violation. That is one big reason India has remained a country with very weak institutions.

A leader's responsibility is to encourage everybody to become open minded, to think deeply, honestly and fairly about issues, to speak out their honest thought, and hold the errant people accountable.

I am a karma yogi. I was influenced by a teacher of mine in middle school. He said, 'You are all judged by your *karma*. You are all going to be judged only by what you do in this life.' So, I decided to observe situations in an honest and unbiased manner; form my ideas and opinions based on data and facts; and act on them quickly. This has helped me to have integrity in my thought and action.

I am known for giving huge equity to youngsters who had hardly completed two years as software engineers. When I founded Infosys, I gave my younger colleagues between 10 and 15 per cent equity each. I am not aware of any other such example of equity sharing. Yes, it is rare, so let me explain my philosophy behind this.

When I decided to start Infosys, I acted on certain principles of fairness and equity. These principles were drilled into me by my parents and early teachers. The cost of following these principles has not seemed much to me. I was never after money. How much equity I held did not mean much to me. The power to do good in Infosys mattered to me a lot, but the power of superior wealth did not mean much to me.

I treated my younger colleagues with respect, dignity and as my equal. I did not want to hide information from my younger colleagues. Because of my lifestyle and because of the simplicity of my life, I did not think it was a big deal to give them such equity. Many people told me that I was being generous. I did not feel I was being generous at all.

What I did was based on my natural instinct. It probably came from my culture. It was how I was brought up by my parents. All along, I had lived in a lower-middle-class family having only minimum needs satisfied. We used to get only one set of new clothes once a year on Diwali day. We were brought up with the concept of sharing. My parents inculcated these values in me. I did not think that I was doing something extraordinary or was being generous. If I did, I probably would not have done it.

I do not say that other businessmen who did not award such equity to younger colleagues were wrong and that I was right. They were acting according to their *dharma*. I was right in my own way. What I did was my *dharma*. It is all a matter of one's own culture.

People say I changed the rules of the game. I do not think I was doing any such thing. I followed what I was most comfortable with. Every decision I took was based on what was natural to me and what kept my mind at peace. And that should be the ultimate goal of all human beings – to seek peace of mind. But it is extremely difficult, not as easy as it may sound.

When a person takes a decision, that person does what he is comfortable with, and what his conscience tells him to do. I took decisions I could live with. I did not know or care what others would have done. Their mindset did not enter my framework of decision-making. All that mattered to me was what my mother would do; what my father would do; and what some of my teachers would do. Fairness has always been very important to me. Was having a large number of shares important to me? Would it have given me more happiness and better sleep? I guess not. Mythologist and writer, Joseph Campbell, once said, 'Follow your bliss and don't be afraid, and doors will open where you didn't know they were going to be'. I just followed my bliss.

I am a manifestation of my culture. Every action that you see from me is a manifestation of my culture. What is culture? Culture is what brings you happiness, what makes you sad, who your friends are, how you spend your time, how you treat strangers, how you react to situations that normally bring out anger, selfishness and desire in people, and how you conduct yourself when nobody who knows you is observing you. Your culture is influenced a lot by your parents, your grandparents, your near relatives, your early friends and, to some extent, by some of your schoolteachers. These are the people that shape your values and your culture. Once your culture is developed, you are not even aware that you act in a particular way. It's like breathing. The day you have to make an effort to breathe, then you have to go under a ventilator! Your actions come from your culture in a similar way. You are not even aware why you behave in a particular way.

When I started Infosys, I said we would be completely merit-driven and there would be no discrimination. At one level, merit is a form of non-discrimination; however, at another level, merit is a form of discrimination. I began selecting Infosys employees based on performance in tests that use certain kinds of puzzles because the job involved using similar skills every day. I needed people who had these skills in order to satisfy our customers and bring in revenue. Therefore, I used these kinds of tests to assess their suitability for the job.

Because only those who could solve these puzzles could join Infosys, we overcame discrimination based on caste, creed, race, class and gender. We did not look at any of these attributes but just their performance in my tests. Therefore, we were totally non-discriminatory.

However, since I chose only those who solved my puzzles, I discriminated. I separated the group of professionals that could solve these puzzles from the group of professionals that could not solve these puzzles. Therefore, you could accuse me of discriminating. Perhaps, I was guilty. This is the dilemma of life. I appeared fair from one angle but totally unfair from another angle. This is almost like the Mahabharata where Krishna advises Arjuna not to refrain from killing one's own relatives to serve the larger task of upholding *dharma*. I knew that foregoing these tests may result in the company delivering poor quality software resulting in loss of business and job losses for our current employees. These employees have families to support. On the other hand, protecting the livelihood of these employees and their families will deprive those who did not pass our tests of jobs. This is a big dilemma.

How do I resolve these dilemmas? Some of these dilemmas are very difficult to solve like the one above. As for me, whenever I come to a fork, I do a very simple exercise. I try and collect data and facts about every issue that I have to solve. I do the analysis in my mind on the pros and cons of each of the decision choices and choose the one with the best benefit to the organization.

For example, one of my colleagues may come to me and persuade me to accept a promotion for a given individual. He or she would say that the individual will leave if we do not give them a promotion. I would model the situation and determine how valuable the individual is. I would ascertain the loss if the individual leaves. On the other hand, I would ascertain the level of dissatisfaction and the resultant loss of morale among the individual's colleagues if we gave him a promotion. I take the path that has a lower loss. So, I deliberately try to reduce every decision to a cost-benefit analysis using data and facts.

But there are certain decisions that must be taken on the basis of one's philosophy and values. Those cannot be supplanted by data and facts. However, most other decisions can be argued on data and facts. For example, in 1990, when we had an offer from somebody to buy us out for what was a lot of money for us at that time, I had a discussion in our Jayanagar office with all my colleagues. My colleagues were quite excited. Even after ten years of founding Infosys, nobody had a car. We were living in rented houses. Our salaries were low. It did not appear like there would be some big improvements in any of our material comfort in the foreseeable future. Perhaps, most of my colleagues felt they could then afford to pursue other aspirations they had.

But my view was different. I felt that I was not short of anything. I was getting my salary, which was not too high, but I was quite content with what I was getting. I had two children. My rental home was near the office. I derived a lot of happiness from my children. So, I did not see anything wrong if I continued with Infosys. Therefore, my opinion was to continue. This decision was not based on data and facts but on my philosophy and values.

What brings you happiness? What makes you sad? How much material comfort are you attached to? Your culture is what will answer these questions. Your culture is what will drive your philosophy and your values. When it is a question of your values, your philosophy and your culture, you cannot use data and facts. Using data and facts to measure benefit in these situations may make you do the wrong things.

A few years later, we again ran into a serious fork where it was difficult to decide purely based on cost-benefit analysis. Though the decision looked like a perfect case for one based purely on data and facts, it was actually based on our values. Our largest customer at that time contributed 25 per cent of our revenues and 8 per cent of our profits. They came to Bangalore to negotiate very hard on rates. But, accepting their demand would have led to serious negative consequences for the company in the long term. It was a situation that would have been unfair to other customers of ours. It was a situation that would have been unfair to our employees whom we could not have compensated properly. We had also gone public just a few years back, and it would have been unfair to them.

It was a question of philosophy for me. If we were to accept this lowering of rates, we could not say no to our other customers if they asked us to lower the rates. Second, this customer, as was his right, was quite demanding in performance. It would have been unfair to the customer if we had to reduce our investments in quality and productivity. If we were fair to him in our investments, it would have been very difficult to make adequate profit. On the other hand, there were many consequences of losing 25 per cent of our revenues, particularly within twenty-four months of going public.

I did not want the cost of this decision to hurt us in the medium term. So, I called my wife that afternoon and I told her that for the next three years I might be travelling 300 plus days in a year. I asked her if she would be in a position to look after the children totally by herself. She was supportive. I took the decision to not sign on the dotted line.

What made me take that decision when others (including other Indian companies working with this customer) did not? Now, we are into a very strange land where I am also confused. It was very easy for me to accept the customer's request and sign on the dotted line because everybody else had signed. Even my colleagues were not sure about walking away. I was the only guy who was saying no. What gave me the courage to say no? Were my confidence and sense of fairness that strong? Would I do the same thing again today? I am not certain.

Maybe my discomfort came from the fact that I did not see fairness in accepting the request of the customer. Therefore, I come back to philosophy and my sense of fairness. It was again about my culture. It was about being yourself. It was about being at peace with yourself. Somehow, God gave me the courage and, more importantly, it worked out! If it had not worked out, I would have been the biggest fool!

It is said that 'chance favours the prepared mind'. To the extent possible, I had done my homework and was prepared for the consequences. I had analysed the downside. I had introspected whether I would be able to replenish the customer business with new business at the required margins. I had spoken to my wife about my prolonged absence from home. I had also spoken to my close friend, Vallabh Bhansali, of Enam about the possible impact of the loss of this business. So, I had done all that I could do.

When we were going back to the office after the negotiations were done, a colleague of mine was very upset that I did not look worried. I told him that as head of the Infosys family, I had to remain calm. I was much more worried than he was, but then again, he had just joined the company only a year ago. I founded this company. We had gone public. Therefore, it couldn't be further from the truth that I was not worried. However, I had already thought about what I should do over the next three years to solve this problem.

The Bhagavad Gita prescribes that you should do what you are supposed to do. It tells us not to worry about what the result will be. In our own case, we had taken a tough decision and we had to work hard to handle the consequence of that decision. When we went back to my office, I behaved as if nothing had happened. I called the head of our planning group and told her that we had to form the 'risk mitigation council'. I told her who the members should be, and what factors we should monitor every week. But that did not mean I was not worried about consequences. Gita says that we should not get attached to the result. But for most of us, it is not possible to be detached from the result! I continued doing what I had to do even though I found it very tough to not worry about consequences.

Any system, any community that makes its people more joyful, more peaceful, more harmonious, more progressive, more transparent, more objective and more prosperous is a good community. Anybody who takes responsibility for that is a leader.

Fairness is perhaps the most important attribute of any human being, not just a leader. I define fairness using the golden rule: *Do unto others what you want them to do unto you.* Fairness is the most important attribute of my *dharma*. I do not know if it is right or wrong. I do not know whether it fits in every context, but fairness is the only *dharma* that I would like to follow.

I believe that every human being can be a leader in a certain context. An office boy working in my office may not get the opportunity to show leadership in the office. But, let us say he is married and has children. He will have certain aspirations for them. He may want to raise his children better than how he was brought up. He may want to give his family a life better than what he got. He will work hard for it. When there is some difficulty at home, he will raise the confidence of his family. He will encourage his children to achieve high targets. He will make huge sacrifices for his family. To me these are all traits of leadership. Therefore, I personally feel that every one of us has leadership potential and we all exhibit leadership in our own ways in different contexts.

I am not a philosopher and I do not have the answer to how we can achieve peace of mind. However, I will tell you what I do to move towards a higher level of peace of mind for myself. I have come to the conclusion that the most important ingredient for peace of mind is self-restraint – self-restraint on anger, self-restraint on desire, and self-restraint on hatred. If we can exercise self-restraint, most of our reactions to external stimuli that cause anger, desire and hatred can be muted.

Mr Narayana Murthy is the founder of Infosys Ltd. He has been honoured with the Padma Vibhushan and Padma Shri.

MR P.C. MUSTHAFA

If I look at my leadership journey, it was abject necessity that brought out leadership qualities in me. And the necessity was for me to feed myself. Many days I used to go hungry to school as my father could not afford to feed us. My biggest motivation for going to school was the midday meal provided there.

Even then, breakfast was a dream. So when I was around ten years old, during summer holidays, I took the lead in trying to solve this problem. During the summer holidays I borrowed some money from my uncle and went to a nearby town. It was around fifteen kilometres away, and I walked there and back alone. In the town, I bought some chocolates, and when I returned, I set up a small makeshift shop in front of our home using my mom's saree and my dad's desk. I started selling the chocolates. That was one way for me to make some much-needed money.

I did not stop at that. I then bought a goat and sold its milk. From that income, I bought a cow. This way, our family income increased. During holidays and weekends, I began working with my father. He used to clean farms on a contract basis. He would 'subcontract' some work to me, and that gave me exposure to taking ownership. I got my sisters involved to take care of cows and goats to generate some more income.

Initially, I had a very bad time at school. I was not good at studies. I dropped out of school when I was in the sixth grade and told my father I just wanted to work with him. One day, my dad asked me, 'Why do you want to become like me? Why don't you study and achieve something more?' With motivation from him and some pressure from teachers, I decided to go back to school.

But then, it was a very humiliating experience. I had to now sit with my former juniors, whom I never respected earlier, as their classmate.

Your old friends are seniors now and will not talk to you. That was probably the turning point in my life. I did not have any friends. I started focusing on the class rather than spending time with friends. Having another chance to study the same subjects meant that things that I wasn't able to grasp the first time became easier.

One day, my Maths teacher was solving a problem on the blackboard. I raised my hand and said, 'Sir, this is wrong.' At first, he was very angry at being challenged. He erased everything he had written on the board and asked me to come and solve the problem. I could do it and prove that he was wrong! Amazingly, that incident got me into his good books. Perhaps he saw some potential in me because he started focusing his efforts on me. He even started teaching me English.

Soon, I was at the top of the class. There was no looking back. From there, I started leading school sports teams as well. Now when I reflect back, I think the biggest leadership lessons that I got in my life was by leading football teams, volleyball teams, etc. Sports is a great teacher of leadership skills. And this happened by chance, not choice.

After school, I studied engineering. After graduation, I got a job with Motorola. I was posted to Ireland for a project, but it was not as good an experience as I had hoped for. This was primarily because I was not able to do my prayers, which are important to me as they give me energy. Besides, I was not comfortable speaking English at that time, and food was an issue. In less than three months, I quit and came back to India.

I was lucky to get another job, with Citibank in Saudi Arabia. The pay gave me a lot of financial freedom. I cleared all my father's debts with my first month's salary. I still remember that he cried when I sent the money home, because he had never seen that much money in his life. I built a new house for my parents and covered the costs of my sisters' weddings. Within a few months, we had become the richest family in the village!

I then moved to Citibank Dubai. I had a very cushy job. The pay was good, and there were no taxes. But when I used to come back to my village on vacation, I realized that my village still had no electricity nor paved roads, and there was only one primary school. To attend high school, children had to walk for miles. This often led them to drop out after the seventh grade and start working in the paddy and coffee farms around or at local teashops. The kids were smart and had good values, but were not getting a break. Their hopeless situation made me think: can I do something for them?

I decided to come back to India from Dubai. I had three objectives. One was to further my education, which I could not do earlier due to financial restrictions. I enrolled at IIM in Bangalore to study for an MBA. Next, I wanted to spend more time with my parents. My third objective was to do something for the youngsters in my village.

I started discussing various ideas with my cousins, who were also my childhood friends. They ran a small *kirana* store in Bangalore, and had a supplier for dosa batter who was inconsistent with his quality. There were many complaints from customers. My cousins had tried to fix the issue with the vendor multiple times, but it did not get resolved. That led to us thinking, why don't we try to make the batter ourselves? That is how iD Fresh Foods was born.

We started very small, in a fifty square-foot kitchen with an investment of 50,000 rupees. We had a grinder, a sealing machine, a mixer, a weighing scale and a second-hand scooty. Every day, we went to the market to buy the raw ingredients, and then we would clean, soak, wash and grind it. After that, we would mix and ferment the batter. The final product was then packed and loaded on to the scooty for selling in the market. We started with twenty stores with the goal to sell 100 packets a day. We wanted to achieve this target in six months, but it took us nine. We did not give up.

At that point, I used the savings I had to start a small factory in Bangalore. That increased our output to 2,000 packets a day. I had invested in property in Wayanad, Kerala, and I decided to sell off that property to put more money into the business. My dad strongly resisted the idea of selling the property at first, but eventually trusting that I would not do anything stupid, he relented.

My decision to quit my job and become a full-time entrepreneur came after attending a session on spirituality in management at IIM Bangalore. In the course, we were asked to write a reflection paper about who we were and what would make us happy on our deathbed. I wrote my reflection paper on just one page. Our professor, D.V.R. Seshadri, read my answers in the classroom. I still remember the points that I wrote.

To the question, 'Who are you?' I answered, 'I am a servant of God.' To 'Why are you are here?', I wrote, 'I am here to serve God.' The third question was: 'How will you achieve that?' and I answered, 'I will have to serve the needy to serve God.' To the last question, 'What will make you happy on your deathbed?' I answered from Quran that I follow.

In it, there is a particular saying, an *aayat*, that states that if you serve God, an angel will come and show you the beauty of heaven even before you die. For me, God's work is to serve the needy. These answers came to me inspired by my own spiritual thoughts.

I believe that all five powers being spoken of in the Mahabharata are required in an organization at all times. What I have also learnt is that while you must continuously improve, you also have to allow for failure. We all celebrate successes but we ignore failures. If you start rewarding people for failures that lead to learning, people start looking at their failures more closely. Only then can we have successful products that were created through countless failures.

Arjuna's *dharma sankata* is something I live with every day. Though I touch the lives of millions of Indian people by offering them healthy food daily, I also feel guilty. That is because I produce millions of plastic bags every month. I keep thinking, am I doing the right thing? On the one hand, I am making nutritious food, but on the other, I am selling it in plastic bags. Does it really balance out? I am determined to find a sustainable solution before I die. The pursuit for ecological alternatives that are widely available, technically feasible and commercially viable is still on.

I came empty-handed into the world, and I know I am not going to take anything with me. Once, I had the privilege to spend some time with Azim Premji and Bill Gates over lunch. I asked Mr Gates what he would have done differently. He told me that he would have started contributing to society much earlier, as there is just so much to do. That gave me the courage to start a different journey.

Today, I run four projects. One is, of course, iD. Second, I mentor around fifteen start-ups. Third, I have a venture capital fund that we created to support such start-ups. And finally, I am part of a not-for-profit organization called Thanal, which means 'shelter' in Malayalam. This is where I spend a lot of my time now.

We have multiple initiatives under Thanal. One of them is low-cost homes. As I did not have a proper home during my childhood days, my father and I are working towards building low-cost homes for less fortunate people. We focus on providing a roof over the heads of needy people in different parts of the country and not just Kerala.

Among other projects, we run a home for over 350 destitute people and thirty-five dialysis centres where we give subsidized or free dialysis. We provide around two lakh dialysis per year. We also have a paramedic clinic for people who have spinal issues. Currently, it caters to around 150 patients. My personal favourite project is our Early Intervention Centre, where we identify children with special needs. We work with hospitals and doctors in northern Kerala and Coorg to identify special needs in kids as young as six months. We provide them free speech and physical therapy for the first five or six years of their life. We have 700 such kids with us today. I am very proud to say that 42 per cent of these kids are able to go to regular schools by the age of six.

The success of these projects gives me the courage and energy to do more. I don't aim to buy a private jet, but to serve more people in need. My companies continue to hire and provide employment to smart kids from rural backgrounds. Today, we have around 1,600 such people working with us at iD.

When we set up iD, we decided to have a few ground rules to help us with decision-making when we hit forks in the road ahead. We want to do what is good for society. We do not want to get into the liquor or tobacco businesses. We promise to keep our food 100 per cent natural, with no preservatives or chemicals. The business has to be profitable, otherwise it is not a business. Also, the business has to have a future. And last, but not least, we want to create employment for smart kids from the villages. When we came to a fork in the road, we always referred to these ground rules to decide what to do.

There was a time when our core values were put to the test. It was 2008 and I had just decided that I would work full-time with iD. We were doing all right but did not want to take loans. I had sold all my property, but there was no way for us to grow the business further. For the sake of innovation, we started selling an interesting snack from our village called 'diamond cuts'. It started doing well.

At that time, I was drawing a meagre salary of 10,000 rupees per month. It was not easy to live in Bangalore with a family on that kind of income. We were literally struggling to pay our kids' school fees. But we were determined and kept all expenses in control.

One day, I got a call from the chef of a popular five-star hotel. He wanted to order thousands of kilograms of diamond cuts from us. That one order value probably would have been more than our total turnover for the year. It was a dream come true for a start-up entrepreneur! I was keen to understand how this hotel would use our product so that I could use the same pitch to sell to other large hotels in different parts of India. I went to meet them with the objective to close the deal.

When they said that the diamond cuts would make for an excellent bar snack, I was confused. 'Bar snack' – I had never heard that term before. It made me uncomfortable and I did not close the deal; I told them that I would get back to them. It was a very tough situation. I called all my partners and we debated for long. Many said that there was nothing wrong with it. If not us, someone else will provide the 'bar snack'. It was very tempting for us to service that order and come out of the difficult times, but somehow our ethics and our values did not agree with the nature of our prospective client's business.

The team left the final decision to me. It was not an easy call to make, especially under those circumstances. It was the light at the end of the tunnel, but our core values did not allow the brand to be associated with the liquor business – even to that minutest extent.

I finally called the hotel, explained my situation and turned down their order. They were not pleased. I apologized again and hung up. I felt like crying. Not because I had to turn down the order, but because the Almighty had given me the courage to take my toughest decision at the most difficult time in my life. It helped us become who we are today.

I pray five times a day. It is designed in such a way that it gives one refreshment at different times of the day. I think it's similar to *dhyaana* in yoga. I do not know the real theory behind it, but what I have experienced is that a few minutes of meditation gives me lots of energy.

I always remember this line from the Bhagavad Gita: Whatever is yours today was someone else's yesterday and will become someone else's tomorrow. Based on these words, I have devised a principle of my own: The more you give, the more you get. I have personally experienced this.

When I was a kid, my dad told me something that I did not understand when I first heard it. We had a small hut. When it rained, a lot of water would leak inside. While throwing out the water, my dad pointed to the mango tree outside our house. There was a particular branch that was always close to the ground. He asked me, 'Why is it close to the ground?' I had no idea! He said, 'It is close to the ground because it has many mangoes.'

At the lunch with Azim Premji and Bill Gates, I finally understood what he meant. The more mangoes on the branch, the more it has to give, and thus, the closer to the ground it is. It is the same with inspiring leaders.

Mr P.C. Musthafa is co-founder and CEO of iD Fresh Foods, a brand worth more than Rs 1,000 crore. He is part of the Prime Minister's 'Champions of Change' team that has a vision to build a new India by 2022.

MR S. RAMADORAI

Leadership does not come from position or rank. Just because you get a fancy job title, it does not mean you suddenly know it all. You have to think hard at every stage and be open to ideas. And those ideas come from your own upbringing, where discussing, listening and observing are a way of life. So, that is what we learnt from our parents: we learnt by listening, and we learnt by reflecting. We must always be willing to learn, to listen, to reflect.

An attitude that is detrimental to good leadership is thinking that what happens after we leave an organization is somebody else's problem and aim to be recognized only for what we did. A CEO should be evaluated not only by what he or she did, but also by what he or she left behind.

Building an organizational culture does not happen overnight. I think it is continuous learning that is very necessary. The bigger purpose emerges a lot more clearly when we are focused on connectivity between the capabilities and the culture, rather than just on what we intend to do.

We used to think that the customer is at the centre of it all. Yes, we work for the customer, but our job is to also challenge them. Where they are not correct, we need to tell them, to challenge them. We can build a lasting relationship with a large number of people than with a single project. Single projects are very transient, whereas a relationship lasts forever. The fact that you aim to build a relationship is recognized, and they will try to solve problems together rather than blaming each other. We build an institution through continuously learning from mistakes, correcting them very quickly, empowering and allocating the responsibility where it rightfully belongs.

There was a time when we had to decide whether we should get computer systems. I am talking about way back in the 1970s with all the licensing procedures and prohibitive duties. We had to think about whether we were going to be viable at all or whether we would sink the organization – it was a very critical point. We had to decide if we wanted to take that risk. These are choices where we say, 'Come what may, I am going to swim or sink with this decision.' Now see how it plays out in a personal context. I had to decide if I am going to be part of this. I was very young. For the organization, a failure is not welcomed, but the board will take care of the long-term consequences. As an individual, we have to face the possibility that our career is endangered if we fail. We made a personal choice and stayed back rather than run away. There was a feeling of being in on a great thing.

There was a time when some joint ventures were being formed at group level. The future of TCS was at stake. Some felt that the company should fold into the JV. Some of us were very clear that it has to be separate. TCS could exist in its own right and it will find its place. Those were very clear positions of survival versus moving on. It was about weighing all the options and finally taking a very clear decision of continuing with TCS the way it was and grow it further. Let joint ventures find their own space, but build capabilities in different areas.

Everyone has a different style of functioning, but we should not confuse style with character. Let's take the example of my boss, Mr Kohli. He very rarely gave you the opportunity to speak, because that was his style of functioning. But a lot of people just thought that he was close-minded. So, they just kept quiet and let him say whatever he wanted. Eventually, some of us discovered how to counter him by expressing our points of view in writing. Kohli would always read it. He was actually very open-minded, which was not obvious to those who could not see beyond his style of functioning. He was a thorough professional and a good mentor.

He was young. He was in his forties (and I was twenty-six), and he was building an institution. He was answerable to the board. He was very impatient, but people saw that impatience as a sign of being tough. So, they would not want to go to his room. They would ask his assistant as to why he was calling them, if he was in a good mood or bad mood. And if they felt that he was in a very foul mood they would probably disappear from the office!

And he knew that. He would laugh it out when we told him this is what they thought. At times he might have even called that individual and told him that he had no such intention.

In my own case, my behaviour was very different: if you wanted to meet me, the door was always open. I never created distance between an employee and myself or showed that I am very tough. If you connect with your boss by understanding and adapting to his methods, you can learn a lot.

But how do we teach observation and listening? I think that comes a lot from your personality. Some people are born with an ability to express their views openly, but others are very reserved. If you are more of an introvert, your ability to listen and reflect becomes a lot stronger. People can mistake an introvert for a person who does not know anything or just has nothing to say. How do you encourage an introvert? In a group setting, have everybody speak up. An introvert may still not say anything in front of others, but if you meet him one-on-one, you find that he has a lot of ideas. There are brilliant people who would not want to speak publicly; we cannot afford to let their intelligence and opinions to not be included in our thinking.

Sometimes we have to shock others deliberately to break any stereotyped image they have of you. But it also works to disrupt the image you have of yourself. For example, I had a serious problem with public speaking. I used to literally shiver when I had to go and speak in public. I overcame that fear through attending theatre workshops. The shock helped in breaking that mental block I had. I chose a public forum to talk about something no one associated with me. In one of the Indo-British events in BKC, I spoke only on cricket, which had nothing to do with IT or anything I am known for. So, you resolved to do something where you completely disrupted the image the other person had of you and the one you had of yourself.

And this applies to organizations also. I will talk about two instances where we worked as a group as soon as I became the CEO in 1996 to change the internal image of who we are. We said we have to specify what is our long-term vision, what we want to do in the next decade.

We deliberated a lot; a simple sentence we could come up with was 'Top 10 by 2010'. It is very easy to understand to start with one line. Now, what does top ten mean is the next question? We decided the parameters to be measured through a third-party assessment would be revenue, profit, quality, sustainability and predictability.

Then we tried to enable every person in the organization to relate to these goals and find a meaning. To drive this strategy, we hired a chief transformation officer. It was a new designation, created for the first time. His job was to align everybody in the organization to the upcoming changes. We put in systems and training modules, and then defined the quality of deliverables. This led to an understanding of a common company culture that all employees must align with or be left behind. It took us three years to deploy, but by 2009, we had achieved all our goals for 2010.

Second change we brought in was automating back-office functions so that we did not have to create separate departments for each function. It was an evolution of a strategy that was simplified so that everybody understood. Of course, there were challenges. We had people who said they did not believe these changes were necessary. We held open discussions and also one-on-one sessions with the employees. The chief transformation officer was given the task of convincing the doubters and the disruptors. If he failed, they were brought to me. I had to take some tough decisions and tell a few senior employees that they would not make it here.

There is always stress, but we should be prepared to take the stress. There are multiple ways to deal with stress. Some take to meditation. My way of dealing with it was to sleep over serious problems. I could sleep without any medication for three to four hours. I would sleep at 10 p.m. and wake up at 2 a.m. with a clearer mind.

Always think about what is the worst that can happen. Is it that you may lose your job? Then, if you are not worried about losing your job, or the embarrassment of being asked to leave, you can achieve a lot. Many people fail at this point. Public perception of you becomes your biggest problem. But your perception of yourself is more important than the public perception of you. This realization sometimes comes very late in life.

A typical modern management model is always to decide quickly with a 'yes' or a 'no' and just get closure. But sometimes patience is the better approach. 'Maybe' is one of the options. Time will tell whether it should have been a yes or a no, but it may suit our purpose right now. Brooding on a decision is not all that bad. At least you are reflecting and taking your time. You can probably come to a clear decision after that. Waiting also allows one to become conscious of one's own thinking process.

Mr S. Ramadorai was CEO of Tata Consultancy Services (TCS) from 1996 to 2009 and its Vice Chairman till 2014. He was the advisor to the Prime Minister of India in the National Council on Skill Development. He was awarded the Padma Bhushan in 2006 and Commander of the Order of the British Empire (CBE) in 2009.

MR VALLABH BHANSALI

Leadership is not an Indian thought. Leadership is not a celebrated thing here. Following one's *dharma* is the Indian thought. The key question for an Indian king has always been: am I entering a Dharmakshetra or a Kurukshetra?

Fundamentally, Western thought has been around empirical knowledge or intellectual knowledge. When you go back to Socrates, he says, 'I will think', and so the focus is on intellect. There is a natural purity in Socrates's thought. It is this paradigm on which the Greek thought and the Roman Empire are built. A lot of scientific discoveries were made through external observation. Examples include gravity, DNA, penicillin. All these are great discoveries.

But in India there was a school of thought that believed it is possible to have perfect knowledge by looking inward. The thought that it is possible to get perfect knowledge, *paraavidyaa,* is the most unique part of India.

The second difference in India is the importance given to *tapas*. We have had all great heroes who have to go and discover great things through *tapas*.

The third great aspect about Indian thought is to look within, more observing self and understanding the observer rather than focusing on the observation.

These three are the most outstanding aspects. Through my reading of the Upanishads, I have realized that only someone who has 'perfect knowledge' can understand *dharma* and the concepts of *isavasyam idam sarvam yat kim ca jagatyam jagat* (Everything in the universe is part of one complete whole that is inseparable from Brahman). I find the *shanti paata* that defines the meaning of *poornatvam* (completeness) very inspiring: *Poornamadah poornamidam poornaat poornamudachyate, Poornasya poornamaadaaya poornamevaavashishyate* (That is complete, this is complete, from the completeness comes the completeness; if completeness is taken away from completeness, only completeness remains). Only someone who has seen *poornata* (completeness) can talk about it. Someone who has done *tapas* and has looked within can talk about *brahmasmi* (Infinite Brahman is me) or *shivoham, shivoham* (Shiva is me).

For me, the two greatest lines of knowledge are found in the Ishavasya Upanishad: *Ishavasyam idam sarvam, tena tyaktena bhunjitha ha ma gradhah kasya svid dhanam* (The universe is pervaded by the Brahman, primordial nature in its turn is also pervaded by Him. Brahman alone is thus the origin of all this. Enjoy whatever is given to you by Brahman with humility, and do not seek any other wealth).

I think the Mahabharata is a unique story. Two parts stand out for me. One is Duryodhana saying, '*Janami dharmam na cha me* (I understand what is *dharmic* action, but I am unable to act in a *dharmic* way).' The second unique aspect is that all the characters face consequences of their actions in their own lifetime – whether it is Kunti, Dhritarashtra, Yudhishthira or anyone else.

In the Mahabharata, there is a scene where Bhishma says, 'Oh, I would give up all my *punya* (merit) if I could hear what Krishna is telling Arjuna.' Some people have commented that Bhishma would not be able to hear, because he does not have the necessary humility. Arjuna had this humility of being a great leader and yet being able to express his vulnerability. Arjuna is being honest to himself. To be able to identify *dharma sankata*, you have to identify that there is a *dharma*. *Dharma* means there are things beyond me, it's just not me.

I do not know for how long I have had this question – 'Who am I?' I am so many different people. Sometimes I behave in this manner and sometimes I behave in that manner, and why does that happen? And then I see my dishful of proclivity, propensities, etc. And then some prevail over the other. When one prevails over the other, some outcome happens, else some other outcome happens. So, I think this possibility of making my field of action a Dharmakshetra or just a Kurukshetra is inside me all the time. Only how one thinks of beyond oneself will make it a Dharmakshetra instead of just being Kurukshetra. This, to me, can happen only when I have the ability to look at the world beyond me.

A lot of human thinking is towards desiring harmony. In *poornamadah poornamidam*, it is captured that there is constant change. There is a disequilibrium, yet an equilibrium. It is a constantly changing equilibrium. So it is inevitable that in day-to-day life, one will be seeing the Dharmakshetra-Kurukshetra dilemma all the time.

I have visited so many companies. We have seen very few companies who have an understanding of 'beyond me'. Beyond me and beyond this moment. The most painful experiences I have had are the ones where we have seen family separations. The Kauravas and Pandavas were also a family. Not accepting that your birth is Nature's plan, whether it is Karna's problem, whether it is Duryodhana's problem, it is not accepting one's own reality. Who am I? Not accepting one's position in life, whether it is within a hierarchy, within a society, within a family, within a relationship, is what causes all the problems.

I was talking to some students from across the world about leadership. I asked them if they would be honest if they started a business. At first, they all said they would comply with all the laws. But then I told them that their competition was cheating to make profits. How long would they remain honest? Most of the students, not all, said that they would not cheat. But then I said, competition has gone and changed the law itself, now what will you do? Now many said they would have to cheat too for their survival. I said that this is the reality, the dilemma faced by Duryodhana when he said, '*Janami dharmam* (I understand what is *dharma*).' So, I think we must inculcate acceptance of oneself and an ability to be anchored in *dharma* as an important part of running a business. I cannot pursue success because I cannot guarantee success. I can only guarantee what Krishna did in the Mahabharata: *yogah karmasu, kaushalam* (excellence and balanced intensity at work). Success is a spin-off that comes from complete focus on one's actions. I would rather teach a class on that philosophy than on leadership.

A person needs to recognize with humility that disproportionate gains may come with disproportionate pains. The acceptance of *dukha sukha same kritva labha alabho jaya ajayau* (acting only after having discovered equanimity in the face of happiness and sadness, gain and loss) comes only if we are not attached to the success. Only in a few companies do we see that the leader understands the power of this truth, that I don't cease to be a businessman if I let go of a business, that I don't cease to be a leader because I am not recognized. Those who deny truth and *tapas* will fail. They may achieve great heights, but they will fall.

Part of one's destiny is to experience failure. Power and wealth can be taken away. There is *karma* (action) and there is *phala* (the fruits of action). *Phala* has its own order. You have to understand the whole order. You have to understand there is trust. I live on trust, others live on trust. I cannot violate it. If you cannot recognize trust in its fullest form, it is because you do not recognize that you are constantly a beneficiary of so much benevolence. Great companies survive because they understand this and have concern for their customers, employees and society.

Once, a large FMCG company felt strongly that they need to do something for communities they sell to, long before CSR laws came in. They retreated and engaged in deep discussions, involving their best managers (this is *tapas*). Something that is not only commercial but also protects margins as they are an A-listed company. They studied

India's problems and found that availability of water is a big issue. They also realized that most of their products cannot be used without water. Since their sales were linked to the availability of water, they decided to make their sales managers responsible for water management in their respective areas. It took them three years to implement, but they got a fantastic ROI for helping villagers manage their water. This is realization that there's something beyond you, but it's also you!

You have to also realize there is moment beyond the immediate. By being patient and transparent, good things will happen. The power of truth is the least-discovered power. It is all right to go with serendipity, and *dharma* will always show you the way. It is easier for people who have faith to build successful organizations. Traditional wisdom says that those who are the ones who endure and prosper.

There was a company that was a leader in its sector in India. They did fabulous work and were extremely fair to their suppliers and to their customers. But then somewhere success got to them. They wanted to go for an IPO, and global investment bankers proposed premium pricing. However, I warned them that companies in their sector in India suffer from a credibility gap. They are not trusted by the people. My advice to them was that they should first build respect in local communities. They heard me out respectfully, but the premium pricing offered by the global banks was too attractive. They could not do an IPO. To raise money, they signed up for many smart structures to protect their equity. But soon they got into deep trouble as the business did not go the way they planned. One day they said, we need peace of mind more than the smart structures: they diluted the equity, cleaned up the company, went back on growth path and did a successful IPO.

There is this saying: *Sadhavo na hi sarvatra chandanam na vane vane.* (Neither are good people seen everywhere, nor is there a sandal tree in every garden.) Unfortunately, only a few people understand that.

Mr Vallabh Bhansali is the founder of Enam Financials, India's leading investment bank. He is also co-founder of Flame University.

MR VELLAYAN SUBBIAH

Fundamentally, I look at leadership and say it stems from how people look at adversity. You could argue that at a certain level it is kind of *karmic*. If I break my life into phases, the first decade was all about chess. Every day after school, I would play three to four hours of chess. I could not even run ten metres, did no physical activity. I just played chess.

The first kind of adversity I faced was when I was about ten years old. I was sent to a boarding school in northern India. First day I went there, one guy comes and he just says '*kaliye tera kya hoga*', which was interesting, and I had not even seen *Sholay*. My Hindi was also not that good. Being one of only two south Indians in a fairly north Indian boarding school brought about a certain amount of 'I need to stand up for myself' learning.

The second challenge that I had to face around that time was that I developed asthma. It got to a point where I literally could not climb a flight of stairs. Asthma made me realize my physical limitations. I began yoga and running and came out of asthma. Now I can just wake up and run twenty-five kilometres. It was so important for me to overcome that physical limitation. That was when I learnt that I had to fight back against adversity. I realized over the years that life is a series of tests. After a while you just start enjoying these tests!

The second decade of my life was spent in education, first at the boarding school and then at IIT. The third decade was spent in the USA, working primarily with McKinsey. I used to love the intellectual part of my job at McKinsey as I enjoyed data analytics. But I hated the selling part. I thought it was such a commercial thing; I had worked to be an intellectual so why should I waste my time with sales? But it was only when I decided to leave McKinsey, that I had the huge realization that if we cannot sell, there is no business at all. It is the most critical part of the business.

In my twenties, I had developed many likes and dislikes, but it was not until a decade later that I understood that there was no basis in rationality at all for those preferences. In my next job, I decided to focus on learning sales and business development. It was an extremely useful education, and also humbling in many ways.

My thirties was also a time when I started pushing both my physical and mental boundaries. I started running marathons. It helped me understand that the physical side helps the mental side and mental side helps the physical side.

My path inwards started at around forty, after I realized that an increase in wealth is not directly correlated to an increase in happiness. That was when it really hit me that all of these things I was looking for, happiness and satisfaction, they do not come from the outside. They can only be generated from the inside. But I still understood that only in theory.

It was in my fifth decade that I started following a spiritual path. It was Sadhguru who made me recognize that it is not just our body and mind that are important, but also our emotions and spirit. He made me realize that the mind is the problem, that the mind is not working for me. This was a huge realization, and a huge challenge. Once the realization comes, we begin to understand that all of us exhibit compulsive behavioural patterns more than conscious ones. Then you can figure out how do you deal with those people differently, and what are your own compulsions. This comes only when you turn inwards.

Call this spirituality if you will. Earlier, I always looked at spirituality as a negative trait. I used to think that you are either a spiritual type or a 'real world' type! Now, what I found is that being spiritual actually makes me phenomenally more capable, both mentally and physically. Through my *saadhana,* I feel I can perform better at pretty much everything I do. Not because I have to prove something to myself, or to others, but just because I enjoy doing it.

You start off on this journey, and it is amazing how what is a compulsive behaviour starts becoming more conscious behaviour. It has changed how I think and how I react. I'm now able to step back into myself and listen to an inner voice and can choose my response. Previously, it was just kind of an action-reaction. And now it is an action where there is cognition, there is internalizing.

The moment we start turning inwards, it kind of automatically also makes you think of an inclusive path. A lot of times, I have been quite happy being by myself. But then I realized that you need a much more inclusive path, what we call *dharmic*. Without that inclusiveness, you cannot move, so you need to be inclusive.

So, this is how I would break up my life into sections: five decades and five different phases.

I have come to realize that we cannot just rely on pure data analytics for decision-making. This so-called 'rational' view of the world is not what works all the time. We have to give instinct and intuition much more importance than what we do. I often think that this data-driven, rational style of work can push us into a safe way of operating. It does not allow us to take the risks that are required for growth. Yes, we must use the data. But we also have to use intuition.

There are a lot of tradeoffs that constantly come up, which effectively come down to risk-taking capability. There are lot of things that push you towards the centre. But the opportunity lies in the circumference. So, how do you keep on pushing yourself out there?

For ten years, my current company's turnover never exceeded 200 crores. But after I joined, it reached 370 crores, an increase of almost 85 per cent. It was achieved through risk-taking, inclusiveness, reflection and listening to my inner self. These are leadership characteristics.

Mr Vellayan Subbiah, a scion of the Murugappa Family, is managing director of Tube Investments of India Ltd.

Appendix

The Toy Story

We will use a case study to help you reflect on your own leadership journey and how you can understand *shakti* and *balam* in your life. As you follow the example, I suggest that you do some exercises for yourself, so that the practices get internalized. In my experience, every person who has internalized these practices has gone on to become very successful leaders.

A young executive by the name of Ranjan was heading the most promising business unit of a large conglomerate, but it held no meaning for him any more. His wife, Sanam, had noticed this and had encouraged him to pause and think about what he would be more passionate about. Ranjan did as she suggested, and it helped make his mind up.

'We will start a toy factory,' he said.

Ranjan had realized that his passion had always been woodcraft. He had learnt it from his father. In his hometown, his father's carpentry unit had been well known. His father prided himself in the revival of the traditional crafts of the area and had travelled to obscure villages to discover old styles and methods. He often found ways to collaborate with local craftspeople. Ranjan had often accompanied him on those trips and would also help his father in the carpentry shop after school hours.

Sanam was delighted when she heard the idea. They began to work on the dream. Ranjan would have to put all his savings into creating the new business. They started a small company called Nava-Rasa and began designing exquisite toys. They wanted to create toys that could have educational value as well. In the beginning, business came mainly from small toy shops. But business remained small. Soon, there was a period when they couldn't find new clients and the old regulars began thinning out.

Sanam was able to find a marketing consultant who helped them with reaching out to a wider public. Soon Nava-Rasa began to get media attention. It took more than two years to become a profitable entity, but business took off after that. New customers came in largely by word of mouth.

An angel investor by the name of Vijay learnt about the venture and became very drawn to the idea. He offered to help them expand by allowing them use of a whole floor of one of his buildings for a toy shop that also had a small carpentry workshop. From twelve people, Nava-Rasa grew to seventy employees. Product design was still managed by Ranjan, but he now had a very able assistant in Raj, a quick learner with a flair for making handcrafted items. Also, a few former teachers had joined Nava-Rasa to take their educational products to schools and train their teachers to use them when teaching.

Soon, there was a pull from the market for Nava-Rasa to expand its business. Its unique product mix, as well as its socially sensitive values, had won it much acclaim. Ranjan and Raj were starting to feel the stress of the changes that were happening as an inevitable part of growth. Exciting new tools and machinery were available, leading Raj to ask Ranjan if they could standardize their methods. 'Those village craftspeople use chemical paints,' Raj complained. 'Organic colours are difficult to get these days. We have to ensure high-quality, reliable products.' But Sanam worried about cutting off their long-term supplies.

Soon, other investors took notice of this upswing in Nava-Rasa's business and saw in it very good opportunities for themselves. They put forward a few ideas:

- One of them owned a chain of large bookstores across the country. 'Make this an exclusive chain of toy shops with an on-premise workshop, the way you have designed this one,' he said.
- Another person came up with the idea of focusing only on the educational toys and suggested they create a large chain of small franchise outfits.
- A third idea was to take their business international and open an Indian toy shop in major capitals around the world.

'What shall we do, Sanam?' Ranjan asked. 'What do these changes mean for us? What will they mean for our idea and for our people? What will it take to make these changes? And what if we don't expand?'

Ranjan and Sanam decided to take a holiday to Bhutan and visit a monastery for contemplation and rejuvenation. They were at a threshold and serious choices had to be made.

Now, back to you.

When was the last time you sat back and really looked at your own life? Does your life have meaning and purpose? What do you stand for? Will you be able to look back at your life with pride when you die? Are you the hero of your life? Did you find peace?

Exercise 1

Step into Ranjan's shoes and try to resolve his dilemma.

1. Take time off from what you are doing and write a retrospective story of your life so far. Make it autobiographical. Try and trace the flow of your life till today. Make sure you capture the critical

turning points. What was the crisis? How did you respond to it? What enabled you to confront the challenge? Who were the people who helped you?

2. What did you learn about yourself from this reflective writing?
3. What are the critical questions or challenges that you face today? How would it change your life if you awakened the Arjuna within, had a dialogue with your Krishna and then charted your future course of action?

Exercise 2

1. Go back to the story of Ranjan. Look at it from the framework of *shakti* and *balam*. What events in the story reflect the three *shakti*s and the three *balam*s?
2. Now look at your own story.
3. What is the nature of your *shakti*? Do you value it? How are you nurturing it?
4. What are the sources of your *balam*? Can you map them clearly? How will you invest in them?

Case Study

We will use the case of Ranjan, who has now become a successful entrepreneur on the verge of consolidating and expanding his business.

Ranjan goes through the Pandava Profile exercise. He realizes that his identification with the Bhima propensity is high. Arjuna and Sahadeva, in that order, are the next propensities he identifies with. The Yudhishthira and Nakula propensities are not natural to him and his identification with them is low. What can Ranjan reflect upon based on this?

Firstly, Ranjan affirms to himself that he is most comfortable with the Power of Action and is driven by passion. He has a high appetite for risk, loves challenges and seeks out the path less trodden. As he reflects on what it means for the Arjuna propensity to be his second preference, Ranjan realizes that his ability for self-reflection is fairly developed and provides a balance to his action orientation. It is this propensity of his that helps him to not keep fighting challenges without introspection when his tactical moves do not fructify. (This is a major derailer of the Bhima propensity.) Ranjan also affirms to himself his respect for research and analysis. Ranjan recollected how he was able to interest a venture capitalist to invest in his idea. He had to do a lot of data-crunching and market analysis to convince the investment company.

As Ranjan looks at the weak Yudhishthira propensity in his profile, it reminds him that he is not good at setting up processes for scaling up operations and creating predictability. He also begins to realize that while he was very inspiring and charismatic, he devalued the Nakula characteristics of inclusivity and compassion. He interpreted them as lack of courage.

We will return to Ranjan and see how he uses the processes described here to grow his organization.

Your Private Green Room

Create your own *saadhana* space where you can turn the Dharma Wheel and prepare yourself before any critical encounter. This space will be like the green room in theatres, where the performers prepare before going on stage. Before you engage in an important event – a team or customer meeting, or before making a strategic decision – take a pause. Revisit the five key questions. Keep a paper and pencil with you.

1. Sit by yourself and ask, 'Where am I? What is the meaning of the context I am in? What does it call for?' Try and describe this to yourself in as much nuance and detail as you can. Write down your answers. Do not be satisfied with the most immediate answer; try and envisage a few possible scenarios.
2. Ask yourself, 'Who am I? What are my propensities? My biases? My derailers?' Put down the most critical ones. Pick out one or

two that are key to the encounter you are preparing for. Write them down.

3. Ask yourself, 'Why am I here? What is the immediate purpose? How does this fit with my larger purpose and the larger goals of the team?' Try and answer these questions from the perspective of the key stakeholders of the encounter. Sit back and decide on what you wish to accomplish. Note this down.

Try and envisage the drama of the encounter as it might play out. Do a few variations depending on the scenarios you have seen. If the encounter is really important, and you have a support group, you could roleplay the different possibilities.

Now you have done your preparation. Next, take time to choose the right weapons to go into the battle with: the right clothes to wear and, if applicable, the right team.

When you are in the thick of the engagement, engage with all your senses and act with great intensity.

After the engagement is over, take a pause again.

1. Describe to yourself what happened after reviewing a slow-motion mental replay of how you played. Then ask yourself, 'In doing what I was doing, what was I really doing?' If this question is answered honestly, you can get past justifications and excuses and go right into your inner motivations and choices.
2. Then ask, 'How am I part of the problem? How can I be part of the solution? Am I being the best I can be?'

Create your 'Discovering my Leadership Style' diary. Use the following simple frame to keep track of the learning:

- Do more of (or start doing)
- Do less of (or stop doing)
- Continue doing as present

Asking yourself these five questions is guaranteed to help you discover your heroic self, your unique leadership style and make you the best that you can be.

Turning the Dharma Wheel

Discover & Embrace			ABCD of Action	Review	
Leadership practices I wish to focus on	Date / Period	What drama am I entering into? Who am I? Where am I? Why am I here? How have I prepared?	What happened? Did I display Awareness, Balance, Conviction and Direction? (Descriptive narrative)	Ask the key questions: In doing what I was doing, what was I really doing? How was I part of the problem? How was I part of the solution?	Learning/ Practices: What do I do more of, or start doing? What do I do less of, or stop doing? What am I doing well and ought to continue to do as I am?

It might help you to read the discussions in the section 'What Does Exile Mean for Leaders in Today's Context?' from Part 3. Go over the steps slowly and contemplate the underpinning philosophy behind the process. To help you internalize the process of using the five key questions and turning the Dharma Wheel, we will go through an illustration of how Ranjan prepares for a board meeting.

Ranjan's Critical Board Meeting

Ranjan's company now has a board of directors. He has to prepare for an important board meeting. He has been studying the market trends and feels that one of the lines of business that has been the foundation of the organization – and been a cash cow so far – is not a good bet for the future. He needs funds to develop a new line of business that will take a few years to mature.

Ranjan writes out a description of the journey that has led up to the current situation. This activity will enable him to start defining the first three critical questions – 'Who am I?', 'Where am I?' and 'Why am I here?' – in clear terms.

Since this is a self-reflective document, Ranjan is brutally honest with himself when he answers the questions.

Who am I? I am a harvester of the seeds sown by me; I am a tactician caught up in the excitement of emerging challenges.

Where am I? I am heading a business that is at a crucial juncture but seem to have captured the trends a little late; I have tested my new hypothesis, and I need to act with urgency.

Why am I here? To take a major step in the growth of my business.

Ranjan goes over the same questions with a more inward gaze: I am a Bhima who tends to get excited with market challenges; I am here because I did not pause to review the strategic directions earlier and was too distracted by tactical wins; I am here to reorient the board in order for them to take a long-term view.

Ranjan then steps into the shoes of his board members. He tries to answer the three questions from their point of view.

- Rita, the chairperson, appointed by their investor: 'I am a conservative; I am being recognized by my organization as a good administrator who can ensure that start-ups get stabilized; I am here to ensure that Ranjan stays grounded; I am here to ensure a steady flow of funds for a new investment that we are planning.'
- Ashok, the independent director: 'I have been invited to the board for my strategic thinking capabilities; I am developing a reputation for being a responsible board member; I wish to

impress the investor community with my capability so that I can be appointed to many more boards.'

Ranjan prepares for the meeting by calling Sara, a strategist he has recently appointed, and Arun, the head of finance, who is known for being conservative. Sara and Arun present the strategy in three different ways by taking different locations: the Yudhishthira location (the stability and solidity), the Sahadeva location (the research that supports the decision) and the Bhima location (the excitement about the new direction). After listening to the roleplays of Sara and Arun, Ranjan works out his preferred way of presentation. He also works on a few other scenarios as a backup.

During the board meeting, Ranjan starts by discussing the business context, and listens very carefully to the way the others on the board discuss their points of view. He makes sure that each of them has a fair amount of time to present their views. Ranjan is also sensitive to his own competitiveness stemming from his Bhima propensity and ensures that he deploys his Arjuna and Sahadeva propensities more by listening with intent when the others speak.

However, when Rita questions Ranjan on some of his projections, he feels challenged. He notices his breath becoming sharper and his stance getting into the familiar 'fight mode'. Having caught the symptoms of the Bhima shadow early, Ranjan takes a pause and asks the board for a five-minute recess. He then re-anchors himself in his larger purpose and asks himself how the challenge could be dealt with in a constructive way. This enables him to really appreciate the point of view of the board members.

Ranjan's Sahadeva propensities come to the fore and his presentation goes well. The board members ask for a review in a few weeks based on a set of pointed questions that are mainly about global trends. Ranjan sees the import of these questions and studies the context with care before reworking his scenarios and suggesting a strategy.

Ranjan puts into practice the 'A, B, C and D of strategic action' that we discussed in Part 3 of this book. He was aware of himself and the context and caught himself becoming reactive; he regained balance by remaining anchored in deep listening; he developed his conviction through rigorous preparation; and he stayed true to the direction he wished to take and invited the others to share his vision of the future.

After the event, Ranjan sits by himself and writes down the flow of events. He asks himself the question: 'In doing what I was doing, what was I really doing?' Especially in the phase when he was feeling provoked.

Ranjan experienced the question as a criticism of his work, to a lacuna in his analysis. If he had responded in his usual way, Ranjan would have ended up converting the board meeting into a debate, splitting the board into taking various stances and positions. Ranjan felt pleased at having caught himself early, given himself breathing time and gone back to orchestrating a healthy enquiry of the merits of each of the scenarios he had presented. He understood that he had made unverified assumptions about a few markets, and it was important for the board to question them.

Ranjan then sits down with Sara and Arun and goes over the board meeting. He first describes it dispassionately like a neutral observer narrating the proceedings. Sara and Arun reflect on what Ranjan did that was enabling a consensus and convergence of views, and what hindered it.

Ranjan sits back and reviews his own style. He sees that his latent Sahadeva propensity has started to balance off his Bhima propensity. His presentations were more convincing since they had passion backed by deep study. His natural ability to approach the meeting in a friendly manner was a great help. However, his eagerness to get into action was making his chairperson nervous, and his impatience was beginning to overshadow his ability to build a consensus. Recognizing this early was the new ability that enabled Ranjan to manage himself well.

Through this process, Ranjan has used the Pandava lens in three ways. Firstly, as a green room, to reflect on his own enablers and derailers and to rehearse the probable drama that would unfold. Secondly, during the board meeting, to understand what propensities the board members were acting from, and therefore how he needed to respond so that the larger good was kept in focus. Thirdly, to develop his own style in a way that reflected his highest potential.

Let us also review what Ranjan did not do. Ranjan does not shape his external expressions or methods based on his green room roleplays. While the green room offers a set of possibilities, it does have a predictive quality. Relying on the green room too much would be a mistake, since we would then be blind to the emerging reality of the actual encounter and in an unintended way, manipulate ourselves and others. An overreliance on the green room roleplays makes one repeat a script like a bad actor who is faking it.

Ranjan uncovers his inner patterns and taps into unused potential by turning the Dharma Wheel. His style will emerge and grow as he repeats this process. Through the use of the five key questions in a disciplined way and by using the 'green room', Ranjan has created a very important resource for himself.

Turning the Dharma Wheel with the Team

You can use these questions to prepare a team to be the best it can be. The process is similar, except that it is done using a team discussion. The team starts by identifying individual propensities. A team comprising members who are able to help each other to understand themselves through sincere self-reflection and honest feedback is already discovering a deep degree of coherence and trust. It is very important that the derailers of the individuals and team are identified and discussed truthfully. After doing some mindfulness practice, each member reflects on their leadership style using the framework of the five seats of power. A team is made more robust when each member accepts not only each other's capabilities but also their own limitations with grace.

The team sets out a feedback sheet with three columns for each member:

- Do more of (or start doing)
- Do less of (or stop doing)
- Continue doing as present

Each member makes a few suggestions and then reviews the suggestions made by the others.

The team now analyses a difficult project they are confronting. This is where they ask themselves the first three key questions. The team members not only describe the tangible aspects of the project but give the critical turning points a subjective description.

If a phase of the project calls for intense planning and discipline to be successful, the group would call it a Yudhishthira moment. If they experience the excitement and anxiety of risk-taking at another phase, it would be a Bhima moment. Similar moments can be experienced for each of the Pandava propensities. Team reflections on their propensities and limitations become crucial to have a meaningful exploration into the possible scenarios.

Such activities create a powerful, shared map of reality and flag possible areas of danger and opportunity. It is then easy to reflect. Who is the best person to anchor each critical phase? Who will play a supportive role? What are our derailers as a team? How can we be mindful of these tendencies? How can we nourish our collective will?

The other steps are similar to the individual process. Engage with the project with intensity and openness. Come back and tell each other how each one saw the whole process unfold. Ask the penetrating question: 'In doing what we were doing, what were we really doing?' – to reveal the gaps between intentions and reality. From this, it is a simple step to asking, 'Which actions were a part of the solution and which ones created problems?' The regular practice of preparation and review based on these questions will make the team extremely cohesive and powerful.

Ranjan Prepares the Team for Deploying the Strategy

After Ranjan has secured the board's commitment to his new strategy, he outlines the strategy and possible timelines to his team. Once the team members are clear about the direction Ranjan wishes to take, they start working out the implementation process.

Every member introspects on the questions posed by each Pandava propensity and writes down their ideas:

Bhima's seat asks, 'How will we ignite and sustain a passion for this strategy?'

Yudhishthira's seat asks, 'How will the process become error-free, efficient and predictable?'

Nakula's seat asks, 'How will the process flow and create value for each member of the system? What infrastructure do we need to build for this to happen?'

Sahadeva's seat asks, 'How do we establish a learning method and create knowledge through the process?'

Arjuna's seat asks, 'How will this project lead to organization-building and evolution while retaining our core values?'

Everyone's answers are gathered and categorized, their suggested actions distilled and arranged across a timeline that coincides with the different phases of the strategy. Now the team ensures that the set of actions is coherent and convergent. Each member of the team takes charge of one aspect of the process. The next step finalizes the action plan.

All members set out work plans to discuss at the next meeting, while asking themselves the three role-preparation questions: 'Who am I? Where am I? Why am I here?' This is the phase where the invisible, but vital, part of the process gets addressed.

'Who am I?' looks at the role we feel inspired to play and how we relate to the other role-holders.

'Where am I?' relates to the throughput that we are accountable for and the situation, the phase of the project, and the assumptions we made at the start.

'Why am I here?' helps to define our role clearly to ourselves and others. The role is not just about the tasks we commit to, but also about how the project is proceeding towards its goals from our vantage point. This helps us make choices to steer the ship towards its intended destination.

The review process at each stage of completion uses the five seats again to ensure that the process is holistic and that it stays on track.

Acknowledgements

I am deeply grateful to Sushil Handa of Core Parenterals, who has been as much a part of my journey as I have been a part of his. Also, Mr Subbiah and the Murugappa family, who have been receptive to my work. I owe a lot to Mr Ramadorai and TCS, who have valued my work for decades. They have given me the space to develop new ways of looking at leadership development and organizational alignment that are based on Indic wisdom.

This book is the result of teamwork. Rajiv Kuchhal's critique of my earlier book, *Leadership Dharma, Arjuna the Timeless Metaphor*, provided the inspiration for this book. His involvement at every stage has been critical. J. Shankar, a dear friend who is passionate about Indian culture, volunteered to read the Mahabharata in its unabridged translation to pick out the stories we discuss in the second chapter. My colleague Sarbari Gomes was part of the discussions and brought in the coaching perspective. Bhavana Issar, Ganesh Chidambara Krishnan and Rajeev Natarajan joined in the conversations from time to time. Gayatri Iyer helped us with the initial collation and editing. Mirra Savara and Venky Ramachandran took on the difficult last mile, reviewing the manuscript, reworking it and editing it to give it its final form.

About the Author

Raghu Ananthanarayanan is one of the chief mentors at Ritambhara Ashram in the Nilgiris. His work involves helping individuals, groups and organizations discover their dharma, and become the best they can be. He has co-founded many organizations focused on inner transformation and its application in various fields. He has also authored several books and papers on yoga, inner transformation and organizational alignment. He can be contacted at raghu.tao@gmail.com.